Digital Education and Learning

Series Editors
Michael Thomas
Liverpool John Moores University
Merseyside, UK

John Palfrey
John D. and Catherine T. MacArthur Foundation
Chicago, IL, USA

Mark Warschauer
University of California, Irvine
Irvine, USA

Much has been written during the first decade of the new millennium about the potential of digital technologies to produce a transformation of education. Digital technologies are portrayed as tools that will enhance learner collaboration and motivation and develop new multimodal literacy skills. Accompanying this has been the move from understanding literacy on the cognitive level to an appreciation of the sociocultural forces shaping learner development. Responding to these claims, the Digital Education and Learning Series explores the pedagogical potential and realities of digital technologies in a wide range of disciplinary contexts across the educational spectrum both in and outside of class. Focusing on local and global perspectives, the series responds to the shifting landscape of education, the way digital technologies are being used in different educational and cultural contexts, and examines the differences that lie behind the generalizations of the digital age. Incorporating cutting edge volumes with theoretical perspectives and case studies (single authored and edited collections), the series provides an accessible and valuable resource for academic researchers, teacher trainers, administrators and students interested in interdisciplinary studies of education and new and emerging technologies.

Karim Sadeghi • Michael Thomas
Editors

Second Language Teacher Professional Development

Technological Innovations for Post-Emergency Teacher Education

Editors
Karim Sadeghi 🆔
Urmia University
Urmia, Iran

Michael Thomas
Liverpool John Moores University
Liverpool, UK

ISSN 2753-0744   ISSN 2753-0752   (electronic)
Digital Education and Learning
ISBN 978-3-031-12072-5   ISBN 978-3-031-12070-1   (eBook)
https://doi.org/10.1007/978-3-031-12070-1

© The Editor(s) (if applicable) and The Author(s), under exclusive licence to Springer Nature
Switzerland AG 2023
This work is subject to copyright. All rights are solely and exclusively licensed by the Publisher, whether
the whole or part of the material is concerned, specifically the rights of translation, reprinting, reuse of
illustrations, recitation, broadcasting, reproduction on microfilms or in any other physical way, and
transmission or information storage and retrieval, electronic adaptation, computer software, or by similar
or dissimilar methodology now known or hereafter developed.
The use of general descriptive names, registered names, trademarks, service marks, etc. in this publication
does not imply, even in the absence of a specific statement, that such names are exempt from the relevant
protective laws and regulations and therefore free for general use.
The publisher, the authors, and the editors are safe to assume that the advice and information in this book
are believed to be true and accurate at the date of publication. Neither the publisher nor the authors or
the editors give a warranty, expressed or implied, with respect to the material contained herein or for any
errors or omissions that may have been made. The publisher remains neutral with regard to jurisdictional
claims in published maps and institutional affiliations.

Cover illustration: Hossein Mahmoodi / Alamy Stock Photo

This Palgrave Macmillan imprint is published by the registered company Springer Nature Switzerland AG.
The registered company address is: Gewerbestrasse 11, 6330 Cham, Switzerland

Foreword

The COVID-19 pandemic has brought death and despair throughout the world. But as old systems have failed or been disrupted, the pandemic has also posed an important question: can we do things better in the future?

Education has not escaped this process of reimagination. As schools at all levels have experimented with emergency distance learning—with millions of teachers and learners engaged in online learning for the first time in their lives—many are asking how this will affect the future of education.

A cottage industry already exists to reimagine education based on the lessons of the pandemic. But very little of that work examines teacher education, a foundational element of the broader educational enterprise.

That is unfortunate, because, as is well known, teacher education is an area badly in need of reform, whether in pre-service education that is too far removed from the actual demands of the classroom or in in-service education that is often taught once and then forgotten.

Many of the problems of teacher education could be partially ameliorated through improved use of technology—by bringing people together in new ways, providing resources at the time of, and providing new tools for reflection and interaction. In this sense, the forced transition to distance learning can be seen as not only a challenge, but also an opportunity—*if* we can learn sufficient lessons from what has occurred.

Fortunately, Sadeghi and Thomas's edited volume takes us a long way in that direction. From conceptual papers, to case studies, to examination of particular sub-topics, it provides a comprehensive view of technology-mediated second language teacher education during the pandemic and what we should (and should not) learn from these experience as we move forward. A particular strength of the book is its inclusion of contributions from many countries, helping ensure that the lessons we gather are informed by a broad array of voices.

If this pandemic had occurred 20 years ago, we would not have had access to the online tools needed to help continue education during a period of forced isolation. Let us hope that, 20 years from now, we can more effectively learn together in a variety of formats and modalities, drawing on the lessons of these last few harsh years. The essays shared in this volume are an important guidepost along that path, not only in the area of second language teacher education but also beyond.

University of California
Irvine, CA, USA

Mark Warschauer

Praise for *Second Language Teacher Professional Development*

"Rarely, in our lifetimes at least, do global circumstances change so immediately and dramatically as they have during this pandemic. Sadeghi and Thomas' book captures this upheaval and innovation in second language teacher education. Their edited volume does an exemplary and geographically comprehensive job of documenting the impacts of pandemic-driven adaptation through technology on second language teacher education. Contributors from ten countries on six continents write about their experiences with 'technological innovations' that have facilitated and extended their work. The collection is as impressive for its breadth as it is timely for its discussions of what can be learned about using technological tools in ELT pre-service preparation and professional development."
—Donald Freeman, *Professor of Education, School of Education, University of Michigan, USA*

"Several books have recently appeared that reflect on the extraordinary shift that took place in second language teacher education in response to the outbreak of COVID-19. This is one of the best. Karim Sadeghi and Michael Thomas have skillfully assembled insights from educators around the world, bringing together the lessons learned while teachers navigated unusually difficult and confusing times. The many practical insights and creative solutions this volume provides will be useful to any astute reader wishing to better understand innovations that emerged during the crisis and the lasting impact that reimagining the use of educational technology may have for our ongoing pedagogy."
—Larry LaFond, *Professor, Southern Illinois University Edwardsville, USA*

"This is a comprehensive volume representing a broad range of cultures and contexts wherein teachers grappled with intelligently responding to the emergency transition to online language teaching. The collected studies provide empirically grounded insights into the talent, resilience and practices of language educators when faced with the challenge of swiftly altering instructional contexts. Research of this kind will lead to better understanding of what it takes to teach languages well online."
—Carla Meskill, *Professor, Department of Educational Theory and Practice, State University of New York*

"This volume provides a set of meticulously curated studies (with multiple conceptual and methodological approaches) on technology-mediated language teacher education from a wide variety of socio-educational contexts around the world. Contributors explore the ways they have used technology to address the unprecedented challenges posed by the COVID pandemic. I believe this collection will be a very important resource for language teacher educators and researchers who study the integration of technology in language teacher education practices."

—Bedrettin Yazan, *Associate Professor, The University of Texas at San Antonio, USA*

Contents

Part I CALL Affordances in Teacher Education   1

1 Introduction: Educational Technology in Teacher Education   3
Michael Thomas and Karim Sadeghi

2 Reimagining Education Is Dead. Long Live Reimagining Education! New Technological Innovations in Second Language Teacher Education and Professional Development   13
John I. Liontas

3 Extending Blended Learning and the Roles of Technology to Meet Teacher-Training Needs in the *New Normal*   37
Martin Mullen, Marta Giralt, and Liam Murray

4 Technology-Enhanced Language Teacher Development During the COVID-19 Pandemic: Experiences of Southeast Asian English Language Teachers   57
Joel C. Meniado

x   Contents

Part II   Reactions to CALL in Teacher Education during the Pandemic   79

5   'We've Been Able to Continue with Our Teaching':
     Technology and Pedagogy in Emergency Remote
     Language Education   81
     Anne Burns, Rebecca Matteson, Kirsty Phease, and Jennifer West

6   Corpus Linguistics in English Language Teacher
     Education During the COVID-19 Pandemic: Exploring
     Opportunities and Addressing Challenges   101
     Vander Viana

7   Digital Competence and Teaching Practices of Language
     Teachers in Sweden in a COVID-19 World   125
     *Jonathan R. White, Tao Yang, Arantxa Santos Muñoz,
     and Man Gao*

8   Assessing Instructional Design During Emergency
     Remote Education   147
     Maria-Elena Solares-Altamirano

9   Technology + Pedagogy in EFL Virtual Classrooms:
     University Teachers' Professional Needs on Technology-
     Enhanced Pedagogy   169
     Li Li

10   A Pandemic to Remember: Best Practices in an Online
     Language Acquisition Methods Course   191
     Kristen Carlson and Ramon Serrano

Contents   xi

Part III   **Emergency Integration of Technology into Tecaher Education Programmes**   207

11   **Enhancing Professional Learning of Primary Student Teachers of L1 and L2 Through a Hybrid Learning Environment**   209
Mirja Tarnanen, Merja Kauppinen, Johanna Kainulainen, Mari Hankala, and Eija Aalto

12   **CALL for Global Learning: Using *World 101* for Teacher Training in an Online TESOL Methods Course**   229
Estela Ene

13   **Learning to Collaborate Through Telecollaboration: Key Knowledge for Novice Teachers in Today's World**   249
Melinda Dooly

14   **Opportunities for Pre-Service Teacher Learning in Video-Mediated Peer Interactions: Focus on Classroom Interactional Competence**   269
Ufuk Balaman

15   **Conclusion: What Did We Learn from the COVID-19 Pandemic?**   289
Karim Sadeghi and Michael Thomas

Index   299

Notes on Contributors

Eija Aalto is Senior Lecturer in Language Education (Finnish and literature) at the Department of Teacher Education, University of Jyväskylä.

Ufuk Balaman (ubalaman@gmail.com) is Associate Professor of Applied Linguistics in the Department of English Language Teaching at Hacettepe University. His research primarily deals with conversation analysis, computer assisted language learning, and language teacher education. His recent publications appeared in *Linguistics & Education*, *TESOL Quarterly*, *ROLSI*, and *Pragmatics*.

Anne Burns (a.c.burns@curtin.edu.au) is part-time Professor of Education at Curtin University and Professor Emerita at Aston University, UK. She is also Honorary Professor at the University of New South Wales, Sydney, the University of Sydney, and The Education University, Hong Kong. She is internationally known for her work in action research.

Kristen Carlson Ed.D. (kristen.carlson@mnstate.edu) is an assistant professor in the Department of Leadership & Learning at Minnesota State University Moorhead. She researches learning design, online learning and authentic assessments. Carlson has experience teaching science grades 5–12, teacher education, educational technology, curriculum & instruction and educational leadership.

xiv   Notes on Contributors

Melinda Dooly (melindaann.dooly@uab.cat) is Serra Húnter Full Professor, Chair in Technology-Enhanced Language & Intercultural Education Department of Language, Literature and Social Science Education at the Universitat Autònoma de Barcelona. She is lead researcher of GREIP: Grup de Recerca en Ensenyament i Interacció Plurilingües (Research Centre for Teaching & Plurilingual Interaction).

Estela Ene (eene@iupui.edu; Associate Professor, Indiana University—Purdue University Indianapolis; Director of the EAP Program; Director of the TESOL MA Program) is an active researcher and practitioner in CALL, Second Language Writing, ESL/EFL teacher education and internationalization. She has published in *CALICO, System,* the *Second Language Writing Journal,* and other books and journals.

Man Gao is Assistant Professor at the Chinese Department at Dalarna University. She received her PhD in Linguistics in 2008. Her current research interests include the phonology and phonetics of Chinese, second/foreign language acquisition of Chinese, teaching Chinese as a foreign language and varieties of English.

Marta Giralt (marta.giralt@ul.ie) is Lecturer in Applied Linguistics and Spanish in the School of Modern Languages and Applied Linguistics, University of Limerick, Ireland. Her research interests are in SLA, computer-mediated communication and language learning and intercultural communication. Recent publications list: https://ulsites.ul.i/la/r-marta-giralt-0

Mari Hankala is Lecturer in Language Education (Finnish and literature) in the Department of Teacher Education at the University of Jyväskylä. Her main research interests are literacies (multiliteracies, media literacy) in digital environments.

Johanna Kainulainen is a university teacher (Finnish and literature; educational science and ICT) at the Department of Teacher Education, University of Jyväskylä.

Merja Kauppinen is Senior Lecturer in Language Education (Finnish and literature) in the Department of Teacher Education at the University of Jyväskylä. Her research focuses on reading and writing literacy, in-service teacher education and literature education from various perspectives (incl. multilingual and -cultural phenomenon) from early childhood to secondary education.

Li Li (Li.Li@exeter.ac.uk) is Professor of Language Education at the University of Exeter. Her research interests include language teacher cognition, classroom discourse, developing thinking skills and the use of new technologies in language learning. She is the author of *Social Interaction and Teacher Cognition, Language Teacher Cognition* and *New Technologies and Language Learning.*

John I. Liontas (liontas@usf.edu) is Associate Professor of ESOL/FL Education (University of South Florida), Editor-in-Chief of the award-winning encyclopedia, *The TESOL Encyclopedia of English Language Teaching* (2018), active member in (inter)national learned societies, distinguished thought leader, and multiple award-winning author, researcher, and practitioner in SLA, idiomatics and emerging digital technologies.

Rebecca Matteson has taught English in three different countries and has been a language learner herself, attending university in Spain and studying beginner Mandarin. She is currently a program coordinator and academic English teacher at UTS College in Sydney. She participated in the English Australia Action Research Program in 2020 and is a strong advocate of reflective practices of professional development. rebecca.matteson@utscollege.edu.au

Joel C. Meniado (joel.meniado@mail.utoronto.ca) is a language specialist at the SEAMEO Regional Language Centre in Singapore, where he teaches a range of courses in Applied Linguistics/TESOL. His research interests are in the areas of language and literacy education, learning design and technology, and teacher development.

Martin Mullen (lead author, martin.mullen@uws.ac.uk) is a lecturer in the School of Education and Social Sciences at the University of the West of Scotland. He has 15 years' TESOL experience in European and Asian contexts. His research interests include CALL, MALL, and specifically, learner uses of and attitudes to smartphones.

xvi   **Notes on Contributors**

Arantxa Santos Muñoz is Assistant Professor of Spanish Linguistics at Dalarna University, where she is responsible for the courses in Sociopragmatics and the Didactics of Spanish, among others. Her research interests focus on digital communication and the use of technology in teaching/learning Spanish as a second or foreign language.

Liam Murray (liam.murray@ul.ie) is Senior Lecturer in French and Language Technologies in the School of Modern Languages and Applied Linguistics, University of Limerick, Ireland. His research interests range from the exploitation of social media and blog writing for SLA to digital games-based language learning. Recent publications list: https://ulsites.ul.i/la/od/101

Kirsty Phease previously worked as Senior Teacher for Blended Learning at Navitas English Australia from July 2019–January 2022, and participated in English Australia's Action Research Program during 2020. She now works as Learning Designer for Online Education Services, Melbourne. kphease@gmail.com

Karim Sadeghi is Professor of TESOL at Urmia University, Iran, and is the founding editor chief of *Iranian Journal of Language Teaching Research*, a Scopus Q1 journal. His recent publications have appeared in *Frontiers in Psychology, Current Psychology, System, ESP Journal, RELC Journal* and *Assessing Writing* among others. His monograph *Assessing Second Language Reading* was published by Springer in 2021.

Ramon Serrano PhD (raserrano@stcloudstate.edu) is currently Department Chairperson of Teacher Development at St. Cloud State University. He teaches elementary education methods courses along with ESL methods. His current interests are investigating school violence, reasons why youth join gangs, the need for mental health training and law enforcement, and using Aikido techniques to control violent situations.

Maria-Elena Solares-Altamirano (solares@unam.mx) works for the Department of Applied Linguistics at Escuela Nacional de Lenguas, Lingüística y Traducción, Universidad Nacional Autónoma de México ENALLT, UNAM. She holds a PhD in Applied Linguistics from

Lancaster University and a master's degree in TESOL from University College London, Institute of Education.

Mirja Tarnanen (mirja.tarnanen@jyu.fi) is Professor of Language Education (Finnish and literature) in the Department of Teacher Education at the University of Jyväskylä. Her recent publications deal with (multi)literacy and assessment practices across curriculum; policies and practices in education for migrant students; teachers' professional development and curriculum reforms in educational communities.

Michael Thomas (M.Thomas@ljmu.ac.uk) is Professor of Education and Social Justice and Chair of the Centre for Educational Research (CERES) at Liverpool John Moores University in the UK and Principal Fellow of the Higher Education Academy. He holds PhDs from Newcastle University and Lancaster University respectively and has taught and conducted research at universities in Germany, Japan, England and Wales over a 25-year period. He is author or editor of over 30 books and peer-reviewed special editions on computer-assisted language learning, digital natives, project-based pedagogy, online education and pedagogical theory. He is founding editor of four book series, including *Digital Education and Learning*, *Advances in Digital Language Learning and Teaching* and *Global Policy and Critical Futures in Education*.

Vander Viana (vander.viana@ed.ac.uk) is Senior Lecturer in Language Education at the University of Edinburgh (UK). His research expertise includes corpus linguistics, TESOL, English for academic purposes and language teacher education.

Jennifer West's most recent experience is as the Subject Coordinator and English teacher in the Foundation Program at UTS College in Sydney. She participated in the English Australia Action Research Program in 2020 and champions quality teaching through best pedagogical practice to ensure positive student outcomes by supporting teachers' professional development. mckee27henricks@gmail.com

Jonathan R. White (jwh@du.se) is Associate Professor of English Linguistics at the English Department at Dalarna University, Sweden. His research interests lie in the effect of Internet language usage on the

English language, including how language is reduced, and how attitudes to grammar norms are changing.

Tao Yang is Assistant Professor of Business Studies and Chinese at the Chinese Department at Dalarna University. Her research interests, among others, lie in Chinese business culture, doing business in the Chinese market, and teaching and learning Chinese as a foreign language.

List of Figures

Fig. 2.1	Digital Storytelling with a Twist (DS+): a rhetorical model of communication	27
Fig. 5.1	Responses to the statement 'I feel that I am receiving the support I need to effectively teach online'	90
Fig. 6.1	CL module configuration	106
Fig. 6.2	Distribution of *pandemic* in NOW across years generated in a smartphone	111
Fig. 6.3	Adjective+*pandemic* sequences in 2020 texts in NOW investigated in a smartphone	112
Fig. 6.4	On-site computer lab	116
Fig. 6.5	Individual chat management in the institution's VLE	118
Fig. 6.6	Concordance lines for *a better future* in the Coronavirus Corpus	121
Fig. 9.1	Teachers' needs during the COVID-19 pandemic. SAGE Open. doi:10.1177/21582440211054491	175
Fig. 11.1	Phases of the hybrid learning environment for L1 and L2 and multiliteracy learning	216

List of Fragments

Fragment 13.1	It's recording now	253
Fragment 13.2	Let's start talking about the collaborative projects …	255
Fragment 13.3	The opportunity to know other cultures	257
Fragment 13.4	Our main goal is to learn	259
Fragment 13.5	We can all be the leader	261
Fragment 13.6	Maybe we can look at …	262
Fragment 13.7	Perfect	263
Fragment 13.8	We were attempting to do too much	264

List of Tables

Table 2.1	Questions Posed since 23 March 2020	17
Table 4.1	Online language teacher development activities engaged in by the respondents during the COVID-19 pandemic	68
Table 5.1	Frequency of themes in our qualitative data	89
Table 6.1	Live online demonstration versus recorded video tutorial	115
Table 7.1	Top three digital tools per language group	134
Table 7.2	Informants' understanding of digital competence	135
Table 8.1	Identified components under epistemic, setting, and social designs	157
Table 9.1	Demographic information	173

Part I

CALL Affordances in Teacher Education

1

Introduction: Educational Technology in Teacher Education

Michael Thomas and Karim Sadeghi

1.1 Introduction

As we are preparing this edited volume in early 2022, COVID-19 has affected over 400 million people and claimed more than 5 million lives worldwide. The pandemic has drastically affected everybody's life, including those of teachers, researchers and students everywhere, in unprecedented ways. The pandemic has refocused global attention on existing social and economic divides and underlined how they manifest themselves in educational inequalities. While too much emphasis is often placed on education to solve these underlying social, economic and health inequalities, education can play a role in widening access to lifelong learning, encouraging more equity of opportunity for learners and teachers and promoting greater social justice in multilingual societies (Kessler,

---

M. Thomas
Liverpool John Moores University, Liverpool, UK

K. Sadeghi (✉)
Urmia University, Urmia, Iran
e-mail: k.sadeghi@urmia.ac.ir

© The Author(s), under exclusive license to Springer Nature Switzerland AG 2023
K. Sadeghi, M. Thomas (eds.), *Second Language Teacher Professional Development,*
Digital Education and Learning, https://doi.org/10.1007/978-3-031-12070-1_1

2021). One such area where digital technologies can play a potential role is in assisting the quality enhancement of pre- and in-service teacher training and continuing professional development, from the use of more flexible forms of online and blended instruction and delivery to massive open online courses (MOOCs) and micro-credentials that challenge selective education policies (Thomas & Schneider, 2020).

The current crisis has directly impacted the way second language teacher educators train language teachers and run professional development programmes involving digital technologies, whether in private language schools or state universities. While many such face-to-face programmes stopped running altogether in technologically deprived or "low-tech contexts" or at the very least, were seriously affected, the role of digital technology has once again come to the fore in helping second language teacher education survive and adapt in challenging times (Karatay & Hegelheimer, 2021). Although technology has long had a place in language education and teacher training (Arnold et al., 2007), the current experience has proved the vital role of digital technology (in its various forms including the Internet, CALL (Computer-Assisted Language Learning), MALL (Mobile Assisted Language Learning), TALL (Technology Assisted Language Learning), TELL (Technology Enhanced Language Learning), social media, to name but a few) in the success of the second language teacher education enterprise. Obviously, interrupted forms of teacher education will impact the subsequent teaching and learning of languages and the facilitation of the learning process for learners, which is the ultimate aim of language teacher education and professional development. Were it not for the vital role of digital technology, L2 teacher education and professional development programmes would have come to a full stop in most parts of the world.

In response to this challenging context, this edited volume containing 15 contributions from researchers in 10 countries brings together documented evidence as well as relevant theoretical work that will help us to understand the essential mediating role of digital technology in L2 teacher education and professional development. The book is international in scope and focus and some of the topics covered include the technological affordances in teacher education; perspectives on CALL in teacher education programmes; response to the abrupt transition from

1 Introduction: Educational Technology in Teacher Education 5

face-to-face to virtual professional development; and the successful practices of online teacher training courses. By bringing together examples from various countries and contexts relating to how L2 teacher trainers and trainee teachers view these forced changes and have been reacting to them, as well as how these programmes are being successfully administered and managed without prior preparation, the volume fills a gap in the use of digital technology in contexts where teacher educators and/or trainee teachers are not technology-literate or prepared for technology-oriented education. Responses to and challenges related to the forced and emergent use of digital technology are therefore the main topics of the volume, and to date no other books to our knowledge have examined the use of advanced technologies in language teaching/language teacher education to this extent.

Some existing research has nevertheless helped to map the landscape of this area pre-pandemic. Indeed, there have been numerous studies of technologies over the last two decades on technologies and practices that are still highly relevant today, and these have led to calls for the professionalisation of CALL teacher technology standards (Hubbard, 2021; TESOL, 2008). Research studies have addressed many apposite areas, including using virtual communities of practice in teacher education (Arnold et al., 2007); integrating electronic portfolios (Cummins, 2007); understanding the importance of situated learning (Egbert, 2006) and establishing communities of practice for teacher educators (Hanson-Smith, 2006). Other studies have carried out extensive reviews of CALL teacher training (Kessler, 2006; Hubbard & Levy, 2006) and explored instructors' attitudes and perceptions of CALL technologies (Wiebe & Kabata, 2010). Equally there have been no shortage of studies exploring how prospective teachers can integrate technology and the challenges they face (Hong, 2010; Shaltry et al., 2013). Previous research has also addressed how teachers can work together to engage in collaborate exchange about technology integration supported by mentoring (Schmid & Hegelheimer, 2014). Likewise, while blended learning has been promoted during the pandemic as a "new" development, previous research has already outlined well-established strategies for this approach (Dudeney & Hockly, 2016; Mononey & O'Keeffe, 2016) and the role of teacher agency in the process in particular (Kitade, 2015).

More recently several studies have explored CALL teacher education with in-depth research that integrates theory and practice. Primary among these studies is Torsani (2016) whose work on CALL teacher education and language teacher and technology integration offers a comprehensive overview of the field, and explores among others the following topics: the relationship between technology and language learning; the integration of technology into language education; theoretical foundations of CALL teacher training; frameworks and standards for CALL education; approaches and processes; CALL training procedures; and curriculum design. While there is significant concentration on both the teaching and learning of languages, as well as on training language teachers, there is a need for more engagement with the implications of training language teachers during a period of disruption rather than during pre-pandemic times. Likewise Pasternak's (2020) study concentrates on strategies for integrating technology in English language arts teacher education in the United States, drawing on findings from extensive longitudinal studies. There are however several limitations to the research in that it does not address the specific needs and practices of ESL/EFL teacher trainers but those teaching English as their L1. Methodological limitations are also evident in that only teacher trainees are surveyed and the views of teacher educators themselves remain under-researched. As was the case for Torsani (2016), while the findings are valuable, they are limited in terms of applicability to help understand the implications during a period of emergency remote teaching. Cutrim-Schmid's (2019) research on teacher education in Germany viewed through the lens of sociocultural theory also elaborates on some of the existing concerns and through deft analysis of longitudinal data begins to piece together a future road map for CALL teacher education. The book adopts a sociocultural approach, based on the principle that teaching (and learning how to teach) is a long-term, complex developmental process that operates through participation in social practices that come with the territory. Cutrim-Schmid highlights the need for situated and localised learning, pre-service and in-service collaboration and collaborative peer-assisted learning. Above all Cutrim-Schmid recommends and proves the efficacy of socially aware and professional reflective practice. This is an essential sociolinguistic take on the computer learning revolution. The book

1 Introduction: Educational Technology in Teacher Education 7

however does not offer technological affordances, options and issues for teacher education at a time of emergency and adopts a more theoretical rather than practitioner-focused position.

In responding to some of the key research studies identified above on teacher education, the vast majority of which are pre-pandemic and therefore disconnected from the scope and depth of disruption encountered by teachers and teacher trainers during COVID, this volume is divided into three parts.

1.2 An Overview of the Book

Following the Introduction to the book, Part I, contains 3 additional chapters and is devoted to defining the scope of the volume as a whole. To accomplish this, the first section identifies the major affordances of digital technology in language teacher education, systematically reviewing a sample of recent research from a variety of contexts including Asian and European perspectives on CALL use, before considering the challenges and the post-pandemic futures of the use of technology in language teacher education. Following this introduction to the volume, in Chap. 2, John I. Liontas explores how to foster sustainable second language teacher education practices in the midst of claims that COVID-19 has successfully led to a process of "reimaging education." Rejecting the notion that emergency remote teaching has fundamentally altered our notions of teaching and learning, Liontas maps out what teacher educators can take away from this experience and how they can produce a more lasting and pragmatic turn in teacher education practices.

Arising from the turn to blended learning during the pandemic in the Republic of Ireland, Chap. 3 by Mullen, Murray and Giralt explores the implications of the transition to online methods of delivery for CALL teacher education theories, processes and practices as well as relevant dedicated and non-dedicated CALL software. Based on a mixed methods approach involving the perceptions of teacher trainers, in-service language teachers, and trainee teachers regarding their state of preparedness for a shift to online learning, findings suggest that changes are required to how teachers are prepared to use digital pedagogies. One solution is the need to incorporate blended learning as an integral element in all future courses to preserve opportunities for on-going professional development.

The focus turns to Asia in Chap. 4, by Meniado which considers how the lack of adequate skills and resources has affected the transition to the "new normal" of online learning. Given this context the paper discusses how teachers developed their own initiatives to develop new approaches to teaching and assessment and how institutional support emerged to aid them in this task to make the new practices sustainable.

Part II, includes six chapters and provides a series of powerful examples and case studies from contexts such as Australia, Mexico, the UK, the United States and Sweden, in which teacher educators/trainee teachers' reactions, responses and attitudes to the sudden shift to virtual teacher education programmes are investigated. The chapters progressively concentrate on a wide range of topics apposite to current debates, including teacher identity and resilience.

Chapter 5, considers the impacts of the pandemic on teacher education in Australia. Burns, Matteson, Phease, and West discuss the impact in particular on language centres and how they adopted strategies in professional development focusing on blended learning arising from an action research project with the English Language Intensive Courses for Overseas Students (ELICOS) organisation.

In Chap. 6, Viana examines an underexplored area in English language teacher education, namely, corpus linguistics. The module aims to provide teachers with a framework for raising awareness of their metalinguistic awareness. The chapter presents a reflective evaluation describing trainee teachers' transition from their traditional approach to that required for the pandemic.

In Sweden, the digital competence and literacy skills of teachers have been prominent since 2006 in particular, following the European Commission's inclusion of these areas in its policy documents on lifelong learning. In Chap. 7, White, Muñoz, Gao and Yang focus especially on the four key elements of digital literacy integrated into the curriculum for compulsory school. These include the implications of digitalisation on wider Swedish society; promoting the use and understanding of specialised digital tools and media; developing criticality and independence of thought; and enhancing problem-solving skills as well as being able to

1 Introduction: Educational Technology in Teacher Education 9

apply what has been learned in practical ways. The research identifies a series of complex challenges related to informal and formal learning, as well as competencies used in teachers' personal and professional lives. In particular the essay explores attitudes and knowledge within the field of digital competence of university level teacher trainees who are training to teach English, Spanish and Chinese. Findings explore differences across the different nationalities and suggest that prominent technologies used by the trainee teachers include instant messaging, blogs, audio-visual resources and websites.

Chapter 8, by Solares-Altamirano explores the implications of the pandemic on teachers in the English Department at the Universidad Nacional Autónoma de México in Mexico. Noting the challenges such as the need for flexible learning design and improved technical competence, the chapter examines the development of a specialised web site offering teachers training and advice on the use of collaborative task-based language teaching during the period of emergency remote teaching.

In Chap. 9, Li explores questionnaire data from teachers involved in a mixed methods study examining their professional learning needs during the pandemic. Over 100 teachers answered a questionnaire and 12 teachers were interviewed to provide data on their understanding of how to teach effectively in online environments. Recommendations from the research explore the types of professional support provided to the participants and the types of support they envisage that they require in order to manage their work during the periods of disruption caused by the pandemic and have clear implications for teachers in pre- and in-service teacher development contexts.

In Chap. 10, Carlson and Serrano share their reflections from teachers at St. Cloud State University in the United States who transitioned to online teaching during the pandemic. Findings from the study suggest that it is essential for teacher educators to combine resilience and cultural competence to support their trainee teachers effectively, alongside a personalised and flexible approach that does not seek to impose one approach on all trainee teachers.

Finally, Part III, brings the volume to a close with the remaining five chapters. It includes a wide range of contributions dealing with important topics such as the successive integration of digital technologies in teacher education and professional development programmes in contexts like Turkey, Spain, Finland and the United States. Instances of various technological tools used during experimental forms of online learning are shared and recommendations are provided on how similar technologies can be used in technologically less-affluent contexts during a time of emergency (UNESCO, 2008a, 2008b).

Chapter 11, by Tarnanen, Aalto, Kauppinen and Hankala discusses how to support the professional development and learning (PDL) of primary teacher students in relation to digital literacies. Focusing in particular on reading, writing and interpreting skills, the chapter examines the role of digital assessments and different approaches to blended learning within the context of lifelong learning via an action research approach.

Chapter 12, by Ene explores a multi-module online material published by the Council of Foreign Relations aimed at training as well as teaching English as a Second Language (ESL). Students on an online TESOL methods course participated in the research to examine an online teaching environment during COVID involving trainees engaged in selecting relevant materials and resources.

The subject of Chap. 13 by Dooly is a network-based exchange between two groups of student-teachers based in Catalunya in Spain and another in Illinois in the United States. As part of an on-going process resulting in two main outputs related to integrating technology into teaching, the chapter explores how the student-teachers mediate their pedagogical interaction in terms of their identity as both current students and future teachers.

In Chap. 14, Balaman discusses findings from a language teacher education project on video-mediated interactional practices of pre-service teachers. Using a multimodal conversation analysis approach, the study examines teacher interactional practices and digital competence and findings will be particularly valuable for trainers and teachers involved in pre-service professional development utilising online and digital pedagogies.

Finally, in Chap. 15, the book's editors, Sadeghi and Thomas, present a conclusion to the volume which reflects on the lessons learned from the pandemic for second language teacher education, and identifies strategies that can be carried forward to make these practices sustainable.

References

Arnold, N., Ducate, L., & Lomicka, L. (2007). Virtual communities of practice in teacher education. In M. Kassen, R. Lavine, K. Murphy-Judy, & M. Peters (Eds.), *Preparing and developing technology-proficient L2 teachers* (pp. 103–132). CALICO.

Cummins, P. (2007). LinguaFolio and electronic portfolios in teacher training. In M. Kassen, R. Lavine, K. Murphy-Judy, & M. Peters (Eds.), *Preparing and developing technology-proficient L2 teachers* (pp. 321–344). CALICO.

Cutrim-Schmid, E. (2019). *Teacher education in computer-assisted language learning: A sociocultural and linguistic Perspective.* Bloomsbury.

Dudeney, G., & Hockly, N. (2016). Blended learning in a mobile context: New tools, new learning experiences? In M. McCarthy (Ed.), *Blended learning for language teaching* (pp. 219–233). Cambridge University Press.

Egbert, J. (2006). Learning in context: Situating language teacher learning in CALL. In P. Hubbard & M. Levy (Eds.), *Teacher education in CALL* (pp. 167–182). John Benjamins.

Hanson-Smith, E. (2006). Communities of practice for pre- and in-service teacher education. In P. Hubbard & M. Levy (Eds.), *Teacher education in CALL* (pp. 301–315). John Benjamins.

Hong, K. H. (2010). CALL teacher education as an impetus for L2 teachers in integrating technology. *ReCALL, 22*(1), 53–69.

Hubbard, P. (2021). Revisiting the TESOL technology standards for teachers: Integration and adaptation. *CALICO Journal, 38*(3), 319–337.

Hubbard, P., & Levy, M. (Eds.). (2006). *Teacher education in CALL.* John Benjamins.

Karatay, Y., & Hegelheimer, V. (2021). CALL teacher training – Considerations for low-resource environments: Overview of CALL teacher training. *CALICO, 38*(3), 271–295.

Kessler, G. (2006). Assessing CALL teacher training: What are we doing and what could we do better? In P. Hubbard & M. Levy (Eds.), *Teacher education in CALL* (pp. 23–42). John Benjamins.

Kessler, G. (2021). Editorial: Current realities and future challenges for CALL teacher preparation. *CALICO Journal, 38*(3), i–xx.

Kitade, K. (2015). Second language teacher development through CALL practice: The emergence of teachers' agency. *CALICO Journal, 32*, 396–425.

Mononey, D., & O'Keeffe, A. (2016). A case study in language teacher education. In M. McCarthy (Ed.), *Blended learning for language teaching* (pp. 176–199). Cambridge University Press.

Pasternak, D. L. (2020). *Integrating technology in English language arts and teacher education*. Routledge.

Schmid, E. C., & Hegelheimer, V. (2014). Collaborative research projects in the technology-enhanced language classroom: Pre-service and in-service teachers exchange knowledge about technology. *ReCALL, 26*, 315–332.

Shaltry, C., Henriksen, D., Wu, M. L., & Dickson, W. P. (2013). Teaching prospective teachers to integrate technology: Situated learning with online portfolios, classroom websites and Facebook. *TechTrends, 57*, 20–25.

TESOL. (2008). *TESOL technology standards framework*. TESOL.

Thomas, M., & Schneider, C. (2020). Language teaching with video-based technologies: Creativity and CALL teacher education. *Routledge*.

Torsani, S. (2016). *CALL teacher education: Language teachers and technology integration*. Springer.

UNESCO. (2008a). ICT competency standards for teachers: Policy framework. *UNESCO*.

UNESCO. (2008b). ICT competency standards for teachers: Competency standards modules. *UNESCO*.

Wiebe, G., & Kabata, K. (2010). Students' and instructors' attitudes toward the use of CALL in foreign language teaching and learning. *Computer Assisted Language Learning, 23*, 221–234.

2

Reimagining Education Is Dead. Long Live Reimagining Education! New Technological Innovations in Second Language Teacher Education and Professional Development

John I. Liontas

2.1 Introduction

This much is true still. The COVID-19 pandemic has caused unimaginable havoc worldwide. Every corner of the world continues to tell its sad story written in businesses closed and lives lost. Numbers need not be mentioned here. Masks, masks everywhere! The halls of education have gone silent—some more than others. Mental anguish is on the rise. Teachers and students alike—from preschools to universities—have long been ordered to stay home. Online learning replaced face-to-face instruction. Remote work is now the new normal. Some cheered, most did not. But all of us, without exception, had to come to terms with the reality of the times staring us in the face. An avalanche of questions followed. Many more questions were professed, few definitive answers given, even

---

J. I. Liontas (✉)
University of South Florida, Tampa, FL, USA
e-mail: liontas@usf.edu

© The Author(s), under exclusive license to Springer Nature Switzerland AG 2023
K. Sadeghi, M. Thomas (eds.), *Second Language Teacher Professional Development*,
Digital Education and Learning, https://doi.org/10.1007/978-3-031-12070-1_2

13

fewer solutions entertained. And so old questions became new again. Some were dusted off and recycled. Others polished on the spot. And still others reimagined without much imagination. This does not have to be so. We simply must do better.

In this chapter, purposefully titled *Reimagining Education Is Dead. Long Live Reimagining Education: New Innovations in Second Language Teacher Education and Professional Development*, I first explain why the mantra of "Reimagining Education" so shamelessly popularized in 2020 is DOA (Dead On Arrival)—plain and simple. This is a strong position from which I propose new arguments in favor of reconfiguring the framework of an existing graduate course on technology applications as an online professional development seminar. I then show how second language teacher education in general and professional development in particular can be imagined on a higher plane of understanding underlying mindfulness and consciousness—the resolute translation of imagination into apposite action—before I endow anew my world of imagination of ideas, thoughts, and conceptions with pragmatic value propositions now befitting wholly the seemingly contradictory phrase and new theatrical mantra, *Reimagining education is dead. Long live reimagining education!*— a playful allusion to another well-established traditional proclamation and chant, *Le roi est mort, vive le roi!* (French for "The King Is Dead, Long Live The King!"), first declared upon the accession to the French throne of Charles VII after the death of his father Charles VI in 1422. I begin by first contextualizing the historical continuum of the practice development that followed in the summer of 2020.

2.2 Reimagining Education Is Dead: The Aftermath of the Transition to Online Education

2.2.1 Historical Continuity Revisited

Not to repeat information covered elsewhere already (Liontas, 2022), but the account presented herein is tied to a sequence of events and causal relations underlying the transition to online learning that started when the University of South Florida first informed faculty and students during Spring Break 2020 to hold classes online henceforward. To no one's surprise, the transition to online learning continued well past the initial two weeks. For the next eight weeks, a dozen doctoral students and I engaged in critical participatory action research (CPAR). Not only were we trying to address the urgency of transitioning instruction from face-to-face to distance learning, but, importantly, we wished to become immersed in the "creation and co-creation of knowledge constructs and meaning-making processes exemplifying the essential mediating role of technology in online instruction" (Liontas, 2022, p. 137). From the outset, such knowledge constructs were singled out as the most desired learning outcome of the entire research enterprise. Applying an informal, qualitative, interpretive, and reflective research design and methodology (Burns, 2010; Niemi, 2019), the CPAR undertaken over the second half of the spring semester 2020 was anchored in the five quality principles of *historical continuity, reflexivity, dialectics, workability,* and *evocativeness* (Heikkinen et al., 2012) through which the theory, practice, and transformation of the relationship and interaction among the people involved in the pedagogical process of building an online Community of Practice (CoP) was subsequently interpreted while employing descriptive, diagnostic, predictive, and prescriptive analytics in the thematic analysis of data collected (Liontas, 2022).

Thereafter, an analysis of the *hermeneutic circle*—the final methodology of interpretation and exegetical understanding—was applied to themes or patterns of meaning within data to elicit an in-depth understanding of meanings produced through systematic interpretation processes (e.g., Gadamer, 1975; Heidegger, 1962; Schön, 1983). Amid a hermeneutic phenomenology steeped in an iterative problem-solving process (i.e., formulation, testing, and evaluation of plan-act-observe-reflect-revise-…), interpretations reached in the formation of new knowledge recognized *user experience* as the engine of the entire CPAR design process, with *community, domain,* and *practice* comprising the three primary features these students learned to embrace ever so skillfully while developing competence with the eLearning technology practices of their community (Wenger, 1998; Wenger-Trayner & Wenger-Trayner, 2015).

The efficacy of the CPAR model heretofore laconically summarized had to be tested anew if firm answers to questions posed as early as mid-March 2020 were to be found in coursework involving technological innovations in second language teacher education and professional development. Table 2.1 presents a network of questions my doctoral students and I posed and tried to have answered since 23 March 2020—the day I first invited all course enrollees to help me explore the transition to synchronous online learning from in-person learning. At that time, said transition was presented to them as the overarching research problem that needed to be solved quickly under the guiding principles of CPAR. The questions reflect the depth and breadth of the conversations I had with these 12 students, 7 of whom also participated in the continuation of the new 11-member (hereafter research-practitioners) CPAR study reported here. The questions also include my personal introspections on these matters at that time. The most critical questions I list below in no particular order, though, I note, they are organized in distinct themes to ease the discussion of them in this chapter. Collectively, however, the questions comprise the organizational framework of inquiry undergirding the contents and the digital technologies discussed in the doctoral seminar I was now teaching online in Summer A 2020 (19 May to 25 June) as a professional development seminar.

A perusal of these queries reveals in no uncertain terms the climate under which these were first cognized. They also shed light into our state of mind that first conceived these thoughts and ideas. The questions speak to the reality on the ground and the conditions and practices under which learning takes place, the perception of success, the stability of programs, the longevity of curricula, the affective state of stress, anxiety, uncertainty, insecurity, frustration, and yes, even acute cases of *xenophobia* (fear of the unknown), and much more. How best to capture the web of ideas in the voice these doctoral students express remains a formidable challenge for sure. The section that follows next addresses one such dynamic and fluid environment that sought to imagine and reimagine the ways we teach and the ways our students learn.

2 Reimagining Education Is Dead. Long Live Reimagining…

Table 2.1 Questions Posed since 23 March 2020

Questions Concerning…

"Me, Myself, and I"
- Where in the world do I start when I do not even know where to start?
- How do I overcome that sinking feeling in quicksand? And how do I crawl out of the quicksand of depression?
- Is there light at the end of the tunnel or is the light I see just the light of an oncoming freight train?
- How do I keep moving forward when the future of learning is not yet imagined—much less reimagined—in paths I can easily follow?
- How do I navigate uncertainty, change, and the complexity of an undefined future?
- How do I empower others to succeed if I cannot even empower myself to be my best self? Is self-agency enough to create meaningful and lasting change?

Students' Mindbody
- How do I reach my students' mind during the coronavirus pandemic? Will they show the resilience needed to continue to learn and thrive under the taxing circumstances of the coronavirus pandemic?
- How do I keep motivating my students to stay the course in the face of adversity amid mutable epidemiological ailments?
- How do I safeguard my students' psychosomatic health and wellbeing?
- How do I help my students cope with post-traumatic stress and other mental health problems when there is nothing normal about our new normal or even the next normal?
- How do I aid my students exhibit credible emotional intelligence and team-building skills for the benefit of all involved in imagining education anew?

Academic Success
- What can I do to ensure students' academic success, and to what standards, benchmarks, behaviors, or desired outcomes?
- Can I inspire my students to express their personalized, mastery-based learning on their own terms without foregoing or minimizing established routines and relationships?
- Is academic success perceived academic success achieved?
- Does attitude toward academic success ensure the altitude of academic success attained?

eLearning Technologies

(*continued*)

Table 2.1 (continued)

- Do students have access to digital technologies and the foundational tools and resources needed to successfully learn in these new virtual and/or hybrid learning environments?
- Which digital technologies or learning-management platforms and assessment tools best facilitate peer-led collaboration, discovery, understanding, planning, and action for quality teaching and learning?
- What are the best practices and conditions for technologically enhanced learning to generate interactive student engagement befitting remote and/or hybrid learning?
- Do I have the needed technical and pedagogical skills to integrate digital experiences into instruction in an efficient and effective manner?
- Can I leverage remote learning or deliver it in ways that help students learn on their own when less screen time, not more, is recommended?

Programs and Curricula

- How can doctoral programs ensure inclusive and equitable quality education in support of every student when reimagining education?
- To what extent will existing curricula, instructional materials, and delivery modes of teaching methods need to be rethought and reframed in research-based structures and practices, respectively, to meet the new demands of learning contexts for a more promising post-pandemic future?
- To what degree must teacher-training programs and professional-development seminars both reflect and embody the new coronavirus realities under which all of us are asked to work and grow as experts in our respective language enterprises or as leaders in our chosen profession?
- Which research frameworks best spearhead new innovations in second language teacher education and professional development?

2.2.2 Reconfiguring Course Structure and Digital Pursuits

As the section heading denotes, both course structure and digital pursuits applied in the six-week course—*FLE 7700: Applications of Technology to SLA and FL Education*—I was scheduled to teach in Summer 2020 had to be rethought given the institutional directive to transition all instruction from face-to-face to distance learning eight weeks earlier. Reconfiguring the framework of the now online course as a professional development seminar added considerable weight to the decisions I had to make time and again. One question in particular kept dancing in my head: Is it possible to reconfigure the framework of a core course offered in the Technology in Education and Second Language Acquisition doctoral program as a professional development seminar without sacrificing quality learning and/or attainment of high standards? How this question is answered would no doubt overshadow the two-dozen questions presented earlier in Table 2.1. Even so, the question had to be asked anew, and answers to questions posed since the onset of the directive to transition from in-person learning to online learning in mid-March 2020 had to found post haste. I begin with the reconceptualizations of the principal imaginations requiring explanation still.

Reconceptualizing Principal Imaginations

As already noted, the arrival of COVID-19 upended every aspect of an educator's life. Having to adapt suddenly to online remote instruction post Spring Break 2020, we had no choice but to ponder, question, and reassess the various facets of our work—from course redesign, pedagogical practices, and assessment tools supporting successful student learning to sustainable support structures and modes of communication ensuring effective instruction. Learning how to manage our own expectations and how best to leverage technology to promote deep learning was a high priority indeed. Reevaluating the affordances-constraints of digital technologies and the instructional practices that help support a new enterprise of synchronous online instruction were pushed to the forefront of concerns we had to address head on in record time. Not only did we have to discover new ways to deliver instruction online, we also had to make sure that the technology we ultimately chose to employ did indeed support effective student learning, engagement, and collaboration. Many of us even had to come to terms with our own relationship with certain computerized technologies, tools, platforms, and resources that collectively exemplify online instruction. Our perceptions of the importance, value, and ease of using them are certain to color our attitude and willingness to see them applied in the online environments we wished to create for our learners and ourselves. Such decisions, manifold as they all surely are, are important in ascertaining how students were expected to process course content and the materials associated in learning the content.

20 J. I. Liontas

Confronted with such raw realities, syllabi had to be revised, lessons adapted, schedules and responsibilities invented anew, mentoring and professional development opportunities reconfigured and scaled again, and, finally, new online spaces for interactive learning fashioned, more often than not from scratch. For better or worse, we had to ask ourselves the hard questions at a time when answers were not so readily available. In fact, we had to deep dive in a short space of time on our own philosophical assumptions (the act of taking something for granted or supposing something, even without proof) and/or presumptions (a belief on reasonable grounds or probable evidence) certain to shape most, if not all, of the decisions we would make throughout the entire research design process and data analysis. In so doing, we also had to take account of our own personal experiences while interacting with other research-practitioners of the practice; that is, *reflexivity* demanded of us that we develop a self-critical approach to how knowledge about specific practices—from transitioning from one state or condition of learning to another—is generated, and, furthermore, how relations of power operate in the analysis of data collected, including those involving assumptions/presumptions, behaviors, and emotions. And because transition is a dynamic process, not a series of discrete events, planning is key to the level of success achieved via different technology means and timeframes. In the end, neither quality learning nor attainment of high standards need be sacrificed when transitioning from in-person learning to online learning—a finding deeply engrained in the de facto transformative change my doctoral students and I experienced first hand. Building upon those key insights, the CPAR research design and methodology involving an iterative problem-solving process had to be tailor-made to suit the specifics of the course structure and the digital pursuits envisaged herein, the most important of which are highlighted next.

Reimagining Course Structure and Digital Pursuits

As specified in the course syllabus, *FLE 7700: Applications of Technology to SLA and FL Education* (13 sections, 14 pages), under *Section 3— Course Goals and Objectives*, the overarching goal was for course enrollees to learn "how to implement digital technology in the FL/SL classroom and apply said knowledge to guide and evaluate both instruction and assessment." Reconfigured as a professional development seminar, the emphasis now was primarily on "practical applications and the development of sound technology skills, with attention to pedagogical justification for choices drawn from applied research" (p. 2). In keeping with best practices in professional development seminars, the 11 research-practitioners (3 national and 8 international students from Cuba, Egypt, Indonesia, Saudi Arabia, and Spain) completing *FLE 7700* were expected to (1) demonstrate knowledge of, and ability in, critically analyzing Second Language Acquisition (SLA) research and Computer Assisted Language Learning (CALL)/Multimedia Assisted Language Learning (MALL) theory and practices in FL/ESOL education across time and space; (2) exhibit operational familiarity with a wide variety of computer software, hardware, and applications in a FL/SL classroom; (3) utilize best practices of digital technology to acquire information that helps accelerate communication and language acquisition in a FL/SL classroom; and (4) exploit digital technology to connect with other disciplines to experience multilingual communities at home and around the world. They all had experience teaching second/foreign languages and displayed varied knowledge of and experience in using educational technology. And nearly half of them were concurrently working as instructors in either TESOL methods or EAP classes. Moreover, the syllabus also provided key information on all emerging educational technology (EdTech) tools and devices gaining much attention in the mass media (e.g., Linear and Non-Linear Multimedia, AI-Artificial Intelligence, AR-Augmented Reality, VR-Virtual Reality, MR-Mixed/Merged Reality, Wearable Devices, Gesture/Haptic Technologies and Display Systems, AR Authoring Tools/SDKs, VR Development Software, VR Content Management Systems, VR Game Engine Software). Class participants were free to choose the tool(s), app(s), or platform(s) they deemed most crucial in their review of immersive multimedia technologies. (A comprehensive account of such EdTech tools, software, and platforms for teachers and students is found in Liontas, 2021b, Table 2, pp. 18–22.) Specific guidelines stipulating the parameters of the critical analysis accompanied this individual assignment, as well as the digital storytelling project *Digital Stories with a Twist* (DS+)—the main group project that would determine the professional growth doctoral students experience over a six-week time period.

In preparation for the first professional development meeting online, the one male and ten female students participating in the professional development seminar hitherto discussed were provided with an introductory handout titled "FLE 7700: A Pedagogical Rationale." Made available online before the first synchronous meeting, the three-page handout was organized in four sections—*Course Devices and Purposes, Course Syllabus, Online Posts, Digital Stories with a Twist* (DS+). Each section informed research-practitioners how learning of course concepts, objectives, and content would be monitored over the next six weeks, and the three main course devices (syllabus, online posts, and DS+) the instructor would employ to assess and evaluate their progress. The importance of these sections was thoroughly explained and the rationale for their inclusion in this professional development seminar explicated, with examples given where required. Several discovery exercises denoting major educational technology acronyms and nomenclature commonly employed in the research literature to date soon followed. Thereafter, the primary theory-to-practice digital construct in this technology-based course first introduced in Summer 2018, DS+, was again described in relatively more detail, and research-practitioners were informed of the project's ultimate outcome: Pending results of data examined and analyzed hermeneutically, record an eight–ten-minute maximum tech-infused digital video story on the impact CALL/MALL technologies can have on SL/FL teaching and learning. The impact of said technologies is to be described in a narrative storytelling style and may employ a tightly curated range of print/digital materials, including audio/video recordings, graphics, photographs, texts, and/or pictures. Serving as a targeted academic commercial, DS+ is to be used with clear intent in teacher professional development events. (For a detailed analysis and discussion of the sets of data collected in Summer 2018, see Mannion & Liontas, 2022.)

Ethos, Pathos, Logos: The Rhetorical Triangle, The Ingredients of Persuasion

Additionally, the 11 research-practitioners were provided with a six-page handout titled "Ethos, Pathos, Logos: The Rhetorical Triangle, The Ingredients of Persuasion." Divided into four distinct sections of information presentation, the handout provided all necessary background information these research-practitioners would need to understand the finer nuances of the method of persuasion and the constructs comprising the three rhetorical appeals—ethical, emotional, logical—speakers and writers have been using since antiquity to convince their audience.

Beginning with *Prolegomena*—a brief introductory section on Plato (a famous Greek philosopher and teacher of Aristotle) and Aristotle's work (a famous Greek philosopher who studied the art of persuasion and who taught Alexander the Great how to properly argue and perform a public speech) and the Methods of Persuasion (the Rhetorical Appeals)—research-practitioners were then instructed on the importance of *Understanding Ethos, Pathos and Logos*, the handout's second section. Here they were provided with copious information and examples of what each rhetorical device means (*ethos*, ἦθος: credibility, disposition, or character of author(s); *pathos*, πάθος: emotion or passion; *logos*, λόγος: argument or discourse, the use of logic to persuade the audience) and entails (appeal, content, techniques, practices, key questions). They were also reminded of the explicit use of *syllogism* (a deductive three-part logic containing two premises and one valid conclusion) and *enthymeme* (a truncated or rhetoric syllogism, an argumentative statement in which one of the major or minor premises is omitted or implied)—two common features in effectual commercials.

The *ART of Persuasion* section followed. Here, Aristotle's Rhetorical Triangle, or the A(ristotle's) R(hetorical) T(riangle) of Persuasion, was explored in more detail. A central argument made repeatedly was that each speech/DS+ project should have a balance of *ethos* (the identity of the speaker/writer as reflected in the speech/writing can be trusted), *pathos* (audience is able to make a connection to speaker/writer and the message communicated), and *logos* (message makes sense). Achieving balance between speaker/writer, audience, and context (rhetorical situation) was highlighted as the key to success. Research-practitioners were informed that Aristotle's Rhetorical Triangle (typically represented by an equilateral triangle denoting the balance ethos, pathos, and logos have within a text) is driven by Purpose (persuade, argue, inform) among Subject/Topic, Reader/Audience, and Speaker/Writer. All additional explanations offered centered on clarifying how (1) the *speaker* is no longer just the speaker but also the writer and rhetor who publicly displays ethos and persona; (2) the *subject* is no longer just a subject but also the message and content the speaker-writer-rhetor wishes to communicate to the audience by using logos, thesis, reason, and invention; (3) the *audience* is no longer just an audience but also the reader/listener who invests in the speaker-writer-rhetor's appeal and pathos; (4) the *context* is no longer just the rhetorical situation in which the speaker-writer-rhetor delivers the speech but also the situation and exigency (condition of urgency) in which the *Kairo*s (Ancient Greek: καιρός, timeliness of an argument) and *Decorum* (dignified propriety) are given full account; and (5) the *purpose* among Subject/Topic, Reader/Audience, and Speaker/Writer is no longer just a purpose expressed but also the unfolding of the speaker-writer-rhetor's ultimate intention and aim that solidifies the rhetorical triangle of *speaker-writer-rhetor, subject-message-content,* and *audience-reader-listener* within a specific *context-situation-exigence.*

Twenty questions addressing said rhetorical triangle followed. The importance of paying particular attention to appeals to *Ethos, Pathos,* and *Logos*—Aristotle's Pillars of Persuasion— was again highlighted in the dialogic interactions that followed, the weekly learning management system (LMS) discussion forums included (Lee, 2016). How to achieve balance among all three rhetorical means was a common thread to these synchronous online discussions. Even when meeting in the breakout rooms the advanced LMS interface functionality of the cloud-based education technology platform *Canvas* provided, research-practitioners were again instructed to reflect deeply upon the *Purpose* of the DS+ projects they were contemplating in creating in their respective groups. Purpose, both real and imagined, was certain to define, and in many respects even circumscribe, the *Tone* (attitude) and *Rhetorical Mode* (style, narrative

2 Reimagining Education Is Dead. Long Live Reimagining...   25

structure) an orator has toward a subject or an audience, and the *Rhetorical Devices* (oratorical strategies are evident) used markedly throughout to create beyond the stated message meaning and emotional intensity. They were further counseled on the enduring effects their "commercials" (aka infomercials) would most likely have on the audiences targeted (i.e., fellow practitioners participating in teacher professional development events over the summer). They were cautioned not to underestimate the significance of their projects' *Purposes*, as said purposes would also showcase their underlying *Assertion(s)* (i.e., the author/writer/speaker's *what* and *why*) and (un)conscious *Bias(es)* (i.e., the perspective an author uses to interpret a story or message for their readers/listeners), both of which should be, to the extent possible, openly harnessed, suppressed, or both. Lastly, they were reminded that in so doing, their art of persuasion would be perfectly balanced and, perhaps, more importantly, their *Ethos, Pathos*, and *Logos*—the triad timeless laws of rhetorical appeals—would positively attain a higher degree of mindfulness/consciousness.

And, finally, the *DS+ Project*, the handout's fourth section, informed these 11 research-practitioners of its purpose as the primary digital pedagogical tool appraising their ability to manipulate the three levels of argumentation (ethos, pathos, logos) to achieve mastery over the *ART of Persuasion*. With the title sequence of the original *Star Trek* science fiction television series (1966–1969) that described the mission of the starship *Enterprise* serving as musical accompaniment in the background, research-practitioners were then prompted to think of their DS+ professional development argument as the starship *Enterprise*—metaphorically that is: *Space: the final frontier. These are the voyages of the starship Enterprise. Its five-year mission: to explore strange new worlds. To seek out new life and new civilizations. To boldly go where no man has gone before!* (To hear the complete introductory speech, spoken by William Shatner as Captain James T. Kirk at the beginning of each episode, visit https://www.youtube.com/watch?v=hdjL8WXjlGI.) Research-practitioners were thus free to determine who among the team members would take on the role of Leonard "Bones" McCoy (*Ethos*: speaker's authority, ethics, expertise, image, intelligence, morals, reliability, reputation, trust/trustworthiness), James T. Kirk (*Pathos*: emotional effect of speaker's words and appeal to beliefs, emotions, feelings, imagination, intellect, motivation, passion, prejudice, sympathy, values), and S'chn-T' Gaii Spock (*Logos*: logical argumentation arrangement, clarity, data, details, evidence, explanations, facts, logic, proof, rationality, reality/reason/reasoning, universal truths, value proposition).

Irrespective of group configurations or *Enterprise* roles assumed, research-practitioners were assured that through their "voice," they would be able to assert their collective agency while also enacting their individual linguistic and sociocultural identities in diverse professional development settings requiring field-based reconceptualizations of pedagogical progress known to transform those learning-oriented practices deemed relevant in English teacher education (Block, 2015; Kanno & Stuart, 2011). And through investment and commitment to ongoing agentive actions taken during discoursal interactions impacting their English teacher education and professional development (Gu & Benson, 2015; Ilieva, 2010; Norton, 2017), akin to the voyages of the starship *Enterprise*, they too would be able to motivate and empower others to seek out new theory-practice constructs and new dialogic spaces in which to explore new digital stories worth reciting again and again. (For a detailed account of discursive spaces reimagined, see Liontas, 2021a, pp. 19–22.) *Taking action for a better tomorrow today*, I asserted in my own strong voice, is the personification of *Telos*, the rhetorical appeal to *Purpose*. Alongside *Ethos* (appeal to credibility), *Pathos* (appeal to emotion), and *Logos* (appeal to logic), *Telos* is the beginning of the end (The Alpha), and *Kairos*, the critical appeal to timeliness (the right place and the right time), is the end of the beginning (The Omega). In what follows next, I discuss additional insights the CPAR model (Fig. 2.1) revealed through purposeful use of "The Dialogic Circles of Digital Pedagogy," the core pentad organizational scaffold I systematically embedded in the course structure in pursuit of dynamic constructs that permeate and mold old and new theories, practices, conceptions, values, and beliefs of identity formation and negotiation in CoP. (For a complete report, see Liontas, 2021a, pp. 22–25.)

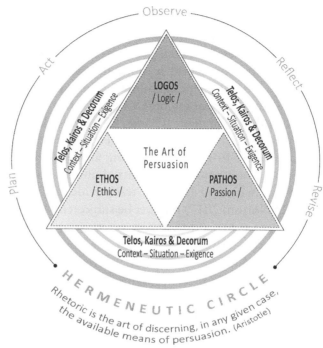

Fig. 2.1 Digital Storytelling with a Twist (DS+): a rhetorical model of communication

2.3 Long Live Reimagining Education! Discoveries Made and Future Directions

From investigating EdTech tools and devices through contemplating the affordances and constraints of digital technologies to creating digital stories worth sharing (Liontas, 2020; Mannion, 2020), such engaging research experiences no doubt will challenge old assumptions and/or interpretations of accepted technological innovations in second language teacher education and professional development. These assumptions, interpretations, or both, are certain to lead to novel reconceptualizations of what it means to attain ever higher levels of what I here now call *mindfulness through consciousness and consciousness through mindfulness.* I characterize said mindfulness-consciousness construct as a fluid core construct that permeates and molds old and new theories, practices, conceptions, values, and beliefs of digital pursuits in CoP, even those created in face-to-face, online, or hybrid learning-to-teach environments, across time and space. Through repeated observations and hypotheses testing in discursive spaces questioning objective-subjective constructs of identity formation and development (Clarke, 2008), the deliberate combination of theory, practice, and experience is likely to permeate every level of macro-micro analysis. In turn, such rolling analyses will result in an intricate blueprint of how common pursuits of understanding the provisional and embryonic nature of language teacher identity (Barkhuizen, 2017; De Costa & Norton, 2017) may yet be subjected to the training of *practicing theory over practice* and *theorizing practice over theory* based on the underlying identity-related notions and the confluence of their synergistic interrelationships now rendered increasingly concrete between and among these notions. Helping teacher-inquirers (aka *Enterprise* explorers) understand culturally relevant pedagogy in classrooms mediated by culture and social interaction through engagement in dialogue oriented toward specific digital skills, strategies, or processes may well epitomize the multi-dimensional character of dialogic exploration and discovery the didactic cycles of critical reflection and informed professional practice seek to attain (Liontas, 2021a).

What becomes abundantly clear from a hermeneutic phenomenology analysis of the themes first uncovered in 2018 (i.e., learning and professional development as a life-long journey; goal setting and knowledge expansion; membership in a community of professionals; roles and responsibilities of educators and other stakeholders; plans to apply new knowledge in future teaching; emotional investment and empathy; self-agency and empowerment; self-reflection and realization; see Liontas, 2021a, Table 2.1, pp. 20–22) and again in 2020 is this: recognizing and seizing upon teachable moments capable of capturing and probing previously held perceptions of digital pursuits within dialogic precepts

2 Reimagining Education Is Dead. Long Live Reimagining... 29

exhibiting critical reflection and informed professional development (see Liontas, 2021a, Table 2, pp. 23–24) is indeed a viable scientific inquiry process of unplanned opportunities. Said inquiry empowers research-practitioners to both cognize and cultivate *mindfulness* (the act of being aware/mindful prior to making thoughtful decisions) *through consciousness* (the state of being conscious or aware of the things surrounding an individual; being privy and knowing with others or oneself), and vice versa. In many ways, the act of being aware and the state of being conscious, respectively, is akin to doing a risky high-wire balancing act in the open air involving a mix of approaches and solutions while also requiring great skill and/or judgment. Carrying a balancing pole (symbolically represented here as understanding the spectrum of knowledge borne out by experience of using new technological innovations in second language teacher education and professional development explicitly, implicitly, and tacitly) at or below waist level not only increases the tightrope walker's moment of rotational inertia, more importantly, the pole also lowers the walker's center of gravity (closer to the ground). Unsurprisingly, the longer the pole, the better it is for the stability of the walker, that is, the length of the pole spreads the combined mass over the rope (the pole's weight + the walker's weight) far away from the pivot point (the walker's feet), thereby reducing significantly the walker's angular acceleration.

Tightrope walking as art personified thus combines with real physical forces to produce novel acts often impossible to realize without advanced planning, proper execution of steps to be taken, and keen understanding of the risks involved in so doing; in short, to acquire *gnosis* (γνῶσις, "knowledge") in many different ways and from many sources either through practical experience or through study, research, investigation, or observation of form of actions in order to know. Experience comes with time, exposure, and (perfect) practice. It is the thoughtful application of knowledge over prolonged periods of time that commands understanding of *knowing how to know*. And it is the combination of experience and depth of knowledge that ultimately produces wisdom, sapience, sagacity, and discernment. The quality or state of being wise (the soundness of judgment in a person), coupled with contextual knowledge of what is perceived to be true, right, or moral, and the ability to think through experiential self-knowledge and act in unbiased, ethical, and benevolent ways inviting renewed imagination, creativity, and self-reflection, is the truest expression of apperception (introspective self-consciousness) and self-transcendence benefiting the pedagogical process of building an online CoP. In the end, *you never know what you think you know until you are able and willing to teach it to someone else.*

The explorations and the many discoveries made in reimagining constructs that previously failed to achieve apposite action provide fresh new evidence in the final DS+ commercials/infomercials the research-practitioners produced. In these technology-based outputs, from new information created as input to a workshop through exhibitions and presentations advertising services and processes to final products in the form of video commercials/infomercials analyzing technological systems featuring unique features and functionality, their value propositions were reweighted and reappraised within the constraints of learning environments supporting online innovations in second language teacher education and professional development. Both individually and collectively, these outputs represent in the stories they tell dynamic constructs that discernibly highlight the efficacy of "The Dialogic Circles of Digital Pedagogy" I methodically applied in the curricular structure of the course when I first engaged in sustainable reconceptualizations of the principal imaginations befitting *FLE 7700: Applications of Technology to SLA and FL Education* as a professional development seminar eight weeks earlier (Liontas, 2020, 2021a). With ethos, pathos, and logos balancing ever so skillfully the *ART of Persuasion*, these outputs also serve as output key results (i.e., tangible products of learning applied) emerging from the inception, conception, and creation of novel paradigms believed to now emend and reform initiatives long known to have failed to produce the desired results. As deliverables, they each attest to the quality of the performance-based milestones these 11 research-practitioners achieved in the process of reaching their prime objective (as noted previously).

How best to create such "toe the line" moments during professional development seminars requiring participants to also "walk the line," infrequent as they likely are, is still open to interpretation and future investigations. Even so, with each new "imagined" or "lived" experience, patterns of interaction and collaboration with other colleagues (and learners), irrespective of the social or professional settings in which these

2 Reimagining Education Is Dead. Long Live Reimagining... 31

exchanges take place, both underscore and regulate in distinct ways how pre-service and in-service teachers (re)assert and (re)position their agency discursively, and, perhaps, more importantly, how they see themselves in relation to others and the world around them (Ellis, 2018; Varghese et al., 2016). Indeed, making sense of self (self-image) necessitates the contemplation of bias-free dialogic events that propagate greater understandings of how to, on the one hand, "theorize practice," and how to, on the other hand, "practice theory."

Irrefutably, remote learning during the height of the global pandemic, even when reimagined as a professional development seminar, has fueled questions few of us felt ready to answer with authority, including those presented in Table 2.1. The way we frame things, as it turns out, can make a big difference in everyone's mood and mental health. Engaging in dialogic interactions promoting psychosomatic health (the state of being healthy) and wellbeing (the state of living a healthy spiritual, emotional, physical, environmental, occupational, social, and intellectual lifestyle), discussing coping techniques, accessing mental health resources, partaking in virtual teletherapy appointments, and so on, has led to more productive, open conversations and broader appreciation for the fact that a healthy, happy sense of physical and mental wellbeing, even under the most strenuous situations, can keep one's soul fulfilled and content as long as the interaction of psychological, social, and biological factors are addressed head on, the combination of which no doubt spearheads informed and responsible decisions.

These decisions, in turn, influence the ways technological innovations in second language teacher education and professional development are imagined and reimagined within the broader parameters of a digital pedagogy. Becoming knowledgeable about how to effectively use digital technology in the classroom is the starting point of many spirited conversations. Expanding said conversations to also include purposeful course design, instructional methods, research-based strategies, and learning activities, to name but a few paradigms worthy of renewed attention in future studies, helps with student satisfaction and academic performance on attaining learning outcomes previously so communicated in the course syllabus and assessment rubrics. And because a one-size-fits-all approach to learning, however sensibly packaged or linked with greater measures of success, restricts team membership and personal engagement, care must be taken to offer a wider selection of choice—one that truly meets the diverse learning needs and interests of students. How instructors are to communicate these choices effectively and persuasively to their students is thus of critical importance.

Evidently, cognizing mindfulness through consciousness, and vice versa, undergirds the learning outcomes attained to date. Consequently, to experience the enduring power dialogic exploration and discovery can have on enriching learning, research-practitioners—from novice to superior levels—must be afforded ample opportunities to exercise choice and cognitive flexibility. *Digital storytelling with a twist*, it is suggested, is one such field-based, multimodal construct language professionals may want to employ in their classrooms and beyond to transform real or perceived realities. Its pedagogical relevance as a rhetorical model of communication is lauded among the linguacultural transactions it now clearly upholds with doctoral students pursuing academic careers in second language acquisition and instructional technology. Each one of these transactions, I assert confidently, provides fertile ground for future investigations and a new round of data analysis and interpretation. "The art of winning the soul by discourse," as Plato proclaims, is the beating heart of rhetoric still.

In closing, the all-embracing nature of the CPAR *hermeneutic circle* reported here, empowering and transformative as it assuredly is, is a value-laden process of relatable interpretations replete with meaning-making systems of knowledge, beliefs, and values in pursuit of practical solutions to theoretical and curricular constraints. Said ongoing didactic process, imagined anew via the *ART of Persuasion* discussed earlier, and probed through the core organizational scaffold the digital pedagogy dialogic circles comprise, allows research-practitioners to think afresh, to step back and look at their thinking, and, deliberately, to reflect critically on their own principles, morals, and attitudes to uncover heretofore unexamined biases and expectations not commonly subjected to a process of continual and substantial reflection, analyses of actions taken to date notwithstanding. And it is this *reflexivity*—the dynamic and iterative process of becoming self-aware—that interlinks with *positionality* (i.e., personal accounts of related but discrete objective-subjective realities assumed in a specific time and space to catalyze the adoption of a particular social and spatial position in relation to others) to produce via *dialectics, workability*, and *evocativeness* ever higher levels of understanding and (re)constructions of identity worthy of future investigations. Mindfulness through the "consciousness of ourselves" (self-consciousness) as a circular relationship involving investments in sensory data alongside questioning, searching, observation, examination, scrutiny, contemplation, introspection, and reflection, when subjected to the broader parameters of thoughtful CPAR constructs exemplifying new technological innovations in second language teacher education and professional development, is a tricky tightrope-walking performance in more ways than one. Most assuredly, imagining anew *mindfulness through consciousness* and *consciousness through mindfulness* reveals pragmatic value propositions now befitting wholly the echoing of the seemingly contradictory phrase and new theatrical mantra, *Reimagining education is dead. Long live reimagining education!*

References

Barkhuizen, G. (2017). Language teacher identity research: An introduction. In G. Barkhuizen (Ed.), *Reflections on language teacher identity research* (pp. 1–11). Routledge.

Block, D. (2015). Becoming a language teacher: Constraints and negotiation in the emergence of new identities. *Bellaterra Journal of Teaching & Learning Language & Literature, 8*(3), 9–26.

Burns, A. (2010). *Doing action research in English language teaching: A guide for practitioners*. Routledge.

Clarke, M. (2008). Language teacher identities: Co-constructing discourse and community. *Multilingual Matters*.

De Costa, P. I., & Norton, B. (2017). Introduction: Identity, transdisciplinarity, and the good language teacher. *Modern Language Journal, 101*(S1), 3–14.

Ellis, L. (2018). Languaged lives: A new perspective on language teacher identity. *Babel, 52*(2), 15–24.

Gadamer, H. (1975). Hermeneutics and social science. *Cultural Hermeneutics, 2*(4), 307–316.

Gu, M. M., & Benson, P. (2015). The formation of English teacher identities: A cross-cultural investigation. *Language Teaching Research, 19*(2), 187–206.

Heidegger, M. (1962). *Being and time.* Harper & Row [Originally published in German, in 1927].

Heikkinen, H. L. T., Huttunen, R., Syrjälä, L., & Pesonen, J. (2012). Action research and narrative inquiry: Five principles for validation revisited. *Educational Action Research, 20*(1), 5–21.

Ilieva, R. (2010). Non-native English-speaking teachers' negotiations of program discourses in their construction of professional identities within a TESOL program. *Canadian Modern Language Review, 66*(3), 343–369.

Kanno, Y., & Stuart, C. (2011). Learning to become a second language teacher: Identities-in-practice. *The Modern Language Journal, 95*(2), 236–252.

Lee, R. (2016). Implementing dialogic teaching in a Singapore English language classroom. *RELC Journal, 47*(3), 279–293.

Liontas, J. I. (2020). Understanding language teacher identity: Digital discursive spaces in English teacher education and development. In B. Yazan & K. Lindahl (Eds.), *Language teacher identity in TESOL: Teacher education and practice as identity work* (pp. 65–82). Routledge.

Liontas, J. I. (2021a). The dialogic circles of digital pedagogy: Reconceptualizing research and teaching practices in ELT. *SPELT ELT Research Journal, Special Issue: Engaging Research in ELT, 1*(1), 17–31.

Liontas, J. I. (2021b). Attaining knowledge of idiomatics in the age of Corona and beyond. In K. Kelch, P. Byun, S. Safavi, & S. Cervantes (Eds.), *CALL theory applications for online TESOL education* (pp. 1–34). IGI Global Publishing.

Liontas, J. I. (2022). Online learning in the time of coronavirus: Paradigmatic lessons learned through critical participatory action research. In K. Sadeghi, M. Thomas, & F. Ghaderi (Eds.), *Technology-enhanced language teaching and learning: Lessons from the Covid-19 pandemic* (pp. 135–150). Bloomsbury.

Mannion, P. (2020). *Digital stories students tell: An exploration of doctoral SLA students' beliefs about storytelling and educational technology* (Unpublished doctoral dissertation). University of South Florida, FL.

Mannion, P., & Liontas, J. I. (2022). On *becoming* language education professionals: Reframing doctoral students' perceptions of language teacher identity negotiations. In L. Klimanova (Ed.), *Identity, multilingualism, and CALL: Responding to new global realities* (pp. 189–217). Equinox Publishing Ltd.

Niemi, R. (2019). Five approaches to pedagogical action research. *Educational Action Research, 27*(5), 651–666.

Norton, B. (2017). Learner investment and language teacher identity. In G. Barkhuizen (Ed.), *Language teacher identity research* (pp. 81–86). Routledge.

Schön, D. A. (1983). *The reflective practitioner: How professionals think in action.* Basic Books.

Varghese, M. M., Motha, S., Park, G., Reeves, J., & Trent, J. (2016). Language teacher identity in (multi)lingual educational contexts [Special issue]. *TESOL Quarterly, 50*(3), 545–571.

Wenger, E. (1998). *Communities of practice: Learning, meaning, and identity.* Cambridge University Press.

Wenger-Trayner, E., & Wenger-Trayner, B. (2015). *Communities of practice: A brief introduction.* Wenger-Trayner. http://wenger-trayner.com/introduction-to-communities-of-practice/

3

Extending Blended Learning and the Roles of Technology to Meet Teacher-Training Needs in the *New Normal*

Martin Mullen, Marta Giralt, and Liam Murray

3.1 Introduction

> If we wait for a pandemic to appear, it will be too late to prepare—George W. Bush, 2005 (Mosk, 2020)

Fifteen years after US president George Bush made these comments while proposing a $7 billion investment on vaccine development and stockpiling of medical supplies, countries across the world showed themselves to be ill-prepared for the COVID-19 pandemic, which had devastating impacts on many aspects of society, from healthcare, to education, to travel, to business. This chapter will limit its focus to the educational impact of COVID-19 on the Irish education system, and in particular, the effects of a sudden and forced switch to online delivery of content on

---

M. Mullen (✉)
University of the West of Scotland, Paisley, Scotland
e-mail: martin.mullen@uws.ac.uk

M. Giralt • L. Murray
University of Limerick, Limerick, Ireland

© The Author(s), under exclusive license to Springer Nature Switzerland AG 2023
K. Sadeghi, M. Thomas (eds.), *Second Language Teacher Professional Development*,
Digital Education and Learning, https://doi.org/10.1007/978-3-031-12070-1_3

modules related to teacher training in TESOL and secondary school teaching at an Irish university. The chapter will first document the tumultuous change to online delivery and the steep learning curves which were associated with it and move on to identify and describe the ways in which different technologies were utilised and how different technological and pedagogical lessons were learned during this period. The chapter will then introduce the research project, which employed a mixed-methods approach, using surveys and reflections of both the teacher trainers and also trainee teachers on the modules, to explore the extent to which these various participants were technologically and pedagogically prepared for this dramatic change to the delivery of content.

Through analysis of the data gathered in the study, the chapter will move on to make various recommendations on how the lessons learned from this period of forced online learning can inform teacher-training curricula in the future and how teachers would benefit from a syllabus which placed greater emphasis on developing the familiarity with the digital tools needed for effective online teaching. These recommendations are made not just within the context of a future pandemic or other event which forces a return to online education, but also as a result of evidence indicating a shift towards increased levels of online learning which both predates and has been notably accelerated by COVID-19. Thus, while these lessons were learned during a particular, and hopefully, unique period in history, they can be applied more widely to the education system. The chapter will conclude by revisiting key points of data and evidence to reiterate the importance of developing teachers who are suitably prepared for the various modes of delivery of educational content that will be prevalent, if not ubiquitous, in the future.

3.1.1 Background to the Project

On March 12, 2020, a press release from the Irish Government's Department of Health announced that, to help contain the spread of COVID-19, a range of measures would be implemented, including a "closure to students of schools, creches, other childcare facilities and higher education institutions" (Department of Health, 2020, para. 4).

Although this closure was initially scheduled for just two weeks, it was later extended until the end of the academic year in June 2020, and although primary and secondary schools did return to classroom-based learning in September for the first semester of the following academic year, a later lockdown brought a return of online teaching and learning at these levels in early 2021 (Flynn et al., 2021), while universities remained almost entirely online for almost 18 months until returning to the campus in September 2021 (Irish Universities Association, 2021).

The announcement caused a seismic shift in the delivery of education in Ireland. At all levels, educators scrambled to identify different platforms for delivering online classes and for suitable Learning Management Systems (LMS), while administrators struggled to communicate how to access these resources to the students. Computer-Assisted Learning (CAL), which had hitherto been an optional niche area which most educators opted out of, was suddenly thrust into the mainstream, necessitating a hasty exploration of and experimentation with resources such as *Zoom, MS Teams*, and *Google Classroom*.

While the shift in delivery of content has often been described as 'online teaching', Milman (2020) noted that, rather than simply being described as online teaching, this period of enforced switch to online teaching by people previously inexperienced in online delivery is better termed Emergency Remote Teaching (ERT), characterised by varying levels of training and preparedness among teaching staff. Similarly, when exploring the response to COVID-19 by teacher trainers at an Israeli institution, Nissim and Simon (2020, p. 13) noted that the main goal of ERT "is not to create a strong, ecological education system from scratch, but to provide quick and readily-available temporary access to teaching, learning, and supervision".

The switch to ERT was far from seamless. Educational disruption affected more than a million children across the country (Flynn et al., 2021). This highlighted not only "a mixed level of readiness among teachers to transition to distance education prior to school closure" (Mohan et al., 2020, p. 13), but also the unequal access to or digital literacy with different devices and resources on the part of Irish students and their families (Darmody et al., 2020). There was an even greater impact on the educational progress of students with additional learning needs, students from disadvantaged backgrounds, and students in their examination years (Doyle, 2020). Teachers suffered also, with more teachers reporting mental health and anxiety issues than in previous years (Dempsey & Burke, 2021).

Moreover, even during the return to classroom-based learning between periods of lockdown and learning from home, the emphasis on restricting exposure to other students, which included not engaging in practical activities with shared resources, increased distance between teachers and students, and student interaction limited to smaller groups, or 'pods' within classrooms, all continued to negatively impact on learning outcomes (Chadwick & McLoughlin, 2021).

Enforced learning at home did bring about some positive outcomes for Irish school students. Primary school students in particular enjoyed the increased levels of project work, and the extra time spent with their family, while for some second-level students, learning from home allowed them to learn at their own pace and, for some, was a welcome escape from in-class disruption or bullying (Flynn et al., 2021). One positive learning outcome of the COVID-19 lockdown was that being forced to remain indoors for hours resulted in an improvement in the reading comprehension of Irish school students. One study of more than one million students in Ireland and the United Kingdom reported that children were reading more frequently, reading more challenging books, and with more enjoyment, than documented in previous iterations of the survey, with Irish primary school students reading at 2½ years above their chronological age (Renaissance Learning, 2021).

Impacts of COVID-19 were clearly felt at Irish third-level institutions also. Hyland and O'Shea (2021), while describing the student response to COVID-19 as 'resilient', reported that 59% of respondents felt it had a negative impact on their ability to learn and also noted that students were affected not only by the lack of ability to communicate with their peers, but also to engage in peer-learning. McFadden et al. (2020) highlight further educational impacts at Irish universities, with students who were midway through work placements or fieldwork unable to complete these assignments and thus experiencing a frustrating delay in earning enough credits to graduate, with some having to wait until the easing of restrictions to complete their assignments.

Moving from the educational to the psychological impacts, Hill and Fitzgerald (2020) reported that the lack of classroom-based learning resulted in a reduced sense of belonging, with negative effects on learner motivation, a finding echoed in a survey of more than 45,000 Irish university students, which reported that the diminishing sense of belonging and growing sense of feeling lost were particularly worrying among first-year students (Studentsurvey.ie, 2021). Hyland and O'Shea (2021) described student uncertainty about the immediate future, in terms of how long they would be online, and how they would be assessed, as factors contributing to increased anxiety and isolation.

Positive outcomes of COVID-19 at third level included the ability for students to learn at a time and place of their choosing (Hill & Fitzgerald, 2020). This was echoed by Yang (2021), who reported on the benefits of being able to pause and review content, which allowed for a more comprehensive understanding than would be possible in live lectures, and who also noted the benefits of online learning for international students in different time zones. One final positive was the lack of time spent commuting which freed up time for study itself (Studentsurvey.ie, 2021). From an academic perspective, one potential positive outcome identified by a participant in Shankar et al.'s, 2021 study was "integration of digital technologies, rethinking of assessment strategies with reduced reliance on final written unseen exams, and more emphasis on pedagogies for greater engagement" (p. 173), with another participant in the same study hoping that "some of the positive contributions of online remote teaching can continue to be integrated in teaching at university level" (p. 173).

3.1.2   Challenges for Teacher-Training Courses

Although it is often assumed that university students are 'digital natives' (Prensky, 2001) or at least, 'tech-savvy' (Hicks, 2011), these assumptions have been questioned among learners in general (Murray et al., 2020), and also among trainee teachers specifically, with a 2019 Organisation for Economic Co-operation and Development report finding that both newer and more experienced teachers can face issues with technology in the classroom. While younger teachers lack the experience to identify pedagogical uses for different technologies, older teachers sometimes lack the technological skills to apply technology to enhance their teaching practices. COVID-19 and ERT presented some challenges specific to teacher-training modules.

In the institution being discussed, only one module of the TESOL programme focused directly on technology, and even then, this module, alongside other modules, was designed with traditional face-to-face in-class teaching in mind, both in terms of the delivery of the module itself and also the environment in which the future teachers would work. Furthermore, in the Professional Master Education-Languages, the language and methodology modules were designed to be taught on-site but were delivered completely online, in alignment with how the trainee teachers started their teaching placement in secondary-level education. All secondary schools, as mentioned earlier in this section, moved to ERT during the two lengthy Irish lockdowns. Micro-teaching training practices during the semester had to be carried out in an online setting, which presented some challenges as most of the content of the syllabus is not designed to develop these types of digital skills or digital pedagogies.

Another challenge on the Master's Degree in Teaching English to Speakers of Other Languages (MA TESOL) programme was the lack of opportunity for traditional teaching practice. In contrast to previous years, in which on-campus face-to-face EFL classes were available for use by trainee teachers, during COVID-19, teaching practice had to be undertaken online. This necessitated some preparation for online teaching, including 6 weeks preparation consisting of training in technology, online delivery of materials, and also observation of online classes. The MA TESOL teaching practice classes themselves were also observed online by the examiners. The main issues reported by MA TESOL staff and students were technical problems such as setting up breakout rooms and sharing sound and screens.

At this institution and elsewhere, the shift to ERT tested the digital literacies of staff and students alike, and the response was far from uniform. Although it is tempting to assume that during this period of online learning, institutions and teachers, in Ireland and elsewhere, developed their digital literacies and competences and arrived at the strong, ecological education systems mentioned above, the reality is somewhat more sobering. Bartolic et al. (2021) surveyed multiple institutions across four continents to explore their reaction to COVID-19 and found little systematic pattern among the reactions, reporting that in one unnamed institution, approximately 30% of courses simply did not transition to online learning, with all students receiving a passing grade, although the use of Learning Management Systems (LMS) prior to COVID-19 by 94.5% of academics surveyed meant that the foundations were already in place for a switch to ERT. The same study reported that almost half of instructors surveyed 'felt overwhelmed' by the sudden shift to online delivery and that 79.7% felt that it took more time to prepare and deliver online classes.

Nevertheless, despite the steep learning curve, teachers did report becoming more confident with technology as a result of ERT (Winter et al., 2021). In our institution, Master's Degree in Teaching English to Speakers of Other Languages (MA TESOL) staff were satisfied with the outcomes, to the point that online teaching practice will remain part of the curriculum. Firstly, future cohorts in the MA TESOL will continue to have online Teaching Practice, in addition to face-to-face classes. Moreover, a new module has been designed, called *'TESOL in Blended Learning Environments'*, which, though primarily developed in response to COVID-19, also serves as a timely step towards preparing for a future in which a blend of online and face-to-face teaching is a permanent feature of education.

3.2   Methodology

The method employed to conduct this research is a mixed-methods one, where qualitative and quantitative data was solicited, respectively, from a questionnaire circulated among students enrolled in a Master's Degree in Teaching English to Speakers of Other Languages (MA TESOL) programme at an Irish University. Additional data was sought from final teaching practice reports and research projects from teacher trainees and interviews with student teachers on a Professional Masters in Education Languages (PME Languages). The differing types of data provided a greater scope to investigate educational issues (Almalki, 2016).

The study is based, in part, on the collection of data gathered throughout a 12-week *Technology and Language Studies* module for MA TESOL students, delivered entirely online due to COVID-19 restrictions. In brief, the aim of this module is to introduce students to the major pedagogical, professional, and research applications of technology in modern languages and to enable students to integrate these into their future teaching practices. Examples of CALLware evaluated by the students over the course of this programme include generic and dedicated language learning websites and apps, automated summarising software, corpus linguistics software, and social media. Those who register on this module are typically novice trainee teachers and CALL users and have limited experience with the integration of either generic or dedicated software into language teaching.

Equally, the data gathered from the PME Languages students took place during a 12-week semester among students that were taking the module *Language and culture in the classroom*. This module focuses on pedagogical approaches to teach languages at the Junior Certificate level in the Post-Primary Irish educational system.

3.2.1 Participants

The participants in this study were trainee teachers from two different training programmes: MA TESOL and PME. The majority of students in both modules were novice teachers with either no or very little experience of teaching. In the case of the PME students, some of the participants had a linguistic background and were competent in two languages. The five students from the PME were graduates from BA Languages Degrees (i.e. BA in Applied Languages; BA Arts with Languages) in most cases, with ages between 22 and 26 years old except for a mature student who was in her 30s. From the five students, three were females and two were males. While these students were all from Ireland and were training to become secondary school teachers in languages, including ESL (English as Second Language), the MA TESOL cohort included both Irish students and students from Brazil, Spain, Italy, France, and China, some of whom were attending online from their home countries, and these students were training to become teachers of English in different settings (adult education, primary school education).

3.2.2 Quantitative Data

A survey was conducted with postgraduate students at an Irish university from the MA TESOL programme. The survey was completed by both novice and experienced language teachers. The data was sourced using questionnaires delivered via *Google Forms*. The survey included a total of 11 questions organised in several sections, including participant teaching experience, participant experience of online learning as teacher or as a student, and perceptions of participants' digital literacy. Questions were multiple choice and for one of the questions, students were invited to elaborate on their answers by leaving an additional comment. This allowed the researchers to explore different viewpoints. The questions were mainly focusing on three important areas: student experiences with online teaching; self-assessment of their ability to use Information and Communications Technology (ICT), and the impact of their teacher training course for future online teaching.

3.2.3 Qualitative Data

Two different sources of qualitative data were used: individual interviews with PME Languages students conducted during the final class of the semester ($n = 5$ participants), and individual teaching reports from students' teaching practicum and research projects on CALL from the cohort of students ($n = 18$) registered in the module *Technology and Language Studies*. The researchers carried out a semi-structured interview where the participants could contribute openly on their perceived effects on their digital skills and their readiness to teach online. All gathered data was analysed following the thematic analysis method in order to identify and map major themes arising from the data (Berger, 2000).

3.3 Data Analysis

Our data revealed that attitudes to CALL and the integration of ICT in teacher teaching practices were quite varied, but nevertheless they were a challenge due to the online setting that teachers and learners were forced to transition to during the pandemic. Analysis of the qualitative data identified three themes which emerged consistently across the various data strands: lack of previous experience using technology; the importance of developing a repertoire of digital teaching resources; online classes affecting engagement and a sense of belonging. These themes will be explored in the following sections.

Theme 1: Lack of Previous Experience Using Technology
Our qualitative data provided from teacher trainees reports delivered after their teaching placements emphasises that during their teaching practices they could witness how in-service teachers had to face several challenges while teaching online due to the lack of preparation and training. In addition, they could observe how the lack of training and experience in online teaching had a negative impact on learners from the motivational point of view and online classroom misbehaviours. The following quotations from student TESOL teaching practice reports illustrate this idea:

> [T]he lack of preparation of these tutors alongside a non-learner tailored learning platform has led many students into becoming demotivated, and as a consequence, unenrolling themselves from these institutions.

Trainees felt that having an online experience—in their teaching placement and in their MA TESOL programme—was fostering the development of their digital skills, most likely making them more digitally literate and prepared to teach online:

> Above all the fact that my placement was held fully online, had contributed to changing my perception about online education. Thus, I was able to learn how to explore the potential that modern technology provides to the ESL field.

Theme 2: The Importance of Developing a Repertoire of Digital Teaching Resources

Regarding the data from the interviews, it could be stated that most of the PME trainees interviewed already had some level of online learning or teaching experience before starting the PME. Although all of them expressed their preference for face-to-face learning and teaching, all of them agreed that having a blended component in their programme was very useful because it made them experience the online learning environment: *"you are learning more about technology at the same time that you are doing it"*. Combining on-campus classes with online classes was perceived as a good option for developing student digital literacies and digital practices (i.e., sharing screens on video-conference platforms; using different apps, e.g., *Padlet*). Furthermore, being students in online components of the MA programme allowed trainees to put themselves in the students' shoes and be more aware of the challenges and feelings that their future students could experience in online teaching environments:

> [I]f they do have to learn online and we'll kind of know what works best as a learner. So then you can use that in your teaching. You know, like if you haven't experienced learning online, it's harder.

Theme 3: Online Classes Affecting Engagement and a Sense of Belonging

Another theme identified was the impact of ERT on students' struggles to feel a sense of community. Some trainee teachers, based on their teaching placement observations, identified with the major barriers for online teaching that Song et al. (2004) describe: learners feeling a lack of community, learners and teachers facing not only technical problems but also issues with motivation, as the following quotation from a student illustrates:

> [N]ot all students felt themselves engaged and motivated to have online classes. It was noticeable how several students used to keep their webcams off and omit themselves from participating in class. Such [an] attitude, which sometimes seemed to be a lack of respect towards the teacher and other classmates, could be linked to the current atypical situation, and also to the lack of preparation of professionals for online teaching.

48   M. Mullen et al.

The difficulties encountered in building a community and a sense of belonging is one of the aspects that appears in the survey data also, which is discussed in the following paragraphs.

As well as the qualitative data described above, quantitative data was also collected in the form of survey data collected from the cohort of 18 students in the MA TESOL programme, which revealed that there was an even blend of students who had no experience of online teaching, students who had limited experience, and students who had regular experience of online teaching. To a certain extent, their prior experience in this area correlated with their responses to survey questions. Teachers with no previous experience were more likely to say that 'I'm not really confident I have the knowledge and skills to do so effectively' when asked how comfortable they felt delivering an online course, while teachers with proper experience were more likely to report feeling confident. In terms of both their own classes, and the classes they observed, the effects of teachers' lack of comfort using technology was keenly felt.

In terms of their prior knowledge of digital resources, none of the respondents reported being familiar with 'a wide range of digital platforms and resources' and, similar to the benefits of online teacher-training highlighted earlier, a majority of survey participants reported that the MA TESOL had done at least a 'reasonable job' of equipping them with these tools for their future teaching, with all students reporting that there had been 'an appropriate focus' on these digital resources across the MA TESOL modules. Similar to the findings of the thematic analysis, the survey respondents felt they benefitted from participating as both teacher and student in a blended learning environment.

When asked what their main issues with adapting to online classes as a student had been, as well as typical responses about mastering new technologies, one noteworthy comment was the 'failure to build relationships'. As mentioned earlier, the same theme was identified during thematic analysis and highlights the importance of recognising and addressing the challenges online learning poses to building a sense of community among students. When asked what their main challenges had been in adapting to online classes as a teacher, a majority noted the difficulties of keeping students' on track, exemplified by a comment that the trainee teacher 'Can't keep all the students focused', and 'student engagement', echoing a theme identified during analysis of the qualitative data.

Overall, the three main themes emerging from the qualitative data analysis were present in the survey data also. It is clear that teachers feel they often lack the resources needed to be confident in their online classes, and curricular reform is needed to address this issue and help them develop their abilities to deliver content effectively and keep students engaged. Moreover, the impact that online classes had on students' abilities to build relationships, and consequently on their sense of belonging, which the participants not only witnessed among their students, but also experienced themselves, is another important finding which must be remedied at curricular level. Recommendations are made later in the chapter in this regard.

3.4   Lessons for Post-Pandemic Teacher-Training Practices

Based on the study and findings derailed in the previous section, the authors operationalise the implications for CALL processes and practices in relation to teacher education and training by making a number of recommendations on how teacher-training curricula can be refined to integrate some of the lessons learned from the response to COVID-19, not only to help futureproof the delivery of content in the event of future public health crises, but also to prepare teachers for a professional future in which online teaching and learning will only increase, a trend which predated and has been accelerated by COVID-19 (Godwin-Jones, 2020; Henriques et al., 2021).

Firstly, rather than returning in relief to the traditional entirely live and entirely campus-based university experience, there is a need for a more permanent blended learning approach, which includes an online presence across modules as a matter of course. Rather than the internet serving as a hastily constructed backup method of delivery, making blended learning a fixed part of the curriculum will allow content, and the delivery of content, to be designed with online delivery in mind, making the teaching and learning process smoother for both educators and students.

As our analysis revealed, trainee teachers, including those with previous teaching experience, report a lack of familiarity with, and consequently, confidence with, digital platforms and resources that can aid their teaching. Thus, it is important for this online element to take different forms and employ different resources and move beyond simply using LMS to make announcements, store files, and submit assignments. From the teacher-trainer's perspective, this could involve online delivery of content, such as recorded lectures or live lectures recorded for re-viewing. From the trainee-teacher's perspective, in addition to engaging with the content mentioned above, there can also be online assessments, such as students' creating, uploading, and delivering presentations, online micro-teaching, use of digital apps, narrated powerpoint files, or even podcasts. In addition, many LMS have a blog function, on which students can reflect on their learning, or a forum function, where discussions can happen. Exposure to and practice with these different digital platforms and resources will help them build the familiarity needed to employ them effectively in their own future teaching practices.

COVID-19 demonstrated the increasing importance of digital literacies and the need for teachers to be able to locate, evaluate, and integrate appropriate digital resources into their teaching practices as teaching and learning aids, which are, in essence, the fundamental elements of digital pedagogies identified by Hauck (2019). As well as ensuring teachers have the competence to deliver content in the 'traditional' forms mentioned above, improving machine translation literacy (Loock & Léchauguette, 2021) is essential for future teachers. Machine translation has moved well beyond pasting sentences into translation software such as *Google Translate* or *DeepL* and now allows translation of audio content in real time and translation of text which is increasingly accurate not only in grammatical but also in context-specific form. During ERT, even 'classroom' time was online, making it possible for students to surreptitiously employ translation resources. Thus, knowing not only how to identify unethical use of machine translation software by students, but also having the competence and confidence to use the software productively as a learning resource in the classroom, is something to be addressed at curricular and indeed at faculty level.

Another literacy whose importance became apparent during the COVID-19 pandemic is information literacy specific to social media content. Media such as *Twitter* and *Facebook* continue to feature prominently during the pandemic, being used to communicate information of all levels of credibility, ranging from mainstream media reporting new government guidelines to self-proclaimed experts promoting conspiracy theories. Thus, teachers should be equipped with the knowledge needed to appropriately and judiciously integrate social media into their classes. This would involve not only a focus on typical information literacy and the extent to which social media can be trusted as sources of information and how claims can be further investigated and verified, but also a focus on how social media can be harnessed as a resource. For learners, this may be by following accounts that will offer authentic second language that can be curated to each learner's interests, and for teachers, as in the MA TESOL, this may occur through sharing useful learning resources and participation in social media-hosted communities of practice.

As highlighted in the methodology and results section, and echoing the findings of previously mentioned research, a sense of not being part of a community, or 'failure to build relationships' impacted on the student learning experience also during COVID-19, as online learning does not allow for the same social interactions and relationship-building that face-to-face campus-based learning affords. This was emphasised recently in a different module currently being delivered by the authors to students of Modern Languages, in which student feedback repeatedly pointed to the return to campus being a central factor in belonging and feeling more motivated in their studies. It is important to be aware of the importance placed by students on this social and relationship aspect of taking a course and that teachers be prepared to offer activities which can mitigate this issue. This might take the form of facilitating face-to-face meetings where possible, integration of social media groups such as Facebook groups, and also informal online get-togethers purely for socialisation, and ensuring that group activities give participants ample time to get to know each other.

Changes such as those recommended here will help to develop not only educators but also students, and by extension, future teachers, who are confident at employing various technologies effectively to create a seamless blend of face-to-face and online delivery. The benefits of this would not only be evident in the event of future crises which prompt a return to online learning, but will also equip students and future teachers with the digital literacies needed to work, learn, and teach in an increasingly online environment. Moreover, as universities become more internationalised, and attempt to attract students paying international fees which are often many multiples of the fees of domestic students, an understanding of the competences needed to facilitate the provision of online delivery which allows for asynchronous learning due to different time zones will also become more valuable.

3.5 Conclusion

The sudden switch to Emergency Remote Teaching (ERT) brought about by the emergence of COVID-19 and consequent public health measures led to a rapid, often panicked scramble for appropriate platforms and resources. The switch was far from seamless, and the impacts on learners and indeed educators at all levels of education, and on teacher-training modules in particular, were documented earlier in this chapter. While there has been an abiding and understandable hope that education can simply 'get back to normal', it seems inevitable that in the future, for different reasons, online teaching and learning will play an ever more prominent role in general teaching and learning practices, and it is crucial that teacher-training programmes revise their curricula to be as up-to-date as possible from both pedagogical and technological perspectives, "in order to be able to adjust pedagogical models and practices to the needs of contemporary and future students, who may even have jobs that do not exist yet" (Henriques et al., 2021, p. 2).

Firstly, in the event of a public health and safety crisis similar to COVID-19, which requires a shift to online learning, it is essential that institutions are better prepared than happened in Ireland in 2020. Thus, it is essential that institutions, and educators, and those undergoing teacher-training, be equipped with the knowledge and competences needed to make a smooth transition to online learning.

Secondly, as already mentioned, online learning was already becoming more common in universities prior to COVID-19, as universities and students alike recognised that online teaching and learning could deliver a suitable standard of education while allowing significant cost savings. This trend will continue in the future, and incorporating aspects of online teaching into regular teaching practices will become normalised in many countries, offering another reason why it is essential that trainee teachers develop the skills needed to ensure they can not only survive but also succeed in this new blended learning environment.

Certainly, the ongoing pandemic has been and continues to be a terrible human tragedy, causing huge loss of life, loss of health, and loss of income and security. Nevertheless, from an educational perspective, the responses by institutions, educators, and students have allowed us insight into which aspects of ERT work, which do not work, and why this is the case. Such insights should not be simply discounted if and when a full return to traditional campus-based education is possible. Rather, these lessons should be heeded, and where appropriate, platforms, resources, and methods of content delivery should be integrated into teacher-training curricula, to produce future generations of teachers who, as and when needed, will have the competence to allow them to teach either online or in class with equal comfort and confidence.

References

Almalki, S. (2016). Integrating quantitative and qualitative data in Mixed Methods Research—Challenges and benefits. *Journal of education and learning, 5*(3), 288–296. https://doi.org/10.5539/jel.v5n3p288

Bartolic, S. K., Boud, D., Agapito, J., Verpoorten, D., Williams, S., Lutze-Mann, L., Matzat, U., Moreno, M., Polly, P., Tai, J., Marsh, H., Lin, L., Burgess, J., Habtu, S., Rodrigo, M., Roth, M., Heap, T., & Guppy, N. (2021). A multi-institutional assessment of changes in higher education teaching and learning in the face of COVID-19. *Educational Review*, 1–17. https://doi.org/10.1080/00131911.2021.1955830.

Berger, A. A. (2000). *Media and communication research methods: An introduction to qualitative and quantitative approaches.* Sage.

Chadwick, R., & McLoughlin, E. (2021). Impact of the COVID-19 crisis on learning, teaching and facilitation of practical activities in science upon reopening of Irish schools. *Irish Educational Studies, 40*(2), 197–205. https://doi.org/10.1080/03323315.2021.1915838

Darmody, M., Smyth, E., & Russell, H. (2020). The implications of the COVID-19 pandemic for policy in relation to children and young people: A research review. *Economic and Social Research Institute.* https://www.esri.ie/publications/the-implications-of-the-covid-19-pandemic-for-policy-in-relation-to-children-and-young.

Dempsey, M., & Burke, J. (2021). *Lessons Learned: The experiences of teachers in Ireland during the 2020 pandemic.* Maynooth University. https://mural.maynoothuniversity.ie/13914/.

Department of Health. (2020, March 12). *Statement from the National Public Health Emergency Team - Thursday 12 March.* Irish Government Department of Health. https://www.gov.ie/en/press-release/96eb4c-statement-from-the-national-public-health-emergency-team/

Doyle, O. (2020). *COVID-19: Exacerbating Educational Inequalities?* UCD Geary Institute for Public Policy. https://publicpolicy.ie/papers/covid-19-exacerbating-educational-inequalities/.

Flynn, N., Keane, E., Davitt, E., McCauley, V., Heinz, M., & Mac Ruairc, G. (2021). 'Schooling at Home' in Ireland during COVID-19': Parents' and students' perspectives on overall impact, continuity of interest, and impact on learning. *Irish Educational Studies, 40*(2), 217–226. https://doi.org/10.1080/03323315.2021.1916558

Godwin-Jones, R. (2020). Building the porous classroom: An expanded model for blended language learning. *Language Learning & Technology, 24*(3), 1–18. http://hdl.handle.net/10125/44731

Hauck, M. (2019). Virtual exchange for (critical) digital literacy skills development. *European Journal of Language Policy, 11*(2), 187–210. https://doi.org/10.3828/ejlp.2019.12

Henriques, S., Correia, J. D., & Dias-Trindade, S. (2021). Portuguese primary and secondary education in times of COVID-19 pandemic: An exploratory study on teacher training and challenges. *Education Sciences, 11*(9), 542–553. https://doi.org/10.3390/educsci11090542

Hicks, S. D. (2011). Technology in today's classroom: Are you a tech-savvy teacher? *The Clearing House: A Journal of Educational Strategies, Issues and Ideas, 84*(5), 188–191. https://doi.org/10.1080/00098655.2011.557406

Hill, K., & Fitzgerald, R. (2020). Student perspectives on the Impact of COVID-19 on Learning. *All Ireland Journal of Teaching and Learning in Higher Education, 12*(2), 1–9. https://ojs.aishe.org/index.php/aishe-j/article/view/459

Hyland, D., & O'Shea, A. (2021). The student perspective on teaching and assessment during initial COVID-19 related closures at Irish universities: implications for the future. *Teaching Mathematics and its Applications: An International Journal of the IMA*, hrab017. https://doi.org/10.1093/teamat/hrab017.

Irish Universities Association. (2021, February 12). https://www.iua.ie/COVID-19/university_updates_faqs/

Loock, R., & Léchauguette, S. (2021). Machine translation literacy and undergraduate students in applied languages: Report on an exploratory study. *Revista Tradumàtica*, n. 19. https://doi.org/10.5565/rev/tradumatica.281.

McFadden, P., Russ, E., Blakeman, P., Kirwin, G., Anand, J., Lähteinen, S., Baugerud, G. A., & Tham, P. (2020). COVID-19 impact on social work admissions and education in seven international universities. *Social Work Education, 39*(8), 1154–1163. https://doi.org/10.1080/0261547 9.2020.1829582

Milman, N. B. (2020, March 25). *Pandemic pedagogy*. Phi Delta Kappan. https://kappanonline.org/pandemic-pedagogy-covid-19-online-milman/

Mohan, G., McCoy, S., Carroll, E., Mihut, G., Lyons, S., & Mac Domhnaill, C. (2020). *Learning for all? Second-Level education in Ireland during COVID-19*. Economic and Social Research Institute. https://doi.org/10.26504/sustat92

Mosk, M. (2020). *George W. Bush in 2005: 'If we wait for a pandemic to appear, it will be too late to prepare'*. ABC News. https://abcnews.go.com/Politics/george-bush-2005-wait-pandemic-late-prepare/story?id=69979013

Murray, L., Giralt, M., & Benini, S. (2020). Extending digital literacies: Proposing an agentive literacy to tackle the problems of distractive technologies in language learning. *ReCALL, 32*(3), 250–271. https://doi.org/10.1017/S0958344020000130

Nissim, Y., & Simon, E. (2020). Agility in Teacher Training: Distance Learning during the COVID-19 Pandemic. International Education Studies, 13(12), 11–26. https://doi.org/10.5539/ies.v13n12p11

Organisation for Economic Co-operation and Development. (2019). *TALIS 2018 results (Volume I): Teachers and school leaders as lifelong learners*, TALIS, OECD Publishing. https://doi.org/10.1787/1d0bc92a-en.

Prensky, M. (2001). Digital natives, digital immigrants part 1. *On the Horizon, 9*(5), 1–6. https://doi.org/10.1108/10748120110424816

Renaissance Learning. (2021). https://www.renlearn.co.uk/what-kids-are-reading-2021-thank-you/

Shankar, K., Phelan, D., Suri, V. R., Watermeyer, R., Knight, C., & Crick, T. (2021). 'The COVID-19 crisis is not the core problem': Experiences, challenges, and concerns of Irish academia during the pandemic. *Irish Educational Studies, 40*(2), 169–175. https://doi.org/10.1080/03323315.2021.1932550

Song, L., Singleton, E. S., Hill, J. R., & Koh, M. H. (2004). Improving online learning: Student perceptions of useful and challenging characteristics. *The Internet and Higher Education, 7*(1), 59–70. https://doi.org/10.1016/j.iheduc.2003.11.003

Student Survey.ie. (2021, May 21). *Results of COVID-19 questions.* https://studentsurvey.ie/blog/results-covid-19-questions

Winter, E., Costello, A., O'Brien, M., & Hickey, G. (2021) Teachers' use of technology and the impact of Covid-19, Irish Educational Studies, 40(2), 235-246. https://doi.org/10.1080/03323315.2021.1916559

Yang, L. H. (2021). Online Learning Experiences of Irish University Students during the COVID-19 Pandemic. All Ireland Journal of Higher Education, 13(1), 1-22. https://ojs.aishe.org/index.php/aishe-j/article/view/499

4

Technology-Enhanced Language Teacher Development During the COVID-19 Pandemic: Experiences of Southeast Asian English Language Teachers

Joel C. Meniado

4.1 Introduction

Language teacher development (LTD) also known as professional development for language teachers, language teacher professional learning, and in-service language teacher training plays a crucial role in promoting quality language education. It is a lifelong, self-directed, collaborative, and reflective process that makes language teachers more effective and efficient in addressing the different learning needs of their students (Johnston, 2009; Maggioli, 2003; Richards, 2008). Carried out in varied forms of formal and informal educational experiences, it provides opportunities for language teachers to learn, reflect, and apply new knowledge and skills that can improve their performance in their teaching contexts (Mizell, 2010). The improved teaching performance as a result of continuing professional learning and development leads to better student

---

J. C. Meniado (✉)
SEAMEO Regional Language Centre, Singapore, Singapore
e-mail: joel.meniado@relc.org.sg

© The Author(s), under exclusive license to Springer Nature Switzerland AG 2023
K. Sadeghi, M. Thomas (eds.), *Second Language Teacher Professional Development*,
Digital Education and Learning, https://doi.org/10.1007/978-3-031-12070-1_4

learning outcomes and institutional performance (Meniado, 2019; Sadeghi & Richards, 2021).

Given the essential role of language teacher development in upholding quality English language education, it is imperative that language teachers have continuing and sustainable access to engaging, useful, and relevant development programs that can prepare them for unprecedented challenges at all times. English language teachers often face challenges in adapting to changes brought by new technologies and innovations, new policies, guidelines, and standards in the educational system, new curricula, evolving social norms and practices, among others; so it is important that they are supported in varied ways to help them succeed and flourish in the profession. Recently, the global COVID-19 pandemic has disrupted educational systems worldwide and changed existing teaching and learning landscapes. In Southeast Asia, countries imposed community lockdowns, school closures, and emergency remote teaching (ERT). Many English language teachers especially in under-resourced areas struggled in transitioning to remote/online teaching due to lack of required resources and skills. They also struggled in learning how to teach remotely/online and how to make themselves more relevant in the new normal. While many studies focused on the impacts of the pandemic on student learning as well as new teaching practices and technologies needed, only few examined how teachers, particularly English language teachers, learned and developed themselves professionally during the pandemic. As of this writing, no study has been conducted at a regional scale on how English language teachers in Southeast Asia leveraged technology for their professional learning and development during the COVID-19 pandemic. This study aimed to address this literature gap. Specifically, it aimed to answer the following questions:

1. What language teacher development (LTD) activities did Southeast Asian English language teachers engage in during the COVID-19 pandemic?
2. What technological tools did they use to engage in these teacher development activities?

3. What factors did they consider in engaging in teacher development activities during the pandemic and in selecting appropriate technological tools for such activities?
4. What challenges did they encounter in their teacher development activities during the pandemic and how did they manage to overcome such challenges?

This study involved English language teachers in Cambodia, Indonesia, Malaysia, Myanmar, Philippines, Singapore, Thailand, and Vietnam. Its findings are useful to English language classroom practitioners as they can learn best practices on technology-enhanced language teacher development that can be adopted/adapted in their own contexts. Moreover, findings of this study can also benefit education leaders and policy makers as they can gain insights that are useful in formulating policies on language teacher development. Lastly, this study is helpful to researchers as it opens opportunities for further investigations on technology-enhanced LTD in the ASEAN region.

4.2 Literature Review

4.2.1 Language Teacher Development

Language teacher development (LTD) as used in this study refers to a continuing process of growth during which in-service language teachers engage in relevant professional learning activities to enhance their knowledge, skills, and dispositions in order to improve quality of language instruction and performance of language learners and learning institutions (Buendia & Macias, 2019; Maggioli, 2020; Meniado, 2019). It is multifaceted, lifelong, and reflection-driven (Hayes, 2019). It can be formal or informal, autonomous or collaborative, work-based or home-based, online or face-to-face (or hybrid), and autonomous or collaborative. Moreover, it can also be teacher-initiated (self-determined) or institutionally mandated (Hayes, 2019).

LTD includes a broad range of professional activities such as self-directed and collaborative learning, coaching, mentoring, work-based projects, personal reflection, and technology-mediated learning (Craft, 2000). Further, it also includes other formal and informal activities such as self-monitoring, journal writing, critical incidents, teaching portfolios, action research, peer observation and coaching, team teaching, workshops, and teacher support groups (Richards & Farrell, 2005). Lastly, it also involves engagements in professional activities such as individual reading of relevant articles, joining study groups and team meetings to plan lessons, solve problems or issues, or learn new strategies, enrollment in online/face-to-face courses, attending conferences to learn from various experts around the globe, and involvement in whole-school improvement programs (Mizell, 2010).

To serve its purpose with lasting impact on practice, LTD activities should be context-based, practical, specific, responsive, engaging, continual, collaborative, sustainable, reflective, and measurable (Hismanoglu, 2010; Maggioli, 2020; McAleavy et al., 2018; Meniado, 2019; Organization for Economic Co-operation and Development [OECD], 2017). LTD programs should also consider teachers' personal and professional backgrounds, existing knowledge, skills and dispositions, experiences, roles, needs, professional goals, capabilities, and available resources. Mizell (2010) claims that teacher development program is most effective when it is embedded in the teacher's teaching context and when professional learning is immediately applied in the teacher's specific context. Hayes (2019) also claims that teacher development is most effective when it is a collaborative enterprise involving teachers, school administrators, and other stakeholders of the institution and when it sustainably improves performance of both teachers and students.

Many studies have proven that high impact teacher development programs can translate to better quality of teaching and learning (McAleavy et al., 2018). For example, in the study by Fletcher-Wood and Zucollo (2020) involving 52 randomized controlled trials evaluating teacher development programs, it was found that high-quality development programs can potentially close the gap between novice and seasoned teachers in terms of teaching performance and can have significant effects on students' learning outcomes. In addition, in a systematic review by Kalinowski et al. (2019) involving 38 empirical studies from 2000 to 2016, it was found that teacher development programs among in-service teachers were effective in improving their teaching performance and students' English language proficiency across curriculum.

Technology-Enhanced Language Teacher Development

In recent decades, social changes and technological innovations have transformed the way people work and learn (Littlejohn & Margaryan, 2014). The changing work systems and the continuous evolution of new technologies have created the so-called technology-enhanced learning where workers learn new knowledge and skills through varied technologies. In the field of education, technology-enhanced learning (TEL) basically refers to the appropriate use of technological tools as mediating devices to support learning that can lead to achievement of optimum outcomes and experiences (International Bureau of Education–United Nations Educational, Scientific and Cultural Organization [IBE–UNESCO], 2021; Kirkwood & Price, 2014; Sen & Leong, 2020).

In the context of English language teaching, technology-enhanced language teacher development refers to the proper use of information and communication technologies to support professional learning and development of English language teachers. More specifically, it refers to a continuing process of growth where English language teachers engage in ongoing meaningful professional learning and development activities that are carried out in web-based, computer-based, or virtual learning environments to improve their teaching performance in order to help their students succeed at learning. In this approach to teacher development, contents are delivered through electronic media (e.g., internet/intranet, audio, video, radio, smart TV, smartphone, Word/PDF documents, PowerPoint presentations), and activities are facilitated through interactive communication and collaboration tools (e.g., Canvas, Zoom, Microsoft Teams, Google Docs, Padlet, WhatsApp, Facebook). Utilizing varied contents and activities available in electronic and online formats, technology-enhanced language teacher development allows teachers to learn and develop, based on their context, at their own time, pace, and space.

Harnessing technology to support language teacher development has practical benefits. As implied in the report of McAleavy et al. (2018), using technology can offer language teachers cost-effective distance models of coaching. Further, it can also provide them opportunities to collaborate with like-minded colleagues/teachers from geographically dispersed locations. Moreover, through videoconferencing and communication tools, language teachers are able to network with experts from around the world. In addition, through videos, they can gain insights from good models of effective pedagogies and reflect on their own practice. Lastly, with the variety and abundance of professional learning resources available online, they can establish ownership of their own learning as they have the freedom to decide what to learn and how to learn.

Some commonly used technological resources to support professional development of language teachers include interactive radio and prerecorded audio contents, web-based and mobile-based videos, open educational resources (OER), mobile/smartphones, computer labs connected to the Internet, online communication/videoconferencing tools, and serious educational games (McAleavy et al., 2018). In addition to these, digital tools like learning management systems (e.g., Canvas, Google Classroom), Massive Open Online Courses (MOOC) platforms (e.g., EdX, Coursera, UDemy), social media (e.g., Facebook, LinkedIn, Blogger), and electronic databases for professional journals are also among the popular resources for formal and informal professional development activities.

Prior to the outbreak of the COVID-19 pandemic, many institutions across the globe used technologies to support their teacher development programs. Technological devices such as mobile phones, tablets, internet, social media, open educational resources (OER), and Apple iPod (iPod Touch) were used and explored to deliver teacher-training contents and facilitate collaboration among teachers (McAleavy et al., 2018; Shohel & Banks, 2012). In Singapore, Hong Kong, Taiwan, and Beijing, online collaboration platforms, file sharing, and communication tools were commonly used to facilitate collaboration and sharing of resources and good practices between and among teachers and educational institutions (Kong et al., 2017).

Language Teacher Development During the Pandemic

The outbreak of the COVID-19 pandemic in early 2020 forced many countries worldwide to impose community lockdowns and school closures. This mobility restriction resulted in sudden and unprecedented shift to remote teaching and learning (distance and online) which caught many teachers unprepared (Muhayimana, 2020). Unfamiliar with the new teaching-learning landscape, many teachers had to find ways to effectively and efficiently deliver online/remote instruction in order to survive in the profession. They had to undergo a series of online trainings and workshops on how to use digital tools in teaching and assessing online, how to motivate and engage learners online, how to create interactive digital materials, and how to promote access, equity, inclusivity, and learner well-being while teaching/learning online. Others also had to engage in professional learning activities that allowed them to deepen their knowledge and understanding of their subject areas.

Aside from participating in online trainings and workshops, teachers also relied on their colleagues to learn new things (Agnello, 2021). Moreover, they also learned through experimentation on their own and by watching model strategies or video tutorials from social media sites like YouTube, Facebook, and Twitter (Agnello, 2021). In the study by Evmenova et al. (2021), teachers learned through an online course with a combination of autonomous (on-demand, self-paced, and unfacilitated) and collaborative (instructor-led with weekly deadlines) features, supplemented by online teaching support group led by previous completers of the course. Further, in the study by Goldsmith (2021), a teacher learned informally through sustained personal communications through email. In the study, it was found that work-based learning is effective in providing individualized, real-time suggestions for teaching moves.

In another study conducted by Gautam (2020), it was found that English language teachers in Nepal learned and developed professionally mostly by attending webinars, online forums, online workshops, online courses, MOOCs, and virtual conferences organized by professional organizations and learning institutions. Among the common digital tools they used for these PD activities were Zoom, Google Classroom, Facebook

Messenger, Microsoft Teams, www.teachingenglish.org.uk, www.americanenglish.state.gov, National Geographic Learning, Ello, and Learning English through Voice of America. Moorhouse and Wong (2021) also examined the professional development activities of teachers in Hong Kong during the pandemic. They found that teachers engaged in school-initiated and teacher-initiated development activities. Under school-initiated program, teachers participated in online workshops and training on using different digital technologies. They also engaged in observations of teachers conducting synchronous online lessons through video conferencing systems (i.e., Zoom, Teams). In teacher-initiated development programs, teachers formed learning circles, working groups, and exploration committees to share skills, experiences, challenges, and solutions using instant messaging platforms such as WhatsApp. Others also conducted their own self-initiated research, watched instructional videos, and joined certification courses.

The study by Yu et al. (2021) also identified some online informal professional learning activities of teachers in China during the pandemic. These included teaching exchanges in reading clubs, delivering talks, and teaching presentations/demonstrations, salons of teaching practice, reflections, among others. The study found that these online activities carried out using technologies had positive impacts on teachers' performance due to three properties: social interaction, autonomous learning, and novelty-seeking. In USA, some teachers also engaged in just-in-time professional development through playlist of videos curated, compiled, and shared online to all teachers in a school district (Neumann & Smith, 2020) and through personalized professional development program with free online resources (Conan, 2020).

Clearly, during the COVID-19 pandemic, new trends and practices in technology-enhanced professional learning and development emerged. According to Alexandrou (2021), these new transformations made teacher learning and development more manageable, accessible, affordable, and efficient. However, in some contexts, accessing professional learning and development opportunities remain a struggle due to internet connectivity issues, lack of required devices, time differences in geographically dispersed locations, lack of time due to work and family pressures, and unsupportive learning environments (Gautam, 2020).

4.3 Methodology

4.3.1 Research Design

This study used a mixed-methods research design, since it involved both quantitative and qualitative data. According to Creswell and Creswell (2018), mixing or integrating quantitative and qualitative data allows better and deeper understanding of a problem or question. In the case of this study, combining quantitative data (e.g., teacher development activities) and qualitative data (e.g., considerations in selecting PD activities and digital tools, challenges encountered, and coping mechanisms used) can allow more holistic understanding of the technology-enhanced professional development practices of Southeast Asian English language teachers during the COVID-19 pandemic.

4.3.2 Participants

Participants of this study were 17 purposively selected English language teachers and lecturers from Cambodia, Indonesia, Malaysia, Myanmar, Philippines, Singapore, Thailand, and Vietnam. They were selected based on their being previous students/scholars at the Southeast Asian Ministers of Education (SEAMEO)—Regional English Language Centre (RELC) in Singapore. The majority of the participants were female (65 percent), 26–40 years old (82 percent), master's degree holders (76 percent), high school teachers (47 percent) and university lecturers (41 percent), and public/government employees (94 percent) with teaching experience over 5 years (83 percent). Though they were purposively selected, their experiences and teaching situations during the pandemic were typical of other English language teachers in the Southeast Asian region.

4.3.3 Data Gathering Instrument

The data gathering instrument used in this study was a researcher-made questionnaire with closed and open-ended questions. It was constructed based on the specific research questions of the study. It was composed of two parts—Part 1, which dealt with the background information of the participants, and Part 2, which elicited quantitative and qualitative data on teacher development activities during the pandemic (covering the period of March 2020 to September 2021), factors considered in selecting development activities and digital tools, challenges encountered, and coping strategies used. To ensure validity and reliability, the researcher had it checked and reviewed by colleagues at work and tried it out among selected teacher-trainees who were taking up a regular course at SEAMEO RELC.

4.3.4 Data Gathering Procedure

Since the target participants of the study were previous students/scholars of SEAMEO RELC in Singapore, permission to conduct the study was sought from the Centre's Research Ethics Committee. After receiving the approval, potential participants were identified using the RELC student database system and through the recommendations of the Centre's language specialists. Then, the invitation to participate in the study along with the consent form was individually sent to each identified participant through email. After receiving the signed consent form from each participant, the questionnaire was then sent as an email attachment. Participants were given 14 days to complete and return the completed questionnaires.

4.3.5 Data Analysis

Quantitative data concerning professional development activities the participants engaged in during the pandemic were analyzed using simple frequency and percentage count, while qualitative data dealing with factors in selecting PD activities and technologies as well as the problems encountered and coping mechanisms used were manually analyzed using inductive thematic approach. The inductive thematic approach is a process where qualitative data are coded without trying to fit them into a pre-existing coding frame or preconceived themes expected to be reflected based on existing theory or knowledge. After coding the data into themes, they were then organized and developed into a new thematic framework.

4.4 Results and Discussion

RQ 1: What language teacher development (LTD) activities did Southeast Asian English language teachers engage in during the COVID-19 pandemic?

To answer this question, respondents were surveyed on the different types of professional learning and development activities they engaged in during the peak of the COVID-19 pandemic. Table 4.1 presents the different types of professional development activities and the frequency and percentage of participants who engaged in each activity.

Table 4.1 shows the common online professional development activities of the respondents during the COVID-19 pandemic. Among the most popular development activities were *meeting with colleagues discussing work-related topics and issues, participation in synchronous webinars with credit or certification,* and *watching how-to videos or lecture videos in YouTube, TEDTalks, and so on* with 16 or 94.11 percent of respondents each. These were followed by *reflecting on new experiences* with 15 or 88.23 percent of respondents, *developing and sharing instructional materials, collaborating with colleagues on a new work-related project, involvement in work-related committees and study groups, attending (virtual) conferences, reading relevant posts/graphics shared through social media (e.g., Facebook, LinkedIn, Blogger),* and *being coached/mentored by others* with 14 or 82.35 percent of respondents each. Then, *peer observation of (online) teaching* and *mentoring or coaching fellow teachers* came next with 13 or 76.47 percent of respondents each. The least popular teacher development activities engaged in by the respondents were *enrolment and completion of relevant Massive Open Online Courses (MOOCs)* with 6 or 35.29 percent of respondents, followed by *involvement as leader or consultant in profession-related projects* and *organizing professional events or forming professional organizations* with 5 or 29.41 percent each, and *keeping a teacher e-Portfolio to monitor progress* with 4 or 23.52 percent of respondents.

68   J. C. Meniado

Table 4.1 Online language teacher development activities engaged in by the respondents during the COVID-19 pandemic

Professional Development Activities	Frequency	Percentage
Work-Based Learning (learning new knowledge/skills at workplace)		
1. Peer observation of (online) teaching	13	76.47
2. Reflecting on new experiences	15	88.23
3. Being coached/mentored by others	14	82.35
4. Reading school manuals and handbooks	8	47.05
5. Developing and sharing instructional materials	14	82.35
6. Experimenting with new resources/ideas in the classroom	12	70.58
7. Collaborating with colleagues on a new work-related project	14	82.35
8. Meeting with colleagues discussing work-related topics and issues	16	94.11
9. Involvement in work-related committees and study groups	14	82.35
Average	13	76.47
Professional Activities (sharing expertise to others)		
10. Giving presentations at (virtual) conferences	7	41.17
11. Giving academic talks/lectures in organized panels or webinars	9	52.94
12. Mentoring or coaching fellow teachers	13	76.47
13. Involvement as leader or consultant in profession-related projects	5	29.41
14. Organizing professional events or forming professional organizations	5	29.41
15. Participation in professional learning communities or communities of practice (CoPs)	9	52.94
Average	8	47.05
Formal and Educational (structured learning offered by educational institutions)		
16. Enrollment in formal distance/online courses	12	70.58
17. Conducting research with mentor supervision	6	35.29
18. Writing articles or papers	7	41.17
19. Attending (virtual) conferences	14	82.35
20. Participation in synchronous webinars with credit or certification	16	94.11
21. Participation in online workshops with credit or certification	12	70.58
Average	11	64.70
Self-Directed CPD (structured but self-paced, independent learning)		
22. Reading journals or articles	10	58.82
23. Keeping a teacher e-Portfolio to monitor progress	4	23.52

(continued)

Table 4.1 (continued)

Professional Development Activities	Frequency	Percentage
24. Reviewing books or articles	6	35.29
25. Completing a mandated training/course online without a strict deadline	6	35.29
Average	7	41.17
Self-Determined CPD (based on self-identified development needs; selective, independent learning)		
26. Enrolment and completion of relevant Massive Open Online Courses (MOOCs)	6	35.29
27. Participation in non-certified webinars which are of topics of interests (or watching recorded versions thereof)	11	64.70
28. Watching how-to videos or lecture videos in YouTube, TEDTalks, and so on	16	94.11
29. Reading relevant posts/graphics shared through social media (e.g., Facebook, LinkedIn, Blogger)	14	82.35
Average	12	70.58

These results are consistent with the previous observations and findings that teachers learned and developed professionally during the pandemic by seeking assistance and guidance of their colleagues at work, experimenting their new ideas, watching tutorial videos from social media sites, observing their fellow teachers teaching online, forming learning circles/working groups, and by conducting independent research (Agnello, 2021; Moorhouse & Wong, 2021). Results also confirm that teachers learned by sharing resources using common online sharing platforms (Conan, 2020; Neumann & Smith, 2020), collaborating with their colleagues, completing an online course (Evmenova et al., 2021), participating in online webinars, forums, workshops, and virtual conferences (Gautam, 2020), self-reflection, and delivering talks and presentations (Yu et al., 2021). Similar to previous studies, the use of teacher e-portfolio as a form of professional development also seemed less popular or less explored among teachers. This variety of online professional development activities during the pandemic implies that while there was mobility restriction, professional learning and development did not stop. As it appeared, technology enhanced the process and provided new pathways and opportunities.

When grouped according to type or category, Table 4.1 also shows that work-based learning (learning new knowledge/skills at workplace) was the most frequently engaged type of teacher development with an average of 13 respondents (76.47 percent). This was followed by self-determined teacher development activities with an average of 12 respondents (70.58 percent), formal and educational type of activities with 11 respondents (64.70 percent), professional activities with 8 respondents (47.05 percent), and self-directed learning activities with 7 respondents (41.17 percent). This result suggests that respondents were more interested in activities that are more relevant, context-based, practical, collaborative, and sustainable. They preferred learning something that they could practically and immediately apply in their own workplace. Results also suggest further that respondents preferred professional development activities that could address their self-determined learning needs. They were more inclined to doing something that is personalized, specific, engaging, and reflective. These inclinations and preferences imply that the respondents were into activities that meet the qualities of impactful and sustainable language teacher development (Maggioli, 2020; McAleavy et al., 2018; OECD, 2017).

RQ 2: What technological tools did the respondents use to engage in these teacher development activities?

The respondents used varied digital tools to carry out their online professional learning and development activities. For example, they used videoconferencing systems and equipment (e.g., Zoom, MS Teams, Google Meet, Webex) to meet with their colleagues discussing work-related topics or issues, to participate in synchronous online course, webinars, trainings, forums, workshops, and virtual conferences, and to observe and coach fellow teachers. They also used communication/messaging tools (email, WhatsApp, FB Messenger, Telegram, etc.) to communicate and collaborate with their colleagues, to share resources, and to seek immediate help and advice on work-related issues. In addition, they also used learning management systems (e.g., Google Classroom, Canvas) to access the online courses they were enrolled in and engagement tools (e.g., Mentimeter, Padlet, Kahoot, Quizziz, Nearpod) to engage themselves in their learning. Moreover, they also used collaboration tools (e.g., Google Docs, Google Jamboard) to work with colleagues and peers and social media (e.g., Facebook, Instagram, Twitter, YouTube) to learn new information, to connect with other professionals, and to share resources such as readings and relevant videos. Lastly, they used Google Search to search resources they need for learning, Google Drive to store and share resources, and ELT websites to learn new strategies and resources in teaching English. This result is similar to findings of previous studies by Gautam (2020) and Moorhouse and Wong (2021). The digital tools had their unique affordances and served various purposes for professional learning and development.

RQ 3: What factors did the respondents consider in engaging in teacher development activities during the pandemic and in selecting appropriate technological tools for such activities?

The respondents considered accessibility, relevance, usefulness, and practicality when deciding to engage in an online teacher development activity. In addition, they also considered timing/schedule, cost, support, and reputation of the speakers and institution delivering/organizing the activity. As one of the respondents shared:

> I prefer the shortened but practical and effective information which helps me improve my teaching performance. I am interested in listening to real experiences of teachers, their own stories and advice. I also like involving in group work/discussion in which I can learn a lot from my colleagues.

Another respondent also shared that she looked into *"who (which university or institution) is going to give the lecture, cost, time, mode of communication, relevance to personal or professional goal(s), and contents/course structure."* These results indicate that the respondents preferred activities that exhibit qualities of good teacher development program which include being context-based, practical, specific, responsive, engaging, continual, collaborative, sustainable, reflective, and measurable (Hismanoglu, 2010; Maggioli, 2020; McAleavy et al., 2018; OECD, 2017).

In terms of selecting and using appropriate digital tools for the PD activities, the respondents considered accessibility, compatibility, familiarity, and cost. They preferred tools that were already available, affordable, easy to use, compatible with their existing devices, and useful for their nature of work. As one of the respondents shared, *"I prefer technological tools that are user-friendly, with minimal issues and requirements in accessibility and internet connectivity."* The results indicate alignment between the considerations for PD engagement and technology use. The respondents considered tools that fit their purpose and existing context.

RQ 4: What challenges did they encounter in their teacher development activities during the pandemic and how did they manage to overcome such challenges?

Common challenges reported by the respondents included unstable internet connectivity, lack of required resources, and lack of time and space. Mostly living in under-resourced areas with limited ICT infrastructure, the respondents often encountered difficulties in establishing and maintaining strong internet connection while attending synchronous sessions. They also reported lack of required hardware/software to access resources and participate in online sessions, lack of skills in using digital tools, heavy course requirements, work pressure, balancing work, studies and personal life, establishing common time to meet and collaborate with learners from different time zones. These results are similar to those reported in the study by Gautam (2020). Results confirm previous findings that connectivity, access to technology, time management, and well-being are issues that need serious attention.

While the respondents encountered many difficulties in participating in online teacher development activities, they were ingenuous enough to find solutions. When they had unstable internet connection during synchronous session, they would ask the lecturer/trainer/organizer to share recorded version of the session. Further, when they did not know how to use specific digital tool, they watched "how-to" videos from YouTube or sought assistance from more digitally literate colleagues or family members. Moreover, when they had many tasks and deadlines on their schedule, they prioritized the more urgent ones and used calendar app to set reminders. They also had to chunk tasks into smaller ones and had short breaks in between. Lastly, they used chat groups in WhatsApp and Telegram to discuss asynchronously when they could not set common time for synchronous discussion. Results show resilience and creativity of the respondents in solving their own online learning problems. These qualities should be cascaded down to their own learners in their online language classrooms.

4.5 Conclusion and Lessons Learned

Findings of this study prove that technology-enhanced language teacher development (LTD) is possible even in the midst of a global adversity like the COVID-19 pandemic. Leveraging available technologies, language teachers can continually engage in various forms of learning and development. Findings of this study also prove that when faced with challenges in emergency situations, language teachers tend to prefer more practical, accessible, responsive, and personalized learning opportunities to enable themselves to solve immediate problems in their own contexts. Lastly, when exposed to various restrictions and difficulties, language teachers develop skills and values that lead to resilience, ingenuity, and commitment to the profession.

The identified patterns of LTD preferences and engagements of the respondents of this study during the pandemic imply a need to revitalize existing school-based LTD programs with the new trends and dynamics of adult/professional learning and development. Work-based LTD programs should be emphasized to foster accessibility, practicality, relevance, responsiveness, personalization, and sustainability. With integration of new technologies, schools should adopt a transformative LTD framework where resources and processes allow intensive, action-driven, personalized, responsive, and focused professional learning and development (Reeves, 2020). To overcome the perennial problems on connectivity and technology access, schools or educational systems should also invest more on ICT infrastructures for language teachers to have wider options of the what, where, and how of their professional learning and development. Technology-enhanced LTD support groups should also be created to facilitate collaboration and guidance for all language teachers.

Though this study yielded findings that provide evidence of technology-enhanced LTD practices of English language teachers in the Southeast Asian region during the pandemic, it acknowledges its generalizability limitations considering its scope and the number of respondents involved. Future studies may consider a more large-scale approach to developing a more comprehensive understanding of technology-enhanced LTD practices in the region. Building on the findings of this study, future studies may consider investigating the impacts of technology-enhanced LTD activities on student learning and institutional effectiveness to identify best practices and inform policies that can help improve language teacher education and development in the ASEAN region.

References

Agnello, E. (2021, October 12). *How professional learning for teachers has changed during the pandemic*. Frontline Education. https://www.frontlineeducation.com/blog/supporting-professional-development-for-teachers-during-pandemic/

Alexandrou, A. (2021). Professional learning and development – Change, conceptualisation, innovation and opportunities. *Professional Development in Education, 47*(5), 725–728. https://doi.org/10.1080/19415257.2021.1966588

Buendia, X. P., & Macias, D. F. (2019). The professional development if English language teachers in Colombia: A review of literature. *Colombian Applied Linguistics Journal, 25*(1), 89–102. https://doi.org/10.14483/22487085.12966

Conan, J. (2020). Personalized professional learning in the move to remote instruction during COVID-19. In R.E. Ferdig, E. Baumgartner, R. Hartshorne, R. Kaplan-Rakowski, & C. Mouza (Eds.), *Teaching, technology, and teacher education during the COVID-19 pandemic: Stories from the field* (pp. 557–560). Association for the Advancement of Computing in Education (AACE). https://www.learntechlib.org/p/216903/

Craft, A. (2000). *Continuing professional development*. Routledge.

Creswell, J. W., & Creswell, J. D. (2018). *Research design: Qualitative, quantitative, and mixed methods approaches* (5th ed.). Sage.

Evmenova, A. S., Borup, J., & Dabbagh, N. (2021). Re-designing professional development to assist instructors' rapid transition to remote teaching during the Covid-19 pandemic. *Teacher Educators' Journal, 14*, 22–42. https://files.eric.ed.gov/fulltext/EJ1296550.pdf

Fletcher-Wood, H., & Zucollo, J. (2020). *The effects of high quality professional development on teachers and students: A rapid review and meta-analysis*. London: Education Policy Institute. https://epi.org.uk/publications-and-research/effects-high-quality-professional-development/

Gautam, G. R. (2020). English language teacher professional development during COVID-19 in Nepal. *Interdisciplinary Research In Education, 5*(1&2), 103–112. https://doi.org/10.3126/ire.v5i1&2.34739

Goldsmith, C. (2021). Navigating pandemic teaching via individualized faculty professional development. *Multidisciplinary Perspectives in Higher Education, 6*(1), 135–141. https://www.ojed.org/index.php/jimphe/article/view/2951

Hayes, D. (2019). Continuing professional development/continuous professional learning for English language teachers. In S. Walsh & S. Mann (Eds.), *The Routledge Handbook for English Language Teacher Education* (pp. 155–168). Routledge. https://doi.org/10.4324/9781315659824-14

Hismanoglu, M. (2010). Effective professional development strategies of English language teachers. *Procedia Social and Behavioral Sciences, 2*, 990–995. https://doi.org/10.1016/j.sbspro.2010.03139

International Bureau of Education–United Nations Educational, Scientific and Cultural Organization [IBE–UNESCO]. (2021). *Technology-enhanced learning.* Retrieved from http://www.ibe.unesco.org/en/glossary-curriculum-terminology/t/technology-enhanced-learning

Johnston, B. (2009). Collaborative teacher development. In A. Burns & J. C. Richards (Eds.), *The Cambridge Guide to Second Language Teacher Education* (pp. 241–249). Cambridge University Press.

Kalinowski, A., Gronostaj, A., & Vock, M. (2019). Effective professional development for teachers to foster students' academic language proficiency across the curriculum: A systematic review. *AERA Open, 5*(1), 1–23. https://doi.org/10.1177/2332858419828691

Kirkwood, A., & Price, L. (2014). Technology-enhanced learning and teaching in higher education: What is 'enhanced' and how do we know? *A critical literature review. Learning, Media and Technology, 39*(1), 6–36. https://doi.org/10.1080/17439884.2013.770404

Kong, S. C., Looi, C. K., Chan, T. W., & Huang, R. (2017). Teacher development in Singapore, Hong Kong, Taiwan, and Beijing for e-Learning in school education. *Journal of Computers in Education, 4*, 5–25. https://doi.org/10.1007/s40692-016-0062-5

Littlejohn, A., & Margaryan, A. (2014). Technology-enhanced professional learning. In S. Billet, C. Harteis, & H. Gruber (Eds.), *International handbook of research in professional and practice-based learning* (pp. 1187–1212). https://doi.org/10.1007/978-94-017-8902-8_43.

Maggioli, G. D. (2003). Professional development for language teachers. *ERIC Digest* (EDO-FL-03-03). https://unitus.org/FULL/0303diaz.pdf

Maggioli, G. D. (2020). Continuous professional development: The seeds of professionalism. In C. Coombe, N. Anderson, & L. Stephenson (Eds.), *Professionalizing your English language teaching* (pp. 253–261). Springer. https://doi.org/10.1007/978-3-030-34762-8_21

McAleavy, T., Hall-Chen, A., Horrocks, S., & Riggall, A. (2018). *Technology-supported professional development for teachers: Lessons from developing countries*. Berkshire: Education Development Trust. https://files.eric.ed.gov/fulltext/ED593386.pdf

Meniado, J. C. (2019). Evaluating the English proficiency of faculty members of a higher education institution: Using results to develop responsive professional development program. *International Journal of English Linguistics, 9*(2), 52–63. https://doi.org/10.5539/ijel.v9n2p52

Mizell, H. (2010). *Why professional development matters*. Oxford, OH: Learning Forward. http://www.learningforward.org/advancing/whypdmatters.cfm

Moorhouse, B. L., & Wong, K. M. (2021). The COVID-19 pandemic as a catalyst for teacher pedagogical and technological innovation and development: Teachers' perspectives. *Asia Pacific Journal of Education*. https://doi.org/10.1080/02188791.2021.1988511.

Muhayimana, T. (2020). Teacher professional learning during the global pandemic: Five critical areas to address. *Journal of School Administration Research and Development, 5*(S2), 66–79. https://doi.org/10.32674/jsard.v5iS2.2840

Neumann, K. L., & Smith, M. D. (2020). Facilitating just-in-time professional development for in-service teachers transitioning to distance learning. In R. E. Ferdig, E. Baumgartner, R. Hartshorne, R. Kaplan-Rakowski, & C. Mouza (Eds.), *Teaching, technology, and teacher education during the COVID-19 pandemic: Stories from the field* (pp. 527–530). Association for the Advancement of Computing in Education (AACE). https://www.learntechlib.org/p/216903/

Organization for Economic and Co-operation Development [OECD]. (2017). How can professional development enhance teachers' classroom practices? *Teaching in Focus, No. 16*. Paris: OECD Publishing. https://doi.org/10.1787/2745d679-en.

Reeves, D. B. (2020, February 1). *Five professional learning transformations for a post-COVID world*. https://www.ascd.org/el/articles/five-professional-learning-transformations-for-a-post-covid-world

Richards, J. C. (2008). Second language teacher education today. *RELC Journal, 39*(2), 158–177. https://doi.org/10.1177/0033688208092182

Richards, J. C., & Farrell, T. S. C. (2005). *Professional development for language teachers: Strategies for teacher learning*. Cambridge University Press.

Sadeghi, K., & Richards, J. C. (2021). Professional development among English language teachers: Challenges and recommendations for practice. *Heliyon, 7*(9), e08053. https://doi.org/10.1016/j.heliyon.2021.e08053

Sen, A., & Leong, C. K. C. (2020). Technology-enhanced learning. In A. Tatnall (Ed.), *Encyclopedia of education and information technologies*. Springer. https://doi.org/10.1007/978-3-319-60013-0_72-1

Shohel, M. M. C., & Banks, F. (2012). School-based teachers' professional development through technology-enhanced learning. *Teacher Development, 16*(1), 25–42. https://doi.org/10.1080/13664530.2012.668103

Yu, H., Liu, P., Huang, X., & Cao, Y. (2021). Teacher online informal learning as a means to innovative teaching during home quarantine in the COVID-19 pandemic. *Frontiers in Psychology, 12*, 596582. https://doi.org/10.3389/fpsyg.2021.596582

Part II

Reactions to CALL in Teacher Education during the Pandemic

5

'We've Been Able to Continue with Our Teaching': Technology and Pedagogy in Emergency Remote Language Education

Anne Burns, Rebecca Matteson, Kirsty Phease, and Jennifer West

5.1 Introduction

The advent of Covid-19 in early 2020 was a time of unforeseen emergency and enormous upheaval for numerous language teachers involved in teaching international students studying in many different countries. Many language centres, some attached to universities and some to private organisations, suddenly lost large numbers of students who were unable to continue their studies or had to return rapidly to their home countries.

A. Burns (✉)
Curtin University, Perth, WA, Australia
e-mail: a.c.burns@curtin.edu.au

R. Matteson • J. West
University of Technology Sydney (UTS) College, Sydney, NSW, Australia

K. Phease
Online Education Services (OES), Melbourne, VIC, Australia

© The Author(s), under exclusive license to Springer Nature Switzerland AG 2023
K. Sadeghi, M. Thomas (eds.), *Second Language Teacher Professional Development*,
Digital Education and Learning, https://doi.org/10.1007/978-3-031-12070-1_5

82   A. Burns et al.

In Australia, the context in which this chapter is set, many of these teaching centres immediately turned to alternative online emergency learning solutions through the use of various forms of technology, in order to maintain enrolments and continue to support their students. For teachers within these institutions, the requirement to adapt their teaching from a face-to-face environment to one where all teaching would be done online was extremely challenging (Burns, 2022). This chapter discusses how the first author amended the facilitation of an action research (AR) professional development programme in which the other three teacher authors participated. The three teachers, two of them working as partners, carried out AR with teaching colleagues in their own centres to investigate how they could respond to these new and unpredictable demands. The chapter draws out the implications for teacher education and professional development.

5.2   The Research Context

At the time of this substantial challenge, the authors of this chapter were all involved in the Action Research in English Language Intensive Courses for Overseas Students (ELICOS) Program. This is a national professional development programme, which focuses on teachers conducting AR, sponsored by Cambridge English Assessment and offered by English Australia, a peak advocacy body for the ELICOS sector. ELICOS is a major Australian educational sector, offering a range of English for Academic Purposes and General English courses for international students, many of them designed for university preparation and entry. Each year since 2010, English Australia has invited teachers to carry out AR over approximately nine months, in order to investigate a research theme relevant to the priorities of the ELICOS sector. Typically, up to 12 teachers participate, conducting six projects focused on topics related to the theme, but selected by the participants for the specific relevance to their own work. For 2020, the theme was Blended Learning (Hockly, 2018), as many teaching centres were moving increasingly towards integrating technology into their courses. However, very rapidly in the early part of the year, with the advent of the Covid-19 pandemic, the research theme extended itself to explore the impact of the use of technology and online emergency teaching and learning (Hodges et al., 2020).

As far as the authors' specific roles were concerned, Anne was the academic facilitator of the AR Program, offering workshops and other forms of support across the year. Rebecca and Jennifer, who were, respectively, Program and Subject Coordinators for courses at their institution in Sydney, worked as research partners, investigating their colleagues' reactions to the rapid change to online teaching, while Kirsty, a Senior Teacher for Blended Learning at her workplace in Melbourne, was a single researcher exploring how to support teachers in this move. In addition, in our collaborative AR group, there were five other teachers, conducting their own joint or individual AR projects focusing on student experiences of this new learning environment. The group received further support and facilitation from the Professional Development Manager of English Australia.

In previous years, the AR in ELICOS Program had always been conducted face to face. Teachers located in different parts of the country valued the opportunity to come to Sydney, to meet with colleagues working in the same sector, and to share their ideas about teaching and researching in their particular context. In 2020 (and indeed in 2021), it was necessary not only for the teachers involved to move their teaching online but also for the facilitators to rethink the way the Program could be offered remotely.

In the narratives that follow, we recount what we did and learned in response to the rapid changes that had to be made, both for the AR Program itself and for the teaching contexts where we worked.

5.2.1 Anne

The face-to-face version of the AR in ELICOS Program typically consisted of two workshops held in Sydney in March and July each year. A third workshop occurred the day before the annual English Australia conference in September in whichever venue across the country this event was situated. At the conference, the teachers had an opportunity to present their research in an AR Colloquium dedicated to the Program. To attend the workshops, the participating teachers flew in from their various cities or towns in order to share their research ideas and activities, and their progress across the year. The workshops offered ongoing collaboration and discussion, as well as support for analysis and for the presentation and writing up of the research. The concept of face-to-face contact is considered to be an integral and very important part of the Program in that the teachers involved can create and experience a close community of practice and gain support from peers through dialogic interaction (Mercer, 2000, 2019). My role in this Program is as a facilitator and guide who introduces teachers to the fundamental concepts and processes of AR and offers support for its continuation (Burns et al., 2022). My assistance also includes one-on-one question and answer Zoom calls as needed between workshops, and input into data analysis. The conclusion of the teachers' research includes opportunities to present and publish their studies, for which I also offer support.

In 2020, eight teachers working in six projects began participating in the Program, with two sets of teachers working as partners for two of the projects. The first workshop was still held face to face over two days in early March in Sydney, although it was becoming very clear that the Covid-19 situation would have an imminent effect on the Program and could even place it in jeopardy. In fact, three of the original group of teachers decided they could not continue because of various pressures emerging in their teaching programmes from the pandemic. At that time, many international students were either returning home, dropping out of courses or were forced to enrol online. In addition, federal government regulations were placing restrictions on international movement and Australian state border closures meant that people could also not travel freely across the country. Thus, the first dilemma was whether the Program could continue at all.

After consultation with the sponsor Cambridge English Assessment, English Australia decided that the Program should proceed and three more teachers, two working as partners, were recruited for the second workshop to replace those who had dropped out. The decision to go ahead meant offering the Program remotely. It also meant renegotiating the structures of the second and third workshops, not only to re-establish new dynamics and different kinds of roles and relationships within the group, but also to experiment with different forms of presentation and interaction.

Although I was relatively accustomed to delivering conference and webinar presentations online, holding a workshop through Zoom across a whole day was another matter, particularly one where there was little focus on presentation of content and much more on participants' interactive sharing and reshaping of their processes of conducting AR.

Some major changes were trialled to accommodate this new professional development situation (see Burns, 2021). For each change that was introduced, feedback was collected from the teachers to evaluate whether the new workshop formats were working for them. The changes comprised:

- contacting the new participants online individually before the second workshop to welcome them and discuss how they could organise their research plans to line up with the other participants. These participants were also sent all the materials and PowerPoints used in the first workshop and any questions or issues they had were discussed;
- in the meantime, making online contact individually with each of the continuing teachers about their projects, to discuss if and how they believed they could proceed and to help develop any revised ideas and directions;
- then, to follow up, convening a short initial online meeting of an hour with all the teachers to introduce the new participants and to briefly explain the major changes in how the Program would proceed for the rest of the year;
- holding each of the second and third workshops over two mornings instead of a whole day and providing several breaks during each session, so that participants could recharge physically and mentally. The workshops included input on data analysis, report writing, and presentation preparation, but also allowed freer discussion time for teachers in each project to update others and seek interactive feedback from the whole group on ways to reshape their research;
- continuing to provide one-on-one sessions for individual projects when the teachers indicated they needed them. These sessions mainly covered areas related to the topics, questions, and directions of their research, data collection tools, and data analysis.

In previous years, the third workshop had always been held the day before the English Australia conference in September, with the aim of giving teachers time to share their findings and rehearse their presentations for the conference colloquium on the Program. In 2020, while the third workshop still included these areas, the teachers' final presentations were not held as part of the (online) English Australia conference. Instead, they occurred the following month in separate sessions offered for 90 minutes over two days, during which each of the three teachers presented their research. As it turned out, this new format worked more effectively than before as a larger national, and even international, audience was able to watch the sessions and there was more time for the teachers to describe their research and answer questions. It was clear too from the online chat comments that other teachers in the audience greatly appreciated hearing about how their colleagues had researched their topics and could offer valuable insights into commonly experienced challenges. Normally this kind of feedback would not have been readily available to the presenting teachers and it served to increase their confidence.

It was very gratifying to discover that changes, which had seemed to have been forced on us by the advent of the pandemic, had in fact led to a valuable renewal of the Program's structure. The teachers involved unanimously indicated that it had been professionally rewarding despite the institutional challenges they were experiencing. One teacher, who had initially been concerned about any additional pressure, commented: 'I'm glad I didn't drop out of the Program as it has provided a sense of continuity and I can feel like I am still accomplishing something during this time'. Another stated: 'It has been a very intense period for me over the last five weeks, but I have always looked forward to the sessions and workshops'.

In the next two sections, three teachers who participated in the Program and whose research focused specifically on the reactions of their teaching colleagues to the dramatic changes brought about by the pandemic, describe the research they undertook through this professional development programme.

5.2.2 Rebecca and Jennifer

We worked as colleagues at a college in Sydney that taught many international students. Since we were both highly involved in training teachers to move to online teaching, we decided that our AR project would investigate teachers' attitudes to transitioning online quickly as a result of the pandemic. Not only did teaching change to being completely online, but during the same time period, the college introduced both a new curriculum and a new Learning Management System (LMS). The fact that teachers had only three days to pivot from a face-to-face classroom environment to wholly online delivery added to the levels of anxiety and stress.

We were particularly interested in the evolving needs of teachers during this time of upheaval. As a result, we developed the following two research questions to capture teachers' feelings:

1. What are teachers' attitudes towards online teaching and learning?
2. How can we adequately prepare teachers for the changes they are experiencing, both with the initial emergency online teaching and with the subsequent online delivery of our courses?

In our investigation, we collected data in two cycles. In the first cycle we developed a questionnaire to collect qualitative and quantitative data after the first six weeks of teaching online. The questionnaire consisted of 17 questions. Some questions were open-ended and structured with sentence stems that asked teachers to complete a sentence with their experience (e.g. 'The thing I like best about online teaching is ___'). Quantitative question types included yes/no (e.g. asking teachers if they had used Zoom before), multiple choice, and rating scales. We received 22 responses to the questionnaire. In the second cycle, we held two focus group interviews with four teachers each. Of the eight teachers interviewed, three had been teaching at our college for between 5 and 10 years, five had been at our college for less than 5 years, four were male and four were female. We recorded and transcribed the discussions. We then conducted a thematic analysis to draw out the main insights.

Initially, teachers expressed both concern that teaching online would not be as effective as teaching in person and excitement at the opportunity to develop new technological skills (cf. Kohnke & Jarvis, 2021). Their concern about using new technologies to teach manifested itself in many ways. In response to a survey question which asked about teachers' feelings when they learned that the school was moving to online teaching, one teacher wrote:

> … nervous because I did not have previous experience of this. I also felt rushed and that there was not enough time to get the hang of it before facing the students, which was a threat to my professionalism.

Another teacher summed up more positive emotions involved in the change, saying:

> I've realised that remote teaching creates many opportunities to leverage new skills and refocus the way we teach to a more blended learning format. It means we've been able to continue with our teaching despite many other organisations closing down.

The training provided to teachers by the college, with our involvement, during the initial phases of emergency remote teaching had focused on the new technologies that teachers needed in order to continue teaching in this new environment. This training included how to use Zoom and other video conferencing tools, using Microsoft applications such as Teams and OneDrive, and demonstrating feedback and assessment marking tools in the new LMS.

However, one of the most important findings of our AR project was that even when the technological demands increased dramatically, the teachers involved maintained a primary focus on pedagogy. As Table 5.1 highlights, thematic analysis of data collected from interviews and surveys showed that references to teaching practice appeared far more often (over 50% of all responses) than any other thematic category.

Our findings indicated that, perhaps contrary to expectations, teachers remained most concerned about the same things they cared about in the physical classroom, such as student engagement, feedback, and monitoring students' progress.

5 'We've Been Able to Continue with Our Teaching'... 89

Table 5.1 Frequency of themes in our qualitative data

Theme	Examples of keywords	Total	Initial questionnaire	Focus groups
Pedagogy	Attendance, classroom management, comparison online vs classroom, feedback, monitoring, student attention/engagement, etc.	156	59	97
Emotion	Anxious, challenge, comparison online vs classroom, confidence, easy, excited, exhausting, isolating, job security, positive, possible, stress, tolerate, etc.	118	78	40
Technology	Breakout rooms, camera, comparison online vs classroom, internet, mistakes, new skills, support, etc.	82	32	50
Physical	Eye contact, comparison online vs classroom, monitoring, physical distance, physical location, time, etc.	44	27	17
Development	comparison online vs classroom, new skills, learning	25	25	0

Noticeably, one major hurdle for our colleagues during this time was related to the confluence of technology and pedagogy. The curriculum and materials teachers were using had been developed for face-to-face delivery, and now suddenly, they needed to use that same curriculum in an online classroom. The materials needed to be adapted urgently to suit the new mode, and this adaptation was being done individually by each teacher. Many teachers struggled with this challenge and found that their work hours were extended well beyond the usual requirements. In the focus group interview, one teacher drew attention to the extra workload and personal demands in this way:

> I think for me, the biggest challenge has been things like, so I don't normally use a lot of PowerPoints, and now we're trying to use all of this other sort of technology which, given enough time I can sit down and work it out. You know, I'm relatively tech savvy. However, I have lost so much time

in my day while my kids are at home when I'm trying to work and in my week that I'm just so stretched in that regard, and I'll end up doing things, trying to work things out at 9:00 o'clock at night. So, although we've had all these trainings available to us, it's like I don't actually necessarily have the time to then do them.

At the time of the interview, teachers were receiving extra training (e.g. through self-help videos) in many different new technologies, but as the above teacher illustrated, many teachers had much less time to reflect on this training and incorporate it into their teaching, so they were often left feeling overwhelmed and under-supported. While around 60% of teachers responded to a survey question saying that they felt they were receiving the support they need to effectively teach online, 40% said they were not, as seen in Fig. 5.1.

Follow-up questions to find out more about the responses shown in Fig. 5.1 revealed that teachers felt they needed more support in the area of pedagogy and in adapting pedagogical strategies to teaching online (cf. Blume, 2020). For example, an open-ended item in the questionnaire asked 'I would like to learn more about___', to which one teacher responded, 'how to marry the teaching pedagogy with the technology tools'. This response exemplifies the pedagogical support needed. Later, in the focus group interview, this need for pedagogical support was

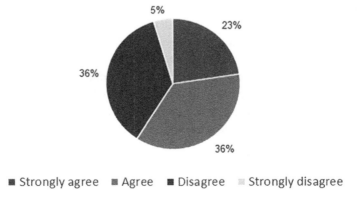

Fig. 5.1 Responses to the statement 'I feel that I am receiving the support I need to effectively teach online'

reiterated. Five out of the eight teachers interviewed said that the area where they most needed further support was in adapting pedagogical strategies to online teaching.

Looking back over the period since emergency remote teaching began, all the teachers at the college have, of necessity, improved their technological skills enormously. There is no doubt that teachers needed training in the use of new technologies to deliver online courses. However, the teachers in this research project clearly maintained a primary focus on teaching and learning. A complicating factor for them was that the materials had been developed for face-to-face teaching and needed to be adapted. A recommendation for future remote teaching is that materials, resources, and curricula need to be curated for online delivery at an institutional level, reducing the stress and inefficiency of each teacher individually re-making materials for online teaching as well as ensuring that students receive quality, standardised opportunities.

It is likely that online teaching will be an ongoing reality for many institutions. Therefore, successful organisations need to consider and plan for the transition from temporary, emergency remote teaching to ongoing online teaching. This will require leadership, investment, and continuing teacher professional development.

5.2.3 Kirsty

In March 2020, in the space of two weeks, my workplace in Melbourne transformed itself from being a large English-language centre to a completely online school. My role as a Senior Teacher for Blended Learning changed from supporting teachers in a gradual shift to technology to something else entirely.

Most teachers had decades of classroom experience and a widespread scepticism of educational technology (Gilakjani & Leong, 2012). Previously, I had supplied live in-class support. Now I had to work out what kind of training and assistance I could offer for an emergency remote teaching environment. The aims of my AR changed rapidly to trying to identify teachers' immediate needs and how to meet them in a timely way. I needed to understand what the teachers were experiencing in their new teaching contexts in order to help them effectively.

To begin to do this, I embarked on my AR by collaborating individually with five teachers. I interviewed them in a series of five recorded half-hour semi-structured Zoom interviews over approximately three months to understand their perspectives and identify a direction for my research. I started out with three general lines of questioning. My first and second questions were:

- What personal observations are you as a teacher making about this transition to online teaching?
- In your opinion, what is and isn't working?

These were intended to lead to my primary question, which underpinned the main part of my subsequent research:

- What training and/or support do you need?

Each set of responses in the initial interviews formed the basis for the guiding questions in the four following interviews. In this way I was able to continue exploring the topics and concerns each teacher raised. A profile of the participants I worked with will help to illustrate their experiences, perspectives, and the kinds of challenges they were facing. The first four teachers were all female, aged 55–65, and had worked at the centre for 20+ years.

1. This teacher identified herself as someone who had not extensively used or pursued educational technology teaching up to this point. She saw the 'emergency' aspect of online teaching as an undesirable but necessary change.
2. The second teacher was already open to using educational technology in her previous teaching. She felt curious and interested about the transition, but unsure how it would unfold.
3. This participant had actively avoided efforts to engage in education technology training up to this point. She felt she could be open and enthusiastic about developing these skills now that the need was clear.

4. The fourth teacher saw herself as someone who had made unsuccessful attempts to use education technology up to now. She acknowledged a sense of anxiety, and after the first two weeks of online teaching took an unpaid period of leave for five weeks. Two final interviews were conducted on her return.
5. The fifth participant was a male teacher aged 35–45 who had worked at the centre for 5–10 years. He saw the benefits and potential of educational technology, but had rarely used it. In the middle of my research, he became a team leader with responsibility for assisting in coordinating a group of teachers in addition to teaching.

After completing five interviews with each participant, I coded their responses to identify common themes for my training interventions. Several topics and issues emerged as key areas.

A Sense of Surprise that Initial Lessons Went Well

The teachers expressed surprise or relief that they had not encountered more problems, even when there were technical difficulties or awkwardness. As Teacher 5 said, 'I couldn't imagine what it would look like. Then you do it and it makes sense … it's surprising'.

A Recognition of Additional Time Needs

The issue of time emerged for most teachers, although they came to similar realisations at different points in the process. One of the first issues was that they needed considerably more time to plan and prepare than in face-to-face teaching. The burden of time was put expressively by Teacher 1: 'I know people who are spending 14 hours a day looking at their screen … planning, preparing, meetings, marking'.

A second dimension was how to divide up and use lesson time. In their first and second interviews some teachers observed that they could not use the same blocks of lesson time as in face-to-face teaching. Teacher 4 reflected the stress of having to allocate time differently: 'After the first day I was just exhausted…they [the students] were very passive…and just wanted to listen to me…but I can't do that anymore. Day two was better…I gave them exercises to do by themselves on Moodle'.

Finally, several teachers pointed to students' changed expectations of how available a teacher should be online, as Teacher 3 reported: 'I had one [student] who messaged me on Saturday night and asked to do some extra speaking exam practice'.

A Sense of Avoiding Being Perceived as Technologically Incompetent

Some teachers worried that their requests for technical assistance were being monitored by senior staff and could negatively affect their professional reputation or even their employment. As Teacher 4 put it: 'Some of us have been here for a long time…they know who we are…we're not used to all this technology…we're expensive for them'.

Seeking One-to-One Help with Specific Technical Questions

After each interview, I asked the teachers if they had challenges that I might help them with. This personalised support seemed rewarding and they frequently had questions saved up. Several teachers scheduled their interview early in order to go over their questions. Teacher 3 told me: 'I'm more than happy to do these [interviews] with you…it gives me a chance to ask you what I'm missing'.

These themes from the interviews led me to three training interventions to better support teachers at my centre.

Mini-tech Workshops

To help teachers' technology skills development I offered a daily drop-in clinic over Zoom, on alternating mornings and afternoons to accommodate their timetables. For these 'mini-tech workshops' teachers signed up via Google doc at their chosen times to a short half-hour session without any pre-determined technology focus, so that last-minute issues affecting them that day could easily be covered. They could ask a question or watch an example of a technical process and then practise it themselves. These workshops were restricted to three teachers. This short, flexible, and rolling scheduling allowed teachers to train in a responsive and safe environment where their concerns could be addressed quickly. Teachers really valued the privacy of the sessions as they did not have to reveal skills gaps to large numbers of colleagues. My observation was that the teachers' questions were overwhelmingly of a 'small' yes/no type. The opportunity to ask questions in an environment where they 'weren't bothering' people struck me as a common theme.

Inspiration Videos

My observations and discussions had led me to understand that although most teachers had some basic technology 'survival skills', they were initially overwhelmed by the sudden requirement for emergency remote teaching. Also, teachers reached a level of comfort with technology at different times. Therefore, any further training needed to be offered in such a way that teachers could access it when they were ready.

To help the teachers further, I began to produce a series of videos. Each video featured one content-creating or content-sharing method. These videos were emailed twice a week to all teaching staff across the larger national organisation to which my workplace belonged. I labelled them 'Inspiration Videos', to avoid giving teachers a sense of obligation to watch them every time they were released, but to enable them to access them later when they felt ready. These videos were always less than eight minutes in length, with a deliberate eye to making each one a manageable timed task that could be fitted into a busy teaching schedule. The videos were stored centrally so that teachers who found themselves needing to upskill quickly in one particular area could access them in a short amount of time.

During my research, I also re-sent videos to teachers who emailed me when they needed demonstrations of particular technical skills for a lesson they were about to teach. This immediate access proved a great source of support for the teachers and a time-saving tool for me.

Assessment Webinar as a Series of Short Videos

From the beginning of the transition, teachers expressed anxiety about how student assessments would be handled. Five weeks into classes I delivered an assessment training webinar which took into account the concerns of senior staff that teachers would need guidance in locating assessments, making them accessible, maintaining academic integrity, supporting delivery and marking, and providing appropriate instructions to their students. The webinar was long and covered a great deal of information. However, I designed the PowerPoint I used as a series of stand-alone videos, with each video modelling the on-screen instructions for a different stage of the assessment process. For example, a screencast video was supplied, from the teacher and student point of view, as to where students would need to click on their screens to accept the terms and conditions of Turnitin when accessing this feature for the first time through the course LMS (Moodle). The videos could afterwards be used for ongoing support, at times when teachers needed immediate access to particular information, which gave them more confidence in successfully delivering online assessments.

Looking back on the whole process, I have reached several personal conclusions on effective teacher education in an emergency remote teaching environment. First, training opportunities need to be discrete, focused, and bite-sized. Teachers take up and use opportunities when they know that time commitments will be limited. Second, video demonstrations are more effective and more immediately successful than email or phone explanations, as teachers soon realise they can re-watch them and even show them to students if necessary. Finally, a recurring theme in my research was that teachers were unsure what help they needed until they needed it. Consequently, opportunities for teachers themselves to guide the training and steer it towards whatever is immediate are more effective and greatly appreciated.

5.3 Implications and Lessons Learned

Like other language educators around the world, we have learned much through the rapid transition to emergency remote teaching (e.g. Davies et al., 2020; Juárez-Díaz & Perales, 2021). Evidence is emerging that the field of ELT will need extensive reconsideration of the kind of professional development needed to support this transition and sustain changes into the future effectively. Here we offer some suggestions from our own experiences.

In order to support teachers (and ultimately students), institutions need to appreciate the need for 'just-in-time' and not merely generalised models of technology training. Training needs to be delivered as and when teachers require it; it should not be assumed that large amounts of technological training input will otherwise be absorbed. Teachers need to be able to engage with technology to meet their own dilemmas and requirements. Institutions need to make available 'go-to' staff, who are skilled at using technology, and who can support teachers quickly. As described above, such staff can also exploit technology to make resources available to teachers that can help them respond to their challenges more autonomously.

Teachers can also benefit from institution-based 'communities of practice' where time is provided for them to come together to share ideas and problem-solve technological and pedagogical challenges. Setting up and supporting a collaborative AR group of the type we have described here is a highly worthwhile institutional investment that can inform future curriculum, materials, and assessment development. Such a group can also form the basis for sustainable critical thinking and creativity for the institution in ensuring students can remain engaged and motivated.

Institutions also need to appreciate that for most teachers, pedagogy drives the use of technology and not the reverse. While there is often great enthusiasm on the part of institutions to incorporate modern technology, this move becomes ineffective without sound pedagogical practices. Teachers can be encouraged to investigate the suitability of different technology platforms (e.g. Quizlet, Mentimeter, or Kahoot!) for their syllabuses and the content they need to cover. They can also explore ways technology might motivate student engagement (polls, screen sharing, breakout rooms, annotations, emojis, chats, etc.) and resources such as Google docs where students can collaborate on activities and teachers can provide feedback.

Teachers should also be empowered to provide feedback and input on the materials they are being asked to use. As we pointed out earlier, assuming that materials designed for face-to-face classrooms will readily translate to online delivery is misguided. Institutions need to provide practical professional development opportunities where collectively teachers can have input into the way such resources can be amended and trialled. Such opportunities need to be ongoing so that amendments and changes can be continued and sustained over time, as well as standardised to provide quality in the way they are presented and delivered. It should not be left to individual teachers to spend hours of their personal time modifying the materials they are required to work with.

5.4 Conclusion

Our research shows that, as elsewhere, in the transition to emergency remote teaching, Australian ELICOS teachers were often overwhelmed and over-worked and were unable to engage with professional development offerings at the times they were offered. Nevertheless, many of them showed that they were able to rapidly extend their skills and knowledge and meet teaching challenges creatively. Renewed forms of language teacher professional development have become, if anything, even more pressing during this time of the pandemic. Clearly, the traditional ways that professional development has been offered in the field of ELT need serious reconsideration if teachers are to extend their technological skills beyond survival mode. At the same time, real change often requires a catalyst in the form of a crisis. It is to be hoped that the Covid-19 pandemic has instigated fundamental movements in thinking in relation to professional development for the integration of technology.

References

Blume, C. (2020). German teachers' digital habitus and their pandemic pedagogy. *Postdigital Science and Education, 2*, 879–905.

Burns, A. (2021). Action research: Transformation in the first year of a pandemic. *Research Notes, 81*, 3–7. Downloadable from https://www.cambridgeenglish.org/Images/630859-research-notes-81.pdf

Burns, A. (2022). More of a fairy godmother type of teacher. In K. Sadeghi & F. Ghaderi (Eds.), *Technology-enhanced language teaching and learning: Lessons from the Covid-19 pandemic*. Bloomsbury.

Burns, A., Edwards, E., & Ellis, N. (2022). *Sustaining action research*. Routledge.

Davies, J. A., Davies, L. J., Conlon, B., Emerson, J., Hainsworth, H., & McDonough, H. G. (2020). Responding to Covid-19 in EAP contexts: A comparison of courses at four Sino-Foreign Universities. *International Journal of TESOL Studies, 2*(2), 32–51.

Gilakjani, A. P., & Leong, L. M. (2012). EFL teachers' attitudes toward using computer technology in English language teaching. *Theory and Practice in Language Studies, 2*(3), 630–636.

Hockly, N. (2018). Blended learning. *ELT Journal, 72*(1), 97–101.

Hodges, C., Moore, S., Lockee, B., Trust, T., & Bond, A. (2020). The difference between emergency remote teaching and online learning. *Educause Review, 3*. https://er.educause.edu/articles/2020/3/the-difference-between-emergency-remote-teaching-and-online-learning

Juárez-Díaz, C., & Perales, M. (2021). Language teachers' emergency remote teaching experiences during the COVID-19 confinement. *Profile: Issues in Teachers' Professional Development, 23*(2), 121–135.

Kohnke, L., & Jarvis, A. (2021). Coping with English for Academic Purposes provision during COVID-19. *Sustainability, 13*, 8642. https://doi.org/10.3390/su13158642

Mercer, N. (2000). *Words and Minds: How we use language to think together*. Routledge.

Mercer, N. (2019). *Language and the Joint Creation of Knowledge: The selected works of Neil Mercer*. Routledge.

6

Corpus Linguistics in English Language Teacher Education During the COVID-19 Pandemic: Exploring Opportunities and Addressing Challenges

Vander Viana

6.1 Introduction

The year 2020 marked a new era in contemporary life: we have had to live with the COVID-19 pandemic, which quickly spread globally. In an attempt to reduce the growing rate of infections and deaths, national/local restrictions such as lockdowns were imposed worldwide. The severity of these restrictions depended on how deeply a geopolitical area had been affected by the coronavirus.

The curbing of free movement has impacted education in numerous ways, and English language teacher education (ELTE) is no exception to this. Before 2020, ELTE was primarily delivered on-site and synchronously, an educational model that was no longer feasible during the

---

V. Viana (✉)
University of Edinburgh, Edinburgh, UK
e-mail: vander.viana@ed.ac.uk

© The Author(s), under exclusive license to Springer Nature Switzerland AG 2023 101
K. Sadeghi, M. Thomas (eds.), *Second Language Teacher Professional Development,*
Digital Education and Learning, https://doi.org/10.1007/978-3-031-12070-1_6

pandemic. Teaching/learning practices had to be reconsidered so that students' educational experiences would not come to a complete halt.

The pandemic has made all ELTE professionals work in difficult circumstances. The phrase 'teaching English in difficult circumstances' has been employed in the literature to refer to contexts where one finds, for example,

> insufficient and/or outdated textbooks, crowded classrooms with limited space, and lack of adequate resources and facilities for teaching-learning, including ICT. These difficult circumstances are compounded, particularly in resource poor environments, if teachers do not have adequate English language and/or pedagogical skills. (Shamim & Kuchah, 2016, p. 528)

There are, however, at least three differences between 'teaching English in difficult circumstances' and the difficult circumstances caused by the pandemic. One difference relates to professionals' lack of awareness of the circumstances being experienced. An educator in charge of a class with 300 students knows the nature of the difficulty to be faced. This was not the case during the pandemic: educators had to navigate uncharted waters and did not know what the short-term future would hold. A second difference is that of scope: the pandemic spread the difficult circumstances worldwide. However, it must be acknowledged that geopolitical contexts across the globe have been affected to different degrees for several reasons (e.g. public health policies). A third difference relates to the academic attention given to these new worldwide difficult circumstances. The pandemic-imposed circumstances could not be neglected in the academic literature contrary to the point made by Maley (2001) in relation to the teaching of English in difficult circumstances. This book is a clear example in this regard.

The present chapter examines the impact of the pandemic in one specific educational context: Master's-level ELTE. This choice of focus is primarily due to my own work in this field, but it is equally relevant from a pedagogical perspective. In many cases, these Master's programs are the means through which novice English language teachers are socialized into the profession. What lecturers do can provide their students with models to be followed or avoided. Tackling pandemic-imposed difficult circumstances in the eyes of current/future English language teachers can teach them about adaptability to uncertain, unknown and undesirable conditions. It can therefore contribute to the call for "teacher education programmes to equip language practitioners with the pedagogic and human skills and attitudes necessary for adapting to the changing dynamics of the world" (Kuchah, 2018, p. 13).

Previous research has considered whether/how ELTE integrates or should integrate fields/topics such as intercultural communication (Nelson, 1998), linguistics (LaFond & Dogancay-Aktuna, 2009), methods (Grosse, 1991), phonology (Murphy, 1997), practicum/microteaching (Cirocki et al., 2019; Papageorgiou et al., 2019) and pragmatics (Vásquez & Sharpless, 2009). However, there is little on the integration of corpus linguistics (CL) as a standalone module in ELTE Master's. A CL module brings a language-oriented focus to ELTE Master's, introducing students to the means through which they can develop their and their students' learning of and about the English language.

Most of the available literature on Master's-level ELTE, understandably, precedes the COVID-19 pandemic. It is unclear whether these findings are valid in the current while-pandemic context and whether they will apply in the post-pandemic world. The present chapter fills this gap: it evaluates the work required to adapt my CL teaching practice to the pandemic-imposed restrictions.

The chapter is divided into six sections. Following this introduction, Sect. 6.2 is dedicated to an overview of CL. The focal educational context is described in Sect. 6.3 before the reflective evaluation is discussed in Sects. 6.4 and 6.5. The latter two sections explore first the opportunities and then the challenges of teaching a CL module to ELTE Master's students during the pandemic. The chapter closes with a summary of the main points as well as a discussion of future directions.

6.2 Corpus Linguistics (CL)

CL is an empirical way of researching language use. Its findings come from computer-assisted analyses of corpora, that is, principled collections of texts which represent a sample of social practice (Tognini-Bonelli,

2001). This may be a sample of an entire language such as English or more specific language uses as in newspaper discourse or Master's dissertations.

The prioritization of performance data over introspective competence in CL constitutes a reappraisal of the importance assigned to knowledge sources. The so-called native speakers are not the sources of linguistic information: their intuitions, as well as those of any other speaker, are not reliable. CL instead favors analyses of examples of language use in naturally occurring texts. This can be summed up in Sinclair's (2004, p. 23) seminal plea that we should "trust the text."

The reliance on principled compiled corpora and the use of computer tools to analyze the textual data contained in these corpora expand the available data for analysis both in language research and in language education. For instance, the Corpus of Contemporary American English (COCA) contains more than 1 billion words (Davies, 2008–) and the News on the Web Corpus (NOW) contains more than 16 billion words (Davies, 2016–). Nowadays there is hardly any shortage of data to investigate language use.

The large amount of data available allows for the investigation of probability, which is a central concept in CL. For instance, even though the adverbs *absolutely*, *completely* and *totally* may be considered synonyms and may be used to modify the adjective *necessary*, *absolutely necessary* is by far the most recurrent combination in both COCA and NOW. This illustrates the notion of collocation, that is, the statistically significant use of one word with another in texts. Collocation is a fundamental notion in CL and "is now part of the stock-in-trade of applied linguistics and language teaching" (McCarthy, 2021, pp. 75–76).

The integration of CL in the ELTE Master's curriculum represents an opportunity to introduce current/future English teachers to the principles of data-driven learning (DDL). Originally proposed by Johns (1991), DDL encourages students to work as researchers: they interrogate corpora themselves to solve their language doubts. DDL has therefore the potential of advancing students' discovery learning skills as well as their linguistic/metalinguistic awareness (e.g. Breyer, 2009; Farr, 2008).

DDL fulfills two main functions in ELTE Master's: (i) it equips current/future teachers with the tools for autonomous learning of the English

6 Corpus Linguistics in English Language Teacher Education... 105

language, and (ii) it introduces these teachers to ways in which they can implement DDL in their own English language classes (see, for instance, Aston, 2011, on the link between DDL and autonomy). In other words, the integration of DDL into the ELTE Master's curriculum has both a primary and a secondary beneficiary group—that is, the ELTE Master's students and these Master's students' English language students, respectively. In the following section, I discuss the integration of CL and DDL in my lecturing practice in ELTE Master's courses.

6.3 Context

As is the case with any evaluation, the reflective evaluation of my pedagogical practice during the COVID-19 pandemic is shaped by specific historical, socio-cultural and professional matters. For this reason, I make these matters visible in the present section. The context described here is inevitably intertwined with my life history. Different from the life histories in Ellis (2016), my aim is to foreground the aspects in my experience that are relevant for the understanding of what has been deemed to be important in the evaluation reported in Sects. 6.4 and 6.5 and why this has been the case.

The evaluation in this chapter focuses on ELTE Master's in the UK, a context in which I have worked for nearly a decade. I have designed, led and taught several modules in both on-site and online ELTE Master's programs. This has provided me with extensive practical experience in ELTE, thus complementing my research experience (e.g. Papageorgiou et al., 2019).

Since my first full-time lecturing appointment, I have always taught CL in addition to other modules like Research Methods, Microteaching and Second Language Education. My CL teaching and research experience (e.g. Viana & Lu, 2021) has equipped me with valuable practical and theoretical knowledge to reflect on how the COVID-19 pandemic has impacted CL teaching to ELTE Master's students.

The CL modules I have offered in ELTE Master's programs throughout my career have three main components—each represented by a circle in Fig. 6.1. The size of each circle visually represents the importance of

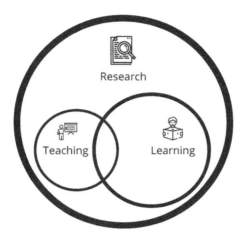

Fig. 6.1 CL module configuration

the component. *Research* is the backbone of my CL modules: it refers to (i) the current academic research which informs the design of the module; (ii) the research discussions in which ELTE students engage throughout the module; (iii) the research skills/techniques to which ELTE students are introduced and (iv) the language research that is conducted by the ELTE students and me. These four aspects correspond to Healey and Jenkins's (2009) four ways of engaging students with research—namely, (i) research-led, (ii) research-tutored, (iii) research-oriented and (iv) research-based. The small-scale language research tasks and projects undertaken during the module feed directly into our collective *learning* of English, a secondary component of this CL module. Since most of the students taking this module are or plan to be English language teachers, the module considers how CL may be used to support English language *teaching*, including the development of pedagogical materials.

All the CL modules that I have taught to date have been optional. This means that the students were potentially motivated to study CL as—at least in principle—they independently decided to study it. These optional CL modules have been attended by a maximum of 15 Master's students in my professional experience, which is a small student cohort in ELTE Master's in the UK.

My CL modules have always been offered in the Spring term, which runs from January/February to April/May. The outbreak of the pandemic in the UK in March 2020 disrupted my ongoing teaching of CL at the time. The institution-wide change from on-site to online teaching was communicated to all staff on Friday, 13 March 2020, and the decision went into effect on the following Monday. There was hardly any time to prepare for the transition even for me, who had had prior experience in online module design and teaching. In 2021, the second pandemic year, there was equally little time to plan since the UK entered a new lockdown just a few days before the start of the Spring term. The reflective evaluation discussed in the following sections considers these two CL teaching experiences disrupted by the COVID-19 pandemic.

6.4 CL Features as Opportunities in While-Pandemic Teaching

The present reflective evaluation starts with a discussion of how the transition from pre-pandemic on-site teaching to while-pandemic online teaching benefitted from CL features. This way, the following three subsections examine CL as a discipline in comparison to practice-oriented modules in ELTE Master's, the advantages brought about by corpus availability and analysis, and the open-access and/or digital availability of pedagogical materials.

6.4.1 CL as a Discipline

The requirements of a CL module differ considerably from those of practice-oriented modules offered in ELTE Master's (e.g. practicum). These practice-oriented modules have traditionally relied on physical presence and synchronous delivery. CL teaching and learning, on the other hand, do not necessarily require the lecturer and the students to share the same physical space at a given time. This has enormously helped the transition to a while-pandemic educational environment.

The comparative ease of adapting the delivery of a CL module during the pandemic can be related to the notion of context. In CL education, one does not need to act on, experience, observe or even be present in the context where the object of study (i.e. the texts that make up a corpus) was produced. This does not mean that context is unimportant in CL: it is indeed highly relevant, and contextual information needs to be captured in corpus compilation. Nevertheless, corpus analysis is (generally) done at least one step removed from the context where the language use took place. The texts included in a corpus are analyzed as standalone products, and this analysis may take place in numerous physical spaces and temporal occasions. All the information needed for the analysis is already captured in the corpus.

In its current form, it is impossible to dissociate CL from computer tools. ELTE Master's students are likely to be aware of the need to be knowledgeable in the use of computers to succeed in a CL module. This is indicated in several CL modules offered in ELTE Master's programs in the UK as exemplified below.

- "Using Technology and Corpora in Learning, Teaching and Research" (an optional module at the University of Portsmouth's MA Applied Linguistics and TESOL—https://www.port.ac.uk/study/courses/ma-applied-linguistics-and-tesol)
- "Using current corpus linguistic software applications and online resources" (a learning outcome in the optional module "Corpus Linguistics for Language Research and Teaching" at the University of Liverpool's MA TESOL—https://www.liverpool.ac.uk/study/postgraduate-taught/taught/tesol-ma/module-details/)
- "This module is aimed at introducing you to the fascinating area of investigating language through computer tools for research, learning and/or teaching purposes" (an excerpt of the module description for the optional module "Corpora in Language Research, Learning and Teaching" at the University of East Anglia's MA TESOL—https://www.uea.ac.uk/course/postgraduate/ma-teaching-english-to-speakers-of-other-languages-tesol#course-modules-1)

ELTE Master's students' familiarity with technology in CL modules has facilitated the transition to a while-pandemic online educational environment. Even though several of them had not previously used the synchronous tool available in the institution's virtual learning environment (VLE; see Fig. 6.5), navigating this new online space did not pose difficulties for these technologically savvy students.

6.4.2 Corpus Availability and Analysis

Several corpora are available online for free, and they can be investigated virtually at any time. The possibility of exploring corpora asynchronously means that time zones are not relevant and that ELTE Master's students—as well as anyone else—can conduct corpus analyses whenever it is most convenient for them. This is a major advantage in a while-pandemic educational context.

Access to research participants during the pandemic has been extremely limited. For this reason, ELTE Master's students have been encouraged to engage in secondary data analysis, "a research strategy which makes use of pre-existing quantitative data or pre-existing qualitative research data for the purposes of investigating new questions or verifying previous studies" (Heaton, 2012, p. 14). In CL, secondary data analysis has been the mainstream practice for a long time. One example is Massa's (2020) Master's dissertation research. It investigated the use of the verb *to get* in the passive voice or as a copular verb in the Michigan Corpus of Academic Spoken English, which was originally compiled to represent spoken academic discourse (Simpson-Vlach & Leicher, 2006). Corpus reuse has been encouraged long before the pandemic, and it has placed CL in an advantageous position within ELTE Master's in the pandemic-imposed difficult circumstances.

Not all possible corpora are available and/or have been compiled; however, compiling corpora is potentially easier than collecting other types of data during the pandemic. Corpora may be compiled without the need of requesting the help of human participants (e.g. a corpus of copyright-free literary works) or with little extra work from research participants (e.g. in a corpus of academic assignments, the participants submit assignments that they have already written). In these cases, the participants do not have to produce anything new for research purposes, thus being in stark contrast with answering a questionnaire and being interviewed, to cite two examples.

Ethical concerns came to the fore during the pandemic. In several contexts, there was an institutional ban on any on-site data collection during the pandemic. One of the solutions was to collect data through online means. For example, an interview which would have taken place in a school context was conducted through Microsoft Teams, thus addressing risk assessment concerns. However, an important question was whether it was ethical to request participants to contribute to a research project during the pandemic. This was especially the case in relation to educational stakeholders, who might have already been suffering with pandemic-related issues (e.g. higher workload and psychological distress). In these difficult circumstances, the corpus option—either reusing available corpora or compiling corpora of previously produced texts—seemed more ethically appropriate as it reduced the burden on the participants.

Corpus analysis does not necessarily require sophisticated technological resources or much Internet bandwidth. Some online corpora have their own search interfaces, which means that ELTE Master's students do not need to install any specialized software nor download data. This is the case, for instance, of NOW (Davies, 2016–), one of the current largest online corpora. Figure 6.2 shows the distribution of the word *pandemic* in NOW across years, generated in an Android smartphone. Unsurprisingly, this word is most frequently found in the texts produced in 2020 and 2021.

In a follow-up query, the same smartphone was used to search for two-word sequences containing any adjective and the word *pandemic* in the 2020 texts in NOW. It took the search interface 7.848 seconds to identify more than 97 k instances of adjective+*pandemic* (over 2.5 k of which are unique combinations) and to list 100 of the unique sequences (see Fig. 6.3). This flexibility of corpus work indicates that nearly anyone, anywhere, under any circumstances can engage in corpus analysis.

6 Corpus Linguistics in English Language Teacher Education...

Fig. 6.2 Distribution of *pandemic* in NOW across years generated in a smartphone

6.4.3 Pedagogical Materials

In addition to corpus availability, CL teaching during the pandemic benefitted from several corpus tools which are freely available online. Two of these resources are AntConc (Anthony, 2021) and #LancsBox (Brezina et al., 2021), programs which allow for the exploration of corpora in multiple ways (see, for instance, Viana & O'Boyle, 2022, on English for

Fig. 6.3 Adjective+*pandemic* sequences in 2020 texts in NOW investigated in a smartphone

academic purposes). A sign of the generosity of the CL community, the free availability of these resources has contributed to the move from on-site to online CL education in ELTE Master's. These resources make it easier for current/future English language teachers to engage in corpus exploration without the need to be experts in, for instance, programming or statistics.

The pandemic has encouraged the reuse of teaching and learning objects. There are numerous YouTube videos on CL-relevant topics such as the software tutorials in the AntLab channel. As the pandemic progressed, new videos were made available like the academic presentations on the YouTube channel maintained by Peter Crosthwaite, one of the organizers of the seminar series "International perspectives on corpus technology for language learning." Altogether, these videos can be reused by either lecturers in their CL classes or students in their learning journeys.

A final consideration in the adaptation of CL education to pandemic times relates to the texts that ELTE Master's students are asked to read. Because the library was not as accessible as in pre-pandemic times, all required reading needed to be electronically available to avoid disadvantaging any student. This was not an issue for recent publications: they were already available electronically. The challenge was in relation to older seminal texts (e.g. Sinclair, 1991, 2003), which are not available electronically or not available for institutional purchase. Adaptations needed to be made in this regard such as the digitalization of individual chapters and the identification of other suitable publications. However, these adaptations had already taken place before the pandemic, given the pre-existing university guidance to prioritize electronic texts as the core reading for modules.

6.5 Pandemic-Imposed Challenges to CL Teaching

Even though CL has presented opportunities for its adaptation to online delivery as described in the previous section, it has also experienced some challenges. In the following subsections, I consider these challenges under three main headings: pedagogical practice, technology-related issues and interpersonal relationships. In addition to discussing the challenges, I present the actual solutions that were implemented or the likely solutions that could have been adopted.

6.5.1 Pedagogical Practice

The move from on-site to online CL teaching during the pandemic demanded a thorough reconsideration of pedagogical practice. The module structure, one of the key considerations in course design (Ko & Rossen, 2017), was kept the same since it had already been carefully developed to meet ELTE Master's students' needs. The module delivery, however, required extensive revision to suit the new online educational environment.

ELTE Master's students' mastery of corpus tools is a must for them to be able to evidence attainment of the learning outcomes of this CL module. In the pre-pandemic on-site classes, live step-by-step demonstrations of corpus tools were conducted, and students had a chance to reproduce these demonstrations synchronously. For the while-pandemic online classes, two alternatives were considered—live online demonstrations and recorded video tutorials, each with pros and cons as summarized in Table 6.1.

Although recorded video tutorials would have been the most appropriate choice, a decision was made for live online demonstrations. The decision was due to the lack of time for appropriate preparation during the pandemic (cf. Sect. 6.3). These demonstrations (and all the classes) were nevertheless recorded so that students could review the classes if/as needed.

Before the pandemic, the CL classes were delivered in an information technology (IT) lab. As can be seen in Fig. 6.4, the students sat in the same direction, facing the whiteboard. This setup was extremely helpful: by standing at the back of the classroom, I could observe what the students were doing and I could identify who needed help. This type of class management was not possible to implement online. Students could share their screens, but only one student could do so at a time, and the screen would be shared with the entire class. Students could be split into individual breakout rooms; however, it would take considerable time for me to move across all breakout rooms and students would not have a chance to interact with their peers. I therefore decided to keep all students in the same online room. I would ask them display and referential questions to

6 Corpus Linguistics in English Language Teacher Education... 115

Table 6.1 Live online demonstration versus recorded video tutorial

	Live online demonstrations	Recorded video tutorials
Pros	Closest alternative to the original pedagogical practice	Asynchronous availability
	Little preparation required of the lecturer	Suitable to students with different levels of technological savviness (e.g. students can increase/decrease the playback speed)
	Students' reassurance of the feasibility of the analysis since it was conducted live	Lecturer's use and reuse of the recording as a teaching object
Cons	Impossibility of editing the demonstration and hence shortening the class time spent on it	Technical expertise required of the lecturer on the use of screen recorders and video editors
	Impossibility of omitting any potential errors made in the demonstration in order not to confuse students	More preparation time required as the lecturer has to record, edit and publish the video ahead of the class
	Students' potential difficulty in reproducing the demonstration while following it in real time, especially if they had a small laptop, tablet and/or smartphone screen	Subject to high evaluation standards (i.e. viewers are more accepting of hesitations, pauses and mistakes in a live demonstration than in a recorded video tutorial)

monitor their progress as well as conduct quick online polls to check whether they needed any support.

In the on-site classes, students could take advantage of the shared physical space to ask quick questions at the end of the class. This type of interaction could take place in while-pandemic online classes, but students did not do so. Instead, they seemed either to keep the doubts for themselves or to rely on e-mail communication. Both options were problematic. The former was worrying because it could hinder their attainment of the learning outcomes; the latter resulted in more work for me because of the time-consuming nature of written communication. Written messages usually need to be more fully developed to ensure that they will make sense to a reader who does not share the writer's context. When these written messages are exchanged on a one-to-one basis, there

Fig. 6.4 On-site computer lab

is the risk of the same information having to be repeated several times. With a view to encouraging students to ask questions and to ensuring a manageable workload, students were provided with anonymous and non-anonymous ways to share their doubts such as writing on an online whiteboard and posting messages on discussion forums.

6.5.2 Technology-Related Issues

Computers can hardly be considered an innovation for Master's students in UK higher education. At the same time, however, computers are not entirely normalized in ELTE. This means that they are not used "without our being consciously aware of its [their] role as a technology, as a valuable element in the language learning process" (Bax, 2011, p. 1; see also Bax, 2003). Different from regular classrooms, the physical arrangement of a lab (see Fig. 6.4) affords diverse interactions, and the objects present in it allow for unique teaching/learning activities. In pre-pandemic times, teaching in an IT lab used to be an out-of-the-ordinary experience for

ELTE Master's students, who were used to other classrooms and who might have been requested not to use their electronic devices in class. The lab environment would work as a motivational source for some students. During the pandemic, the situation seems to have reversed. Because all classes had to be delivered online, the potential novelty of relying on computer tools for a CL module seemed to have been lost. As a matter of fact, the use of computers may have even become a negative aspect for some ELTE Master's students during the pandemic since the CL module extended the time that they had to spend in front of a screen.

The pandemic has made socio-economic inequalities amongst ELTE Master's students even more visible. One must not take for granted that all students will have access to the hardware required to participate in online classes, that they will have the means to pay for reliable Internet connection and that they will be able to afford electricity costs. These three aspects are not specific to the CL module under evaluation. They instead relate to student participation in online education in general, especially in lockdown when students cannot leave their houses to use campus facilities. All university staff must keep these issues in mind: we cannot overlook or underestimate the negative effect that the lack of access to resources, one of the features in digital exclusion (Helsper, 2012), may have on students' learning. We must additionally remind ourselves that it is not easy for students to admit that they do not have the financial means for what may be perceived to be the basic needs in contemporary education.

6.5.3 Interpersonal Relationships

The outset of the pandemic seemed to impact negatively on the support that ELTE Master's students would offer privately to one another in class. Students' physical proximity in the on-site lab (see Fig. 6.4) facilitated knowledge/experience sharing. Before the pandemic, a student could turn to the side and ask a question to a peer, thus solving their doubt on the spot. In the while-pandemic online class, students have had fewer chances of approaching their peers individually. This one-to-one chat amongst students can be set up in some VLEs—with or without the lecturer's supervision, but it requires skill on the students' part to engage cognitively in class, complete the tasks which are required of them and communicate with other peers. An additional challenge is that students need to ensure that they are using the appropriate channel to reply to their peers. They should not reply to a private question in the chat that is open to all students. Managing several individual chats may be challenging as illustrated in Fig. 6.5, which has been designed for this chapter.

For me, one of the main challenges in establishing and maintaining interpersonal relationships in synchronous online classes during the pandemic is the lack of visual contact with the students. Being able to read ELTE Master's students' in-class reactions provides me with first-hand, empirical evidence of how the class is progressing and allows me to make any necessary adjustments on the spot. In a while-pandemic online space, it is more difficult to tell students' reactions, especially given their unwillingness to turn on their cameras. This difficulty is widespread across different subjects, but it affects CL teaching considerably. The teaching of corpus techniques (e.g. the compilation of word lists) is a means to an end. It is vital that, early in the module, students understand what these corpus techniques are, how they are implemented and when they should

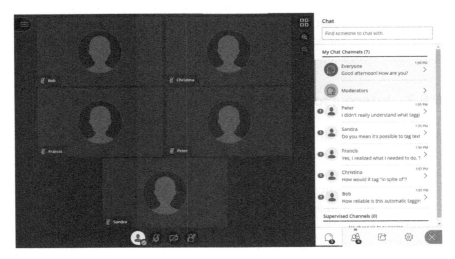

Fig. 6.5 Individual chat management in the institution's VLE

be conducted. Only then will ELTE Master's students be able to make informed use of these techniques to evidence attainment of one of the learning outcomes for this module—to be able to analyze language use as a way of developing their linguistic/metalinguistic knowledge. It is therefore vital to find ways to gather evidence of students' understanding during online classes.

6.6 Looking Back and Looking Ahead

The chapter has reported on my reflective evaluation of the impact that the pandemic has had on my teaching of CL to ELTE Master's students in the UK. The evaluation indicates how the focal CL module has been disrupted by the pandemic; however, solutions were found to minimize or, in some cases, overcome the disruption. These solutions drew heavily on the available technology, which made it possible to continue to teach CL during the pandemic. The points discussed in this chapter cohere with Shamim's (2018, p. 248) conclusion that "technology, if used with a clear understanding of contextual constraints, can go a long way to ease some of the difficult circumstances in teaching and teacher development."

The experience was deemed successful from a teaching perspective. The learning outcomes did not have to be changed, and the ELTE Master's students were able to evidence their attainment of such outcomes. The end-of-module summative assignments provided students with a chance to evidence their engagement with the available literature, conduct a small-scale corpus research and/or design pedagogical activities to bring CL to the language classroom.

The development of ELTE Master's students' corpus research skills helped them to learn more about language use and/or teaching-related matters. For example, one student explored the differences in the use of the synonymous verbs *collaborate* and *cooperate*, another decided to investigate the noun collocates of *cause, create* and *provide*, and a third developed materials to teach reporting verbs to students of English for academic purposes. These newly acquired skills supported students' autonomous language learning, one of the advantages associated with the pedagogical application of CL. Given the transferrable nature of these skills (e.g.

quantitative data analysis), they were also helpful later in students' Master's journeys even if students decided not to undertake corpus research for their dissertations.

The reflective evaluation discussed in this chapter cannot be dissociated from the following contextual factors:

(a) It focused on the UK, one of the world's advanced economies.
(b) It was historically situated after the UK-wide second lockdown.
(c) It was conducted from a teaching perspective.
(d) It drew on my lecturing experience of working with on-site and online ELTE Master's students.

The present evaluation cannot be generalized to other contexts—nor is it the aim of this chapter. The evaluation stands as an example of how I, a university lecturing staff member, responded to the constraints imposed by the pandemic in my ELTE practice. The points made here may resonate with ELTE professionals in other geopolitical contexts, at other times and in charge of modules other than CL. In this sense, the lessons learned during the pandemic—both the opportunities and the challenges—may be relevant in other contexts.

In going forward, the above-mentioned contextual factors provide useful pointers for follow-up evaluations.

(a) Further geopolitical contexts must be investigated, including those eligible to receive official development assistance, where ELTE is likely to have faced more challenges.
(b) Ongoing evaluation is a must: the opportunities and challenges may change as the pandemic unfolds (and hopefully ends).
(c) Other ELTE stakeholders' perspectives need to be considered such as those of students.
(d) ELTE colleagues should evaluate their teaching contexts with a view to observing whether/how the opportunities and challenges discussed in the present chapter resonate with their experiences.

In closing this chapter, I draw on one of the developments in CL during the pandemic: the Coronavirus Corpus (Davies, 2019–), a

6 Corpus Linguistics in English Language Teacher Education... 121

```
01 AU  How COVID-19 could inspire us to a better future # COVID-19 created new ways of
02 BD  m the COVID-19 pandemic and build a better future for all. # " Let's resolve to
03 CA  fight against COVID-19 and build a better future for everyone. " # As the Star
04 GB  ge caused by Covid-19 and prepare a better future for coming generations. Member
05 IE  . # Budget 2021 is a bridge to that better future . # COVID-19: GOVERNMENT RESPO
06 IN  wheels of commerce and help build a better future . Like the Covid-19 shots, the
07 NG  o the COVID-19 crisis and prepare a better future for all segments of society, i
08 PH  he objectives of giving Filipinos a better future after the COVID-19 crisis. Phi
09 US  respond to COVID-19 and reimagine a better future , with sustained peace, includ
10 ZA  strong recovery from COVID-19 and a better future for all on a safe and healthy
```

Fig. 6.6 Concordance lines for *a better future* in the Coronavirus Corpus

1.5-billion-word corpus of online newspaper and magazine texts that deal with the coronavirus. A search for the two-word sequence adjective+*future* in this corpus reveals hopeful views[1] as indicated in Fig. 6.6 containing data from ten different countries (AU = Australia, BD = Bangladesh, CA = Canada, GB = Great Britain, IE = Ireland, IN = India, NG = Nigeria, PH = Philippines, US = United States and ZA = South Africa).

In line with the optimism expressed in these concordance lines, I hope that the knowledge that we have gained throughout the pandemic may help us build a better educational future. In practice, this means using this knowledge to help us navigate the pandemic, which is still not finished by the time of writing, and (re)build a positive educational context in a post-pandemic world.

References

Anthony, L. (2021). *AntConc (Version 4.0.0)*. Waseda University. https://www.laurenceanthony.net/software/antconc/

Aston, G. (2011). Applied corpus linguistics and the learning experience. In V. Viana, S. Zyngier, & G. Barnbrook (Eds.), *Perspectives on corpus linguistics* (pp. 1–16). John Benjamins.

Bax, S. (2003). CALL: Past, present and future. *System, 31*(1), 13–28. https://doi.org/10.1016/S0346-251X(02)00071-4

Bax, S. (2011). Normalisation revisited: The effective use of technology in language education. *International Journal of Computer-Assisted Language*

---

[1] The sequence *better future* is the third most frequent one in the Coronavirus Corpus; the first two are *near future* and *foreseeable future*. The fourth sequence is *uncertain future*, though.

Learning and Teaching, *1*(2), 1–15. https://doi.org/10.4018/ijcallt.2011040101

Breyer, Y. (2009). Learning and teaching with corpora: Reflections by student teachers. *Computer Assisted Language Learning, 22*(2), 153–172. https://doi.org/10.1080/09588220902778328

Brezina, V., Weill-Tessier, P., & McEnery, A. (2021). *#LancsBox* (Version 6.0). http://corpora.lancs.ac.uk/lancsbox

Cirocki, A., Madyarov, I., Baecher, L., & (Eds.). (2019). *Current perspectives on the TESOL practicum: Cases from around the globe*. Springer.

Davies, M. (2008). *The Corpus of Contemporary American English (COCA)*. https://www.english-corpora.org/coca/

Davies, M. (2016). *Corpus of News on the Web (NOW)*. https://www.english-corpora.org/now/

Davies, M. (2019) *The Coronavirus Corpus*. https://www.english-corpora.org/corona/

Ellis, R. (2016). *Becoming and being an applied linguist: The life histories of some applied linguists*. John Benjamins.

Farr, F. (2008). Evaluating the use of corpus-based instruction in a language teacher education context: Perspectives from the users. *Language Awareness, 17*(1), 25–43. https://doi.org/10.2167/la414.0

Grosse, C. U. (1991). The TESOL methods course. *TESOL Quarterly, 25*(1), 29–49. https://doi.org/10.2307/3587027

Healey, M., & Jenkins, A. (2009). Developing undergraduate research and inquiry. *The Higher Education Academy*. https://www.advance-he.ac.uk/knowledge-hub/developing-undergraduate-research-and-inquiry

Heaton, J. (2012). What is secondary analysis? In J. Goodwin (Ed.), *SAGE secondary data analysis – Volume I: Using secondary sources and secondary analysis* (pp. 1–20). SAGE.

Helsper, E. J. (2012). A corresponding fields model for the links between social and digital exclusion. *Communication Theory, 22*, 403–426. https://doi.org/10.1111/j.1468-2885.2012.01416.x

Johns, T. (1991). Should you be persuaded: Two examples of data-driven learning. In T. Johns & P. King (Eds.), *ELR Journal 4: Classroom concordancing* (pp. 1–16). CELS, The University of Birmingham.

Ko, S., & Rossen, S. (2017). *Teaching online: A practical guide* (4th ed.). Routledge.

Kuchah, K. (2018). Teaching English in difficult circumstances: Setting the scene. In K. Kuchah & F. Shamim (Eds.), *International perspectives on teaching*

6 Corpus Linguistics in English Language Teacher Education... 123

English in difficult circumstances: Contexts, challenges and possibilities (pp. 1–25). Palgrave Macmillan.

LaFond, L., & Dogancay-Aktuna, S. (2009). Teacher perspectives on linguistics in TESOL teacher education. *Language Awareness, 18*(3–4), 345–365. https://doi.org/10.1080/09658410903197348

Maley, A. (2001). The teaching of English in difficult circumstances: Who needs a health farm when they're starving? *Humanising Language Teaching, 3*(6). http://old.hltmag.co.uk/nov01/mart4.htm.

Massa, B. (2020). *Get-passive and copular get in university classroom discourse and EAP textbooks: A corpus-based comparison* [Unpublished Master's dissertation]. Swansea University. https://www.teachingenglish.org.uk/sites/teacheng/files/Get-Passive%20and%20Copular%20Get%20in%20University%20Classroom%20Discourse%20and%20EAP%20Textbooks.pdf

McCarthy, M. (2021). *Innovations and challenges in grammar*. Routledge.

Murphy, J. M. (1997). Phonology courses offered by MATESOL programs in the U.S. *TESOL Quarterly, 31*(4), 741–764. https://doi.org/10.2307/3587758

Nelson, G. L. (1998). Intercultural communication and related courses taught in TESOL Master's degree programs. *International Journal of Intercultural Relations, 22*(1), 17–33.

Papageorgiou, I., Copland, F., Viana, V., Bowker, D., & Moran, E. (2019). Teaching practice in UK ELT Master's programmes. *ELT Journal, 73*(2), 154–165. https://doi.org/10.1093/elt/ccy050

Shamim, F. (2018). Conclusion: Teaching English in difficult circumstances – Lessons learnt and the way forward. In K. Kuchah & F. Shamim (Eds.), *International perspectives on teaching English in difficult circumstances: Contexts, challenges and possibilities* (pp. 243–253). Palgrave Macmillan.

Shamim, F., & Kuchah, K. (2016). Teaching large classes in difficult circumstances. In G. Hall (Ed.), *The Routledge handbook of English language teaching* (pp. 527–541). Routledge.

Simpson-Vlach, R. C., & Leicher, S. (2006). *The MICASE handbook: A resource for users of the Michigan Corpus of Academic Spoken English*. University of Michigan Press.

Sinclair, J. (1991). *Corpus, concordance, collocation*. Oxford University Press.

Sinclair, J. (2003). *Reading concordances: An introduction*. Pearson Longman.

Sinclair, J. (2004). *Trust the text: Language, corpus and discourse* (Edited with Ronald Carter). Routledge.

Tognini-Bonelli, E. (2001). *Corpus linguistics at work*. John Benjamins.

Vásquez, C., & Sharpless, D. (2009). The role of pragmatics in the Master's TESOL curriculum: Findings from a nationwide survey. *TESOL Quarterly*, *43*(1), 5–28. https://doi.org/10.1002/j.1545-7249.2009.tb00225.x

Viana, V., & Lu, L. (2021). Corpus linguistics and continuous professional development: Participants' prior knowledge, motivations and appraisals. *Revista de Estudos da Linguagem, 29*(2), 1485–1527. https://doi.org/10.1785 1/2237-2083.29.2.1485-1527

Viana, V., & O'Boyle, A. (2022). *Corpus linguistics for English for academic purposes*. Routledge.

7

Digital Competence and Teaching Practices of Language Teachers in Sweden in a COVID-19 World

Jonathan R. White, Tao Yang, Arantxa Santos Muñoz, and Man Gao

7.1   Introduction

For the European Union (EU), digital competence was marked as being of great importance when it was included as one of the important skills for lifelong learning in 2006 (European Parliament and the Council, 2006). The DigComp project led to a framework to map and describe digital competence, which was itself described as the "confident and critical use of ICT tools" (Vuorikari et al., 2016, p. 5). Such skills are also discussed in the curriculum for compulsory schooling in Sweden as vital

---

J. R. White (✉)
Department of English, Dalarna University, Falun, Sweden
e-mail: jwh@du.se

T. Yang • M. Gao
Department of Chinese, Dalarna University, Falun, Sweden

A. S. Muñoz
Department of Spanish, Dalarna University, Falun, Sweden

© The Author(s), under exclusive license to Springer Nature Switzerland AG 2023   **125**
K. Sadeghi, M. Thomas (eds.), *Second Language Teacher Professional Development*,
Digital Education and Learning, https://doi.org/10.1007/978-3-031-12070-1_7

general skills for pupils to develop. Because of this, it has been noted in reports by the Swedish Education Agency that there is a pressing need for training in the use of digital tools for teachers (cf. Skolverket, 2018, among others).

Reports on the use of digital tools in Swedish schools (such as Skolverket, 2018) acknowledge that language subjects lag behind other subjects like Mathematics and Natural Science in the use of digital tools. Thus, it is important to understand why teachers of foreign languages, including English, are not using tools to the same extent as their counterparts in other subjects. This was a major reason why the authors decided to investigate attitudes to digitalisation and the use of digital tools among practising teachers in language subjects in Swedish schools.

This has become an even more pressing issue due to the COVID-19 pandemic. From 17 March 2020, upper secondary/senior high schools in Sweden went over to more or less complete distance teaching, as did universities. The same was allowed (although not required) at a later date for lower secondary/junior high schools. Thus, teachers had to adapt, with basically one week's notice, all their planning for online environments. In order to answer the question of whether the teachers were prepared for this change, and whether they received enough support, we will first present some background on digitalisation and digital competence in Swedish society and in Swedish school contexts, and in particular how it is presented in regulatory documents and reports from the Swedish Education Agency (Skolverket).

7.2 Digital Competence and Schools

7.2.1 What Is Digital Competence?

In their synthesis of research and policy documents, Gallardo-Echenique et al. (2015) note that the concept of "digital competence" has changed over the years from describing being able to use a computer to referring more now to skills in information-searching and source criticism. Martin (2009) described three levels of digital knowledge: "digital competence" is the lowest level which includes skills and concepts. Level two is called "digital usage" where these skills are used in professional contexts, and level three is called "digital transformation" where the user becomes innovative and creative in digital contexts. Käck and Männikkö-Barbutiu (2012) instead discussed technical, theoretical, and didactic digital competence, referring to competence in the technology, and its pedagogical and practical applications, respectively. We will look here at whether this is reflected in teachers' perceptions of digital competence.

7.2.2 Digital Competence in Sweden

Digitalisation is described as a driving force in knowledge societies, which changes how individuals think and work (Regeringskansliet, 2015b, p. 57). It affects all areas of society, and therefore, it is vital for all societies to ensure that all citizens can cope with such changes. As a result, the Swedish government proposed, and parliament adopted, a Digitalisation Strategy for the whole of Swedish society in 2017 (Regeringskansliet, 2017a). The overall vision was for everyone in Sweden to have trust in a digitalised society (p. 8), and for Sweden to be the best in the world when it comes to using digital tools (p. 10). Five sub-goals were defined in order to achieve this vision. These are related to digital competence, safety, innovation, leadership, and infrastructure (p. 11).

The role of schools in Sweden is mentioned specifically only under the first sub-goal of the strategy: digital competence. Digital competence as a concept is defined in relation to, among others, the European Union's definition. It spans the broad picture mentioned above, that is, skills in using digital technology and tools, an awareness of different digital tools and services, and what is referred to as "media and information knowledge" (Regeringskansliet, 2017a, p. 12). The latter refers to having a critical attitude towards the information presented online.

One very important reason for adopting this strategy is the aim for equality (Regeringskansliet, 2017a, p. 13). Everyone should have equal access to digital knowledge and be able to take part in a digitalised society, regardless of their gender, ethnicity, social class, education level, and so forth.

7.2.3 Digital Competence in Swedish Schools

Schools are seen as a crucial area for individuals to develop skills that are important in a digital society (Regeringskansliet, 2015a, pp. 126–127). There are great demands for flexibility and critical thinking, which are mentioned as fundamental skills to be developed throughout the schooling process.

Digitalisation is viewed as one theme which should be taken up throughout a child's schooling in Sweden (others include equality, democracy, and sustainability). Thus, commentary material was provided by the Swedish Education Agency (Skolverket) for all levels of schooling from pre-school to compulsory schooling, to upper secondary/senior high school. A basic principle regarding the focus on digital competence in schools is defined as "digital competence for everyone in schools" (Regeringskansliet, 2017b, pp. 5–9).

Four themes regarding digital competence are mentioned in the Swedish curriculum for compulsory school, special education, and the Sami school (and are carried over to upper secondary/senior high schooling as well). The following specific skills are discussed in the commentary material for the curriculum (Skolverket, 2017, pp. 10–11):

- The effect of digitalisation on society
- Being able to use and understand digital tools and media
- Having a critical and responsible approach
- Being able to solve problems and put ideas into practice

From a schooling perspective, the first point relates to the effect of digital tools on pupils' development and learning. An important question to be asked is, therefore, do the tools used in the classroom contribute to pupils' learning (Diaz, 2019, pp. 31–46). This is something which is addressed in the interviews described later. The second theme relates to having skills in using the technology. There is often a misconception among teachers that their pupils are, by definition, much better than them at using digital tools, but there is a great need on both sides for basic training in using technology. The third point refers to being able to critically sort through the mass of information available online, and the final one can relate to solving problems using technology, or solving problems caused by technology.

Specific needs are mentioned for staff in the commentary material: "personnel who work with children and pupils should have the competence to choose and use appropriate digital tools in education" (Regeringskansliet, 2017b, p. 6). According to Skolverket (2016), teachers feel a continued need for personal development within Information Technology (IT). As written in Käck and Männikkö-Barbutiu (2012), digital competence is continuously changing; technology moves forward constantly, and research is needed into its effects and pedagogical implications. For users of such technology, knowledge of didactic, theoretical, and technical digital competence is needed (p. 62).

Much research points towards differences between the private and personal lives of pupils and teachers, as there can be a gulf between what teachers and pupils do inside and outside of school. For example, Burnett (2011) describes the situation that teachers have different identities linked to digital competence. Even if you use digital tools much in your private life, this is sometimes not visible in school practices, and this is something that we specifically addressed in our interviews.

7.2.4 The Effect of Digital Competence on the Work Environment

Research has also discussed the effect of digitalisation on teachers' work environments. Skolverket (2018, 2019) points out that digitalisation affects how teachers work, for example, by breaking down the dividing line between teachers' professional and private lives. Foldspang et al. (2014) have argued that even though there are positive effects of digitalisation on the physical environment, many negative effects have been mentioned in relation to stress, in particular. This can clearly be connected to the COVID-19 situation, which forced many teachers to move to completely digital teaching environments with very little time to adjust. Training in digital competence is a clear way of reducing stress among teachers (cf. the proposals in Willart, 2019).

Macintyre et al. (2020) carried out a study of stress during the pandemic among language teachers. They reported that the biggest causes of stress were the workload, family health, blurred lines between private and working lives, and a loss of control. The teachers dealt with these stress factors in a number of ways, including psychological acceptance of the situation, advanced planning, and support.

Moser et al. (2020) also reported the perceptions of language teachers regarding online teaching during the pandemic. Although their perception was generally positive towards online teaching, the teachers acknowledged that synchronous interaction between students was harder, that more contact was needed between teacher and student, and that significant changes needed to be made to course design.

7.2.5 Research Aim and Questions

As a result of the COVID-19 pandemic, the Swedish government made the decision to stop all face-to-face teaching at firstly upper secondary/senior high school and then subsequently made it an option at lower secondary/junior high school, and so during the Autumn semester of 2020 until Spring 2021, all courses and programmes at upper secondary/senior high school were only offered online. Subsequently, the digital competence of teachers and pupils became a hot topic for debate nationally.

Although the effects of the COVID pandemic have begun to be the subject of research, the effect of this on language teaching, as well as the preparedness of teachers for the change-over, has not been discussed. Therefore, we decided to take up the issue as part of the project we were running on language teachers' digital competence. Specifically, we wanted to deal with the following research questions:

- How digitally competent are language teachers in Sweden in their private lives?
- How does this competence translate into the use of digital tools in the classroom?
- How much has the need to move to online teaching affected the teaching practices of language teachers?

7.3   Method

In our study here, we have mapped attitudes towards and the use of digital competence among practising high school teachers of English, Spanish, and Chinese. We employed the following research procedure:

- Contact was made with working teachers to get their consent to participate in the project.
- A digital questionnaire was sent to all participating working teachers (based on the questionnaire used in Santos Muñoz & White, 2020).
- We went deeper into the topic through interviews with working teachers.

The questionnaire developed by Santos Muñoz and White (2020) was originally in Swedish and contained sections on teachers' private use of digital tools, the use of digital tools in the classroom, attitudes to what digital competence meant, and the need for support regarding the use of digital tools in the classroom. The questions were then translated by authors Yang and Gao for the Chinese teachers. It was known by the authors that the majority of Chinese teachers in Sweden had only recently arrived in Sweden and therefore did not yet have the competence in Swedish to answer a questionnaire. Since the questionnaire had already been piloted in the earlier study, it was felt that it was already reliable enough to be used here in the larger study.

In total, 73 questionnaires were completed, with 26 by English teachers, 28 by Spanish teachers, and 19 by Chinese teachers (an additional 16 were completed by teachers of other languages, but these were discarded from the results presented here). Fourteen teachers were male, and 59 were female, which is in line with the gender distribution among language teachers in Swedish schools (Skolverket, 2021). Forty were in the age group 31–45; 25 were 46–55; and 6 were over 55 (this is in line with the age distribution of the senior-middle school teachers in Swedish schools, where nearly 80% are aged 30–60; Skolverket, 2021). The informants are therefore representative of the Swedish school teacher population.

The interviews took place from June to September 2021. Fifteen language teachers were interviewed, five from each language selected from the pool of those who answered the questionnaire. Those who had filled in the questionnaire were asked to give an email address if they were interested in taking part in an interview. They were then contacted, and the interview was arranged. In that sense, they were self-selecting. The interviews were conducted in English or Swedish for the English teachers, in Spanish for the Spanish teachers, and in Chinese for the Chinese teachers. Our aim here was to have the interview in the teachers' mother tongue, in order to avoid linguistic misunderstandings as much as possible.

The informants were aged from 30 to 55, with only one male in the group. The average years of teaching experience was 10–20 years, with three Spanish teachers having under 10 years' experience. Each interview lasted between 30 and 50 minutes, and was recorded and transcribed. Consent was obtained orally from interviewees to use their answers in this chapter. In the interviews, we mainly addressed the following basic questions, and some follow-up questions were added when needed:

1. How much has the use of digital tools been affected by the pandemic?
2. What is the greatest barrier to using digital tools/resources in teaching?
3. Do the digital resources they use in their private life influence their digital competence in language teaching?
4. "Cooperate with a mentor who can help me to develop my teaching": do they support this statement, and why?
5. What should be included in the teacher's programme regarding digital competence?
6. What is (are) their most often used digital resource(s) in teaching? Why did they choose them?
7. What is the influence of using digital resources in their teaching?
8. "To create digital content": what does this mean for you?

Now, we present the results of the questionnaires.

7.4 Survey Results

In the questionnaire, 5-point Likert-scale questions were used to address to what extent the respondents agree or disagree with statements regarding digital competence, the influence of digital tools on language teaching, and what affects digital competence. To test their statistical significance, the Z value of the sign test[1] was adopted. When the Z value of a certain statement is larger than 1.64, the statement could be regarded as statistically significant, meaning this statement has enough support to be accepted. In addition, in order to compare the differences between the respondents in the three language groups, the Kruskal-Wallis test[2] was adopted. When the P value of the Kruskal-Wallis test of a certain statement is smaller than 0.05, the difference between the three groups is significant. The mean rank of the Kruskal-Wallis test shows from which teacher group a statement gets more support; in our case, the smaller the mean rank, the stronger the support. This was only calculated when the original P value showed a significant difference between groups.

The results from the survey are summarised in Tables 7.1 and 7.2. Table 7.1 shows the top three digital tools for each language group:

As we see from Table 7.1, similar digital tools appear among the top three tools for all three language groups, although the ranking is different. In particular, Instant Messaging and Facebook were common to all three groups. When it came to the tools they used in the classroom, there was no overlap between private and public lives. The tools used in the classroom were uniformly specialist tools for learning, and in particular language learning. Thus, classical learning tools like dictionaries and the learning platform itself come high on the list, and the only non-specialist

---

[1] The sign test is the simplest way to analyse data from paired samples (i.e. agree/disagree with a certain statement). The null hypothesis is that the total cases that agree with the statement are equal to that who disagree with it. The Z value is adopted to compare the numbers that agree with and disagree with a statement. It is calculated by using the formula: $Z = P_{obs} - 0.5/$square-root of $(0.5 \times 0.5)/n^*$, where P_{obs} = number of answers with the value of either 1 or 2 (i.e. positive attitudes to the statements)/n^* and where n^* = the total number of answers except value 3 (i.e. neutral attitude to the statements).

[2] The Kruskal-Wallis test is a test for between-group analysis and is used to compare the scores on a certain variable for three or more groups. Scores are converted to ranks and the mean rank for each group is compared.

134   J. R. White et al.

Table 7.1 Top three digital tools per language group

Item	Chinese	English	Spanish
Most commonly used digital tools in private life	1. Instant messaging	Facebook	Instant messaging
	2. SMS	Instant messaging	Facebook
	3. Facebook	Instagram	Apps for daily transactions
Most commonly used digital tools in teaching	1. Audio-video resources	Language learning tools	Dictionary
	2. Learning platform	Learning platform	Audio-video resources
	3. Dictionary	Dictionary	Language learning tools

tool would be audio-visual resources, meaning typically YouTube videos. Therefore, we see a focus on specialist tools, and tools which have been discussed in relation to language learning like Facebook and worlds like Second Life, among others, are not mentioned at all.

Next, in Table 7.2, we see the informants' answers to the different skills involved in digital competence.

7.4.1   What Is Digital Competence?

Respondents were presented with a number of possible skills that could be considered a part of digital competence, such as using a computer through to being critical of online sources. They indicated that all options were relevant, with a Z value for all the statements being much greater than 1.64, but source criticism gained the strongest support, while creating digital content was the least popular option. Teachers of Spanish and English were most positive towards source criticism as being an important part of digital competence, while Chinese teachers were much less positive. The same was also true for creating digital content, which suggests that Chinese teachers were less sure whether these generic skills were part of digital competence. As well as testing whether the language group was the cause of the significant difference, age was also tested as it can be surmised that younger teachers would be more interested in using digital

7 Digital Competence and Teaching Practices of Language... 135

Table 7.2 Informants' understanding of digital competence

The understanding of digital competence		
To be digitally competent means being able to:		
	Z value	Kruskal-Wallis test (P value) mean rank of Kruskal-Wallis test
Use a computer	8.49	0.227
Handle digital information	8.49	0.187
Communicate in a different digital context	8.19	0.000 (Ch = 51.11/En = 30/ Sp = 33.93)
Create digital contents	8.13	0.014 (Ch = 46.35/En = 35.77/ Sp = 31.66)
Critically source the digital contents	8.49	0.016 (Ch = 43.16/En = 34.88/ Sp = 34.79)
Handle the digital information in a secure way	8.43	0.378
Use digital tools for problem solving in teaching	8.25	0.314
The influence of using digital teaching and learning tools in language teaching		
Using digital tools in language teaching means that:		
	Z value	Kruskal-Wallis test (P value) mean rank of Kruskal-Wallis test
The time needed for preparing the teaching increases	2.48	0.056 (Ch = 45.74/En = 36.67/ Sp = 31.38)
The time needed for teaching increases	−0.82	0.854
Pupils have more fun in classes	5.91	0.000 (Ch = 19.95/En = 42.92/ Sp = 43.07)
Teaching materials become more practical	7.5	0.856
Language teaching is influenced positively	7.42	0.788
Language learning is influenced positively	6.86	0.297
Pupils' learning becomes broader	5.66	0.001 (Ch = 21.66/En = 42.92/ Sp = 41.91)

(*continued*)

136   J. R. White et al.

Table 7.2 (continued)

The understanding of digital competence		
Factors helping to build digital competence		
As a language teacher when it comes to digital competence I expect:		
	Z value	Kruskal-Wallis test (P value) mean rank of Kruskal-Wallis test
The textbook would contain digital resources	7.94	0.084
In teaching materials there would be several examples of the target language in different digital contexts	8.06	0.677
To have the opportunity to develop my skills in this area	7.52	0.106
To be able to participate in practical workshops to get tips that can be used in language teaching	7.65	0.918
To get tips on reading simple and interesting digitised literature	7.70	0.554
To collaborate with a mentor who can help me develop my digital teaching	4.28	0.051 (Ch = 26.87/En = 36.35/ Sp = 41.38)
To participate in formal meetings and discussions with other language teachers/language teacher students	7.18	0.390
To deepen my theoretical knowledge of digital competence	5.17	0.748
To deepen my technical knowledge about the use of digital tools	6.79	0.157
To deepen my didactic knowledge in digital competence	7.18	0.508
To be able to evaluate and assess my own use of digital tools in language teaching	6.97	0.231

tools. However, age was not found to be a factor, and in fact, younger respondents were less positive than older ones. It seems that language teachers' understanding of digital competence focuses mainly on selecting and using the available digital resources.

7.4.2 Influence of Digital Tools on Language Teaching

When we asked what sort of digital tools, if any, they used in teaching, respondents mentioned classic tools like learning platforms, dictionaries, and audio-visual resources. What was not frequently used, somewhat surprisingly in relation to the importance of oral interaction for language learning, were communication tools like Facebook, Skype, and WeChat.

Respondents were also given a number of statements about the effect of digital competence on teaching. They were clearly very positive about the positive effect of digital tools on language learning. The statements that language learning and teaching were positively affected were strongly supported, as was the statement that teaching materials would become more up-to-date if digital tools were used. Once again, teachers of Chinese were less positive, although this was not as strong as the differences reported above. However, the Chinese teachers showed a significantly positive attitude towards pupil's experience. If they had more fun in classes because of digital tools, their learning became broader compared with the English and Spanish teachers. Respondents also recognised that digital tools brought extra work with them, as more planning would be needed.

7.4.3 What Affects Digital Competence?

The final theme to report here regards what respondents thought would help to build their digital competence. The strongest support went to the need for practical workshops with tips on what tools to use in language teaching, and for including digital language use in textbooks. The least support went to the idea of having a mentor who could help to develop new teaching ideas. In this case, unlike the previous ones, teachers of English were less positive than those of Chinese and Spanish.

7.5 Interview Results

The interview results are organised based on the same themes as the survey results earlier.

7.5.1 Digital Resources in Teaching

The lack of digital resources in online teaching seems to be caused by the availability of online resources; teachers mentioned that there are well-created online resources for teaching and learning English but less for Chinese. This implies that language teachers' digital teaching resources are largely limited by their availability.

According to the teachers, they spent more time on teaching preparation only in the initial period when they changed from campus teaching to online teaching. Once they were familiar with the online teaching tools and online teaching environment, the preparation time was shortened. Online exams also took a lot of time for the Chinese teachers in particular since they had to create exams on a platform that is not very user-friendly to the Chinese language.

Teachers from all three languages would create digital resources on their own. In addition to the basic type of teaching materials such as Word and PowerPoint, they also mentioned word sets in Quizlet (quizlet.com) and games in Kahoot (kahoot.it). However, none mentioned other types of materials such as videos or animations that would require more time and specific computer skills from the teachers.

Another interesting finding related to this is the teacher's competence at creating digital resources. They reported that they themselves had seldom tried to create digital resources except for PowerPoint slides since they believe they lacked the knowledge of how to do this. English teachers added that an important factor when choosing digital tools in general was whether the tools added anything to the learning of pupils. Pupils are in these classes to learn language, and not digital tools. Therefore, the tools should be easy enough for the pupils to learn and apply so that they can concentrate on language learning.

7.5.2 What Is Digital Competence?

According to the interviewed teachers, all the elements of digital competence that have been mentioned in our questionnaire are important. A knowledge of the function of digital tools and the integration of digital tools in teaching is basic. As one teacher said: "The most important part in digital competence is to grasp the knowledge of the digital teaching and learning tools, and next is to use them according to our teaching tasks", to critically evaluate digital resources and create one's own digital resources "depends also on the knowledge of the digital teaching and learning tools". Another aspect mentioned is the pupils' acceptability, as the same teacher mentioned:

> When we think of digital teaching, digital competence we always discuss it from the teacher's perspective, the pupil's acceptability is an important reference for teachers, especially the long-term effect of a certain tool or method on pupil's learning. So far this discussion is also missing

In this sense, Spanish teachers also mentioned the necessity of being aware of the difficulties and needs that pupils have when using digital tools, which also came up in the interviews with English teachers. As one of the interviewees mentioned, "we used to think that pupils are used to the use of technology, but many of them lack competence when it comes to basic tasks such as finding a file in Google Classroom". It is a frequent stereotype that younger students are "digital natives", but this seems to be a myth, as all interviewees noted.

7.5.3 Influence of Digital Tools on Language Teaching

The interviewed teachers believe that the shift to digital teaching is irreversible, and that the COVID-19 pandemic was only a catalyst. It was felt by the interviewees that this practice would spread after the pandemic into the future, as one of the Chinese teachers pointed out: "before the pandemic online teaching was like sparks, after the pandemic this has become a tendency". This tendency makes digital competence a necessary competence for teachers to develop. However, some of the digital teaching and learning tools have already been used in language classes as teaching supplements before the pandemic.

A positive part of digital online teaching, as mentioned by the Chinese teachers, is that some shy pupils who find it difficult to practise in front of their classmates would have more opportunities to practise in an online environment where a pupil could only face the teacher alone. However, Spanish teachers also mentioned that teaching online lessons in larger groups could result in less pupil-teacher interaction since many students are unwilling to speak up in front of a larger peer group and also since there are few opportunities for asking questions privately. This makes it more likely for the teacher to fall back on more teacher-led pedagogical practice with fewer opportunities for small-group interaction. Another positive influence of digital online teaching is that some digital resources such as video clips and Kahoot exercises could make the pupils experience more fun in class. This could also provoke their interest to continue.

The change from classroom teaching to online teaching and learning has caused both positive and negative effects. For teachers, the time spent on preparation has increased, especially when teachers are not familiar with the digital tools and there are fewer digital resources available for them. In-class and after-class language training, as well as the checking of pupils' assignments, also have proved to be more time-consuming in a digital teaching and learning environment.

All the interviewed Chinese and Spanish teachers have mentioned the lack of face-to-face interaction between the teacher and pupils as a problem in online teaching environment. This causes them to feel a lack of control of the classroom. This is shown to be a specific problem in White's (2020) survey of language learning through Adobe Connect.

7.5.4 What Affects Digital Competence?

Many English and Spanish teachers mentioned that teacher training programmes should include some elements of basic digital competence, such as the basic learning platforms that most schools in Sweden use: Unikum, SchoolSoft, or Google Classroom. Similarly, a mentor who can help them to develop digital teaching is more welcomed by the Chinese teachers, while other teachers, feeling that they already have a quite good level of digital competence, prefer to have workshops focusing on good practices for online teaching.

7 Digital Competence and Teaching Practices of Language...   141

One of the interviewed Chinese teachers pointed out the importance of the theoretical basis of digital competence and the systematic training to develop it:

> I believe digital teaching and learning is the future of education, unfortunately the trainings so far are mainly short-termed, practice centered.... When we get to know a new tool, what we think most is whether it is suitable to my class, and how to use it? The theoretical basis is missing....The thinking of long-term effect is also missing.

For her, this should be included in the discussions of digital competence.

To summarise, according to the interviewed teachers, the biggest barriers to carrying out online teaching are lack of experience, knowledge, and training. This indicates training and experience sharing are very important. As another interviewed teacher said: "I would prefer workshops where teachers could share their experiences to each other; I would like to hear what others have done, and what the effect is".

7.6 Discussion and Conclusions

In this chapter, we have mapped the attitudes of three different groups of language teachers (Chinese, English, and Spanish) towards digital competence in Sweden and the effect of digitalisation on a COVID-19 world, showing that the shift from traditional teaching to online teaching in Sweden has affected teachers' performance (Skolverket, 2018) from different perspectives and to different extents.

In general, all the teachers considered themselves digitally competent to some extent, having stated that they used digital tools in their private lives. When asked about the barriers that they found, a lack of time and lack of preparation were pointed out as main barriers within the three groups, although there are also some differences to consider among the languages. Chinese teachers stated that their lack of knowledge was the biggest barrier, while English teachers, who already considered themselves competent before the pandemic, and Spanish teachers mostly focused on the fact that they did not have enough time to try new tools.

These differences might be due to the fact that in practice, there are not only more digital tools available for teaching English than Spanish or Chinese but also more tutorials in English about the use of digital tools in teaching. This is not something mentioned in previous research and therefore can be considered an important lesson to take from the pandemic.

If we compare the results of the survey answered before the pandemic (as presented in Santos Muñoz & White, 2020) with the answers given during the interviews in this study, Spanish teachers seem to have started visiting more blogs and websites in their search for advice and tips on how to use digital tools. They have started working with more online resources and creating more digital content. Even if, before the pandemic, most of them stated that there was no connection between the digital tools used in their private lives and the tools used at work, the lack of time during the pandemic has shortened the distance between their private identity and their professional identity (Burnett, 2011; Skolverket, 2018, 2019; Macintyre et al., 2020). However, all teachers seem to agree with the fact that while the beginning of the pandemic was harder in terms of workload, this might be seen as positive in the long run, since nowadays they have created their own set of digital content. This supports the results in Moser et al. (2020) that teachers felt that online teaching content was often very different from face-to-face content.

In summary, compared to traditional teaching, online teaching has been more time-consuming, especially in terms of preparation and requiring teachers to dedicate more time to digital resources, as well as trying new communication tools. However, this has improved teachers' digital skills, but at the same time their private identity has also been affected (Burnett, 2011; Macintyre et al., 2020). On the other hand, the pandemic situation has caused a bigger opening to the world. Teachers have contacted other colleagues and teachers around the world trying to learn and find good practices to bring to the online teaching. In this sense, English teachers seem to be a step ahead, in part, surely due to the fact that there are more digital tools and resources available online, which reflects in part that the use of digital tools can also increase the digital divide.

7.7 Lessons for a Post-COVID World

On the one hand, the implementation of online teaching at schools has improved the awareness of how important *digital competence* is for teachers and pupils nowadays; on the other hand, it has raised different issues related to digitalisation in schools in practice.

One of the main issues is the need of investing more resources for training, taking into consideration that language teachers need to acquire not only theoretical competence but also didactic and technical competence (Käck & Männikkö-Barbutiu, 2012; Diaz, 2019). Especially for Chinese and Spanish teachers, the school system was not prepared to adapt to online courses. Keeping this need in mind, most teachers agreed with the fact that teacher programmes and schools should include more content and practical workshops focusing on digitalisation. This need to improve knowledge and skills seems to be something that even students and parents might have experienced during their online learning, something that it would be interesting to address in a new study.

The most relevant changes for teachers, no matter what their target language, are, first, that preparation for the lessons has been more time-consuming and, second, that most teachers have also experienced problems related to classroom interaction itself (as supported by Moser et al., 2020); technical problems, or a lack of control over what the pupils are doing, have affected both teachers' and students' performances. Additionally, for some teachers, assessment has also been one of the most challenging issues while teaching online.

Teachers' experiences with oral interaction seem to have been double-edged: while some teachers pointed out that online lessons have been positive for increasing shy pupils' interaction, some Spanish teachers have underlined the fact that many pupils did not dare to ask questions during the videoconferences because they did not feel comfortable with the whole group listening to them.

To conclude, the COVID-19 pandemic has opened into new ways of teaching and learning, and the situation has only acted as a catalyst, underlining what previous research had already shown: digital competence changes constantly according to the society and its needs (Käck &

Männikkö-Barbutiu, 2012) and consequently teachers' needs within IT also change and develop over the years. The major lesson we see coming out of this research is that teachers need to have the time to collaborate and explore the possibilities of using digital tools, which is a clear lesson that schools can take into account.

References

Burnett, C. (2011). Pre-service teachers' digital literacy practices: Exploring contingency in identity and digital literacy in and out of educational contexts. *Language and Education, 25*(5), 433–449.

Diaz, P. (2019). *Digitala verktyg för språkutvecklande undervisning* (Digital tools for language teaching). Lund. Studentlitteratur.

European Parliament and the Council. (2006). Recommendations of the European Parliament and of the Council of 18 December 2006 on key competences for lifelong learning. *Official Journal of the European Union.* Report L394/310.

Foldspang, L., Spejlkavik Mark, M., Rants, L., Hjorth, L., Langholz-Carstensen, C., Poulsen, O., Johanson, U., Ahonen, G., & Aesnaess, S. (2014). Working environment and productivity. A register-based analysis of Nordic enterprises. https://doi.org/10.6027/TN2014-546.

Gallardo-Echenique, E., de Oliveira, J., Marqués-Molias, L., & Esteve-Mon, F. (2015). Digital competence in the knowledge society. *MERLOT Journal of Online Learning and Teaching, 11*(1), 1–16.

Käck, A., & Männikkö-Barbutiu, S. (Eds.). (2012). *Digital kompentens i lärarutbildningen. Ett integrationsperspektiv* (Digital competence in teacher education. An integration perspective). Lund. Studentlitteratur.

Macintyre, P., Gregersen, T., & Mercer, S. (2020). Language teachers' coping strategies during the Covid-19 conversion to online teaching: Correlations with stress, wellbeing and negative emotions. *System, 94.* https://doi.org/10.1016/j.system.2020.102352.

Martin, A. (2009). *Digital literacy for the third age: Sustaining identity in an uncertain world.* ELearning Papers (12). Available from http://www.uh.cu/static/documents/AL/Digital%20Literacy%20for%20the%20Third%20Age.pdf.

7 Digital Competence and Teaching Practices of Language... 145

Moser, K., Wei, T., & Brenner, D. (2020). Remote teaching during COVID-19: Implications from a national survey of language educators. *System, 97*. https://doi.org/10.1016/j.system.2020.102431.

Regeringskansliet. (2015a). *Gör Sverige i framtiden – digital kompetens* (Take Sweden into the future – digital competence). Report SOU 2015:28. Available from https://www.regeringen.se/49bbaa/contentassets/e0acd9a7659d4c138c6666d2d5e21605/gor-sverige-i-framtiden%2D%2Ddigital-kompetens-sou-201528.

Regeringskansliet. (2015b). *Digitaliseringens transformerande kraft – Vägval för framtiden* (The transformative power of digitalisation – A path to the future). Report SOU 2015:91. Available from https://www.regeringen.se/4add1a/contentassets/b69dac4f05d44e8d836cdd91a5a7401b/digitaliseringens-transformerande-kraft%2D%2Dvagval-for-framtiden-sou-201591.

Regeringskansliet. (2017a). *För ett hållbart digitaliserat Sverige – En digitaliseringsstrategi* (For a sustainably digital Sweden – A digitalisation strategy). Report N2017/03643/D. Available from https://www.regeringen.se/49adea/contentassets/5429e024be6847fc907b786ab954228f/digitaliseringsstrategin_slutlig_170518-2.pdf

Regeringskansliet. (2017b). *Nationell digitaliseringsstrategi för skolväsendet* (National digitalisation strategy for schools). Report xxx. Available from https://www.regeringen.se/4a9d9a/contentassets/00b3d9118b0144f6bb95302f3e08d11c/nationell-digitaliseringsstrategi-for-skolvasendet.pdf

Santos Muñoz, A., & White, J. R. (2020). Digitalisation in schools in Sweden: Needs and experiences of trainees teachers of languages. *Lingua, 2*, 28–31.

Skolverket. (2016). *IT-användning och IT-kompetens i skolan (IT use and IT competence in school)*. Report 2015:00067. Available from https://www.skolverket.se/getFile?file=3617

Skolverket. (2017). *Få syn på digitalisering på grundskolenivå. Ett kommentarmaterial till läroplanerna för förskoleklass, fritidshem och grundskoleutbildning (A view of digitalisation at compulsory school level. Commentary material for the syllabus for pre-school class, after school class and compulsory schooling)*. Report 2017:3783. Available from https://www.skolverket.se/getFile?file=3783

Skolverket. (2018). *Digitaliseringen i skolan. Möjligheter och utmaningar (Digitalisation in school. Possibilities and challenges)*. Report 2018:3971. Available from https://www.skolverket.se/getFile?file=3971

Skolverket. (2019). *Digital kompetens i förskola, skola och vuxenutbildning (Digital competence in pre-school, school and adult education)*. Report 2019:476. Available from https://www.skolverket.se/getFile?file=4041

Skolverket. (2021). *Pedagogisk personal i skola och vuxenutbildning läsåret 2020/2021 (Pedagogical personnel in school and adult education in the academic year 2020/2021).* Report 2021:433. Available from https://www.skolverket.se/getFile?file=7908

Vuorikari, R., Punie, Y., Carretero Gomez, S., & van den Brande, G. (2016). *DigComp 2.0: The Digital Competence Framework for Citizens. Update Phase 1: The Conceptual Reference Model.* JRC Working Papers. JRC101254. Joint Research Centre (Seville). <https://publications.jrc.ec.europa.eu/repository/handle/JRC101254>

White, J. R. (2020). A case study of student experiences of multi-modal net-based language learning. *International Journal of Online Pedagogy and Course Design, 10*(2), 1–20.

Willart, M. (2019). *Det akademiska skruvstädet – Om IT-stress och all annan press (The academic vice – About IT stress and all other pressure).* SULF report.

8

Assessing Instructional Design During Emergency Remote Education

Maria-Elena Solares-Altamirano

8.1 Introduction

The Escuela Nacional de Lengua Lingüística y Traducción (ENALLT) is part of the Universidad Nacional Autónoma de México (UNAM), the largest public university in Latin America. Besides two bachelor programs, ENALLT has a foreign language teaching center which offers students courses in 15 foreign languages. English proficiency is a graduation requirement for students at UNAM. Students are Spanish speakers and come from multiple fields of study. English as a Foreign Language (EFL) courses run in two-hour sessions three times per week. Courses focus on intermediate and advanced levels, taking learners from A2 to B2 levels of the Common European Framework of Reference (CEFR). As the English Department syllabus at ENALLT is under construction, the series *New Language Leader* (intermediate and upper intermediate) has been used for the last five years. The COVID-19 outbreak began when the first of two

---

M.-E. Solares-Altamirano (✉)
Universidad Nacional Autónoma de Mexico, Ciudad de México, Mexico
e-mail: solares@unam.mx

© The Author(s), under exclusive license to Springer Nature Switzerland AG 2023
K. Sadeghi, M. Thomas (eds.), *Second Language Teacher Professional Development*, Digital Education and Learning, https://doi.org/10.1007/978-3-031-12070-1_8

terms a year was running in 2020. Three things became clear while facing this crisis: (a) many teachers were inexperienced in Online Education (OE), (b) others were technically unskilled, and (c) there was an immediate need for free online ready-made educational materials and resources for language teaching fitting the school 'program'. Available technological tools such as Zoom, Skype, and Google Meet allowed teachers all over the world to cope with emergency remote education (ERE). However, an educator's job goes beyond meeting students synchronically online. Expeditious creation, selection, adaptation, and digitization of available teaching materials on the Web were also crucial. The greatest challenge, however, lay in being able to combine technology and available online resources within effective instructional designs. The above demands did not come on their own. Opening the classroom door made evident already existing problems such as the digital divide, teachers' poor familiarization with the latest SLA research, students' lack of autonomy, poor infrastructure, bias against OE, and, above all, a lack of time and of human and technological resources. ERE presented ENALLT teachers with very specific demands: (a) the urgent design of EFL lessons that could be delivered online and that met the minimum requirements of OE; (b) flexible lesson designs that could be used with different communication tools (Zoom, Skype, Google Meet) and learning management systems (Google Classrooms, Moodle, Edmodo, etc.); (c) minimum dependence from personnel at the Distant Education Department who had to support the whole school with the transition to online. Given these demands, the researcher opted for the construction of a website.

The website was named 'TBLT lessons for EFL teachers'. It offered ENALLT teachers and students ready-made technology-mediated TBLT lessons to ease the teaching-learning process during ERE. Hence, the objectives of this chapter are (a) to explore the ongoing design and implementation of technology-mediated TBLT lessons specifically addressed to ENALLT students; (b) to report students' assessment of such lessons implemented via Moodle in the researcher's EFL groups. Word constraints oblige the researcher to leave the target teachers' assessment of the lessons on the website for a future paper.

8.2 Theoretical Framework

Three theoretical pillars support this study: online education, technology-mediated TBLT, and a framework to analyze learning networks. Online education[1] (OE) was not new when the pandemic emerged. OE has advanced greatly in recent decades. Those who have been involved in OE know about the systematic instructional design it requires, its theoretical bases and the constructivist principles it develops from in order to guarantee meaningful learning in participative and transversal environments (Bezanilla & Arranz, 2016). The advantages and effectiveness of OE are supported by much research (Patrick & Powell, 2009; Schachar & Neumann, 2003). Despite this, OE was viewed as low-quality instruction among language teachers at ENALLT. The low popularity of English hybrid courses available in the English Department before the pandemic was evidence of that. Serdyukov (2021) assertively signals that the coronavirus pandemic became 'the biggest distance learning experiment in history' (p. 1). The experimental nature of this experience lay in the fleetness with which this transition was implemented. It is vital, therefore, to understand that what people experienced during the pandemic was not online distant education but rather ERE. Bozkurt et al. (2020) explain that the implementation of distance education 'is grounded in theoretical and practical knowledge which is specific to the field and its nature. On the other hand, emergency remote education is about surviving in a time of crisis with all resources available, including offline and/or online' (p. 2).

The technology-mediated TBLT framework proposed by González-Lloret and Ortega (2014) constitutes the second pillar of this chapter. Their framework suggests that educational and language developmental rationales such as task-based language teaching should guide the 'design, use and evaluation' (p. 3) of new technologies for language learning. These researchers believe that the theoretical principles of TBLT enlighten, reinforce, and expand the potential of technologies. Tasks in this framework are defined by five features: meaning-focused, goal-oriented, learner-centered, including real-world processes of language use and encouraging experiential learning. González-Lloret and Ortega advise

---

[1] Online Education, Distant Education, and E-learning are used synonymously in this paper.

using the above task features to build, examine, adapt, and assess technology-mediated designs.

The third theoretical pillar corresponds to Carvalho and Goodyear's (2014) framework to analyze learning networks. This framework distinguishes three types of design in learning networks: the epistemic, the setting, and the social. The design of learning environments is not constrained in this framework to 'the design of instructional sequences or textbooks or learning materials [but embraces] anything that can be designed with the goal of supporting somebody's learning' (p. 57). Epistemic design refers to the designer's efforts to create knowledge-oriented activities. Understanding the way epistemic choices influence learners' subsequent activities is essential. The designer may engage learners in investigating, planning, hypothesizing, or reflecting. However, the way in which the designer communicates the epistemic component (e.g., proposed tasks and resources) will also indicate the participants' choices about sequencing, pacing, and selection of what will be shared and will also include other participants, interests, and objectives. The setting design refers to the scenery or physical conditions in which learning occurs, for example, rooms, furniture arrangement, computers, but it may also include non-material tools such as webpages, videos, e-books, or light. Social design refers to the way learners' learning is influenced by people around them, including their assistance, support, guidance, or instruction. The roles assigned to participants, their organization in pairs or teams, are included in this social design.

8.3 Instructional Design

8.3.1 Procedures

The design and implementation procedures of technology-mediated lessons are now described. The teacher-researcher designed nine of the lessons on the website. Two ENALLT colleague teachers revised and enriched each lesson. Each revised lesson was implemented via Moodle in the teacher-researcher's EFL group. Students' feedback was incorporated into the lessons. Only then were lessons published on the website. This procedure was repeated for each lesson. Available lessons on the website were few at the beginning of the pandemic. However, their number increased after each term as the project progressed.

The Moodle learning management system (LMS) was used for lesson implementation because, when adequately implemented and exploited, its characteristics allowed it to be used so as to go beyond being a mere repository of content. The ease of integrating images, audio, video, or links to useful websites with interactive and multimedia material let the implemented Moodle lessons act as hypertexts, potentially enriching each lesson. Written paper lessons were turned into written dialogues with the students, who were also able to incorporate links to texts, videos, recordings, and other types of material. Moodle offers forums which were considered during lesson design to promote interaction. Recording students' assignment submission, an important part of process evaluation, is another Moodle advantage.

8.3.2 Task-Supported Language Teaching

Previous research (Solares-Altamirano, 2010, 2014) has described the EFL educational context in Mexico as 'task-supported' rather than 'task-based'. Samuda and Bygate (2008) describe the former as a context where tasks are 'used to enrich the syllabus or to provide additional learning opportunities. However, tasks are not used for assessment purposes and the syllabus may be defined by categories other than tasks' (p. 59). In the same research, ENALLT's EFL program was identified as being textbook-bound. In such settings the textbook syllabus is used as a basis for standardization and accountability (Waters, 2009). Considering this and other contextual constraints, Solares-Altamirano (2020) makes it clear that pure TBLT was not viable in ENALLT's context and that only task-supported language teaching with mainly *focused tasks* that matched the textbook syllabus was feasible. Incorporating technology into instruction, on the other hand, was not a choice during the confinement. If on-site EFL lessons had to move to online education immediately, it was better to do it in the most principled way. Exploring the design of technology-mediated task-supported lessons was deemed an opportunity.

The way TBLT principles were integrated into lessons' instructional design is now explained. First, the objectives of each lesson stage are stated. Then, the way *rich input, incidental learning*, and utilized *noticing* techniques were nurtured through lessons stages is explained.

The *pre-task stage* introduces the task. Students watch a video, read a text, or discuss questions that offer plenty of language and content input. Promoting opportunities for noticing is crucial in this phase.

In the *during-task stage*, learners do something concrete, something 'worth doing' in Carvalho and Goodyear's (2014) words. Learners use the target language to launch a new product or service; to inform classmates about different processes everyday products or services go through before or after they reach users; to solve a mystery case based on collected evidence; to participate in a trivia about modern world inventions. Task completion engages learners in learning by doing and incidental learning. Focus on language may be incorporated at this stage by means of *focus-on-form* techniques. This means that while students' attention remains on the task, they simultaneously and incidentally give attention to language as well.

In the *post-task stage*, students' reflecting on their experience is encouraged. Students are engaged in language-focused activities or what Long (1991) refers to as focus-on-formS activities. These may target linguistic features which seemed problematic during task performance. Language analysis becomes explicit. TBLT, Skehan (2003) points out, is 'the major current implementation of focus on form concepts' (p. 391). Noticing techniques used in the pre-task stage are picked up here to allow for focus-on-formS through discovery learning. At this point, as Rod Ellis (2003) notes, there is no longer a threat that focusing on language will undermine the integrity of the task.

As can be observed in the lesson stages above, *plentiful input, noticing opportunities, and incidental learning* are promoted in all lesson stages. Where in the task sequence focus-on-form should be dealt with is an open question for TBLT researchers. Long (2016) states that 'attention to grammar [in TBLT] is not carried out … as an end in itself (focus-on-formS), but during (and if necessary after, but not before) task work' (p. 17).

Plentiful input and incidental learning were promoted in these lessons via listening, reading, and video materials which were used to introduce the lessons but also as sources of linguistic input to promote incidental learning. Exploitation of texts and videos concentrated on their content and the message they conveyed, that is, they were used as ends in themselves rather than to develop reading or listening skills. Paran (2003) explains that from a TBLT perspective, (a) reading must focus on the meaning of the text, (b) the text should encourage learners to communicate to each other about the text, and (c) reading tasks should make learners identify reading as something enjoyable that contributes to their understanding of the world. Texts in this approach are used to implicitly learn the language. Some lessons included both video and reading sources about the same topic. Although this might seem repetitive to some teachers, the rationale for doing so was the designer's aim to provide rich instruction. Nation (2014) explains that rich instruction involves meeting the same word [or structure] in several sentences and contexts. Learners also appreciated (see Results section) having exposure to the same information via different channels. Comparison of content in both video and reading sources is a cognitive skill commonly used to exploit these materials in lessons. Selection, organization, analysis, and synthesis were also used.

Noticing opportunities, as explained above, were also promoted in all lesson stages for incidental learning. The noticing techniques the researcher utilized in reading texts and video transcripts were *'input enhancement'* and *'glossing'*. These are both textual modification techniques commonly used in reading research to encourage incidental focus-on-form. Sharwood Smith (1993) describes *'input enhancement'* as making target language items more salient through typographical manipulations such as coloring, underlining, capitalizing, or bold-facing. Input enhancement was used to make grammar structures more noticeable. *'Glossing'*, Sharwood Smith adds, refers to linguistic information about an item in a text which is generally inserted in the margin. Glossing was mostly used in these lessons to explain vocabulary. Providing a word's meaning first facilitated learners' text comprehension while also enabling bottom-up reading processes; secondly, it allowed learners to notice glossed items while their attention remained on processing the text. In this way, tasks kept learners' focus on meaning, while textual modification techniques occasionally drew their attention to grammar and vocabulary.

8.3.3 Lesson Components

Technology-mediated task-supported lessons were implemented in the researcher's groups as hybrid courses. 'Hybrid' means that Zoom synchronic sessions and Moodle asynchronic lessons were combined. The latter constituted the hub of the course. Students in the researcher's groups did not buy the textbook adopted by the school, though the same linguistic content was addressed. Each lesson had four components:

A lesson presentation where the objectives, task, task outcome, potential linguistic output, and the way the lesson fits ENALLT's language program were specified.

A lesson where content was organized as 'pre-, during and post-task' stages. The lesson assembled instructions, tasks, and links to pre-selected learning websites in an easy-to-navigate structure.

Learners' printable handouts accompanied each lesson. Printable PDF versions were especially important for learners with a poor Internet connection as it allowed them to work offline. They were also easy to store and retrieve for students' further study. Handouts also allowed the designer to manipulate the input students were being exposed to.

Transcripts and answer sheets for different learning activities were sometimes included.

The above components were enhanced with a private Facebook group and email communication. Internet free-access videos were important components, too. Videos were used for different purposes: to introduce topics, to explain grammar and vocabulary, and to practice pronunciation. Included videos came from personal non-profitable channels whose authors beg users to subscribe to their channels. Learning tasks were created to pedagogically exploit those videos. The designed lessons were created for educational non-profitable purposes. Authorship of websites, videos, or other types of resources was properly acknowledged, so they could be uploaded to the open access website https://sites.google.com/enallt.unam.mx/tbl/inicio (currently restricted to ENALLT personnel until is fully developed).

8.4 Data Collection and Analysis

8.4.1 Participants

Sixty-two students from three intact classes at intermediate EFL level (*B1, CEFR*) taught by the teacher-researcher assessed the instructional design. Students were 34 females/29 males, with an average age of (+/-) 22 years. They came from different academic fields (Science, Engineering, Social Sciences, Economics, Medicine, and Humanities). Teaching the same level in three consecutive terms (a different group at each stage of the ERE period) allowed the teacher-researcher to distinguish three periods: August–December 2020 (Group 1), January–June 2021 (Group 2), and August–December 2021 (Group 3).

8.4.2 Method

Students' assessment was collected via an open-ended questionnaire delivered at the end of each term in each group. The questionnaire included three open questions. Each question corresponded to each of the three types of design Carvalho and Goodyear's (2014) framework suggests: learning activities (Q1-epistemic design), the resources and tools utilized (Q2-setting design), and the course's social atmosphere (Q3-social design). The questionnaire was piloted, refined, and validated in an additional similar group that did not participate in this study. First, analyses of students' responses were conducted to confirm the questions elicited the desired information and to identify the components of each question mentioned most. Repeated topics were categorized, reclassified, and better defined after each analysis. New categories were also created while much less frequent ones were discarded. The final version of the questionnaire with the identified components may be found in the Appendix.

Collected data from groups 1, 2, and 3 (G1, G2, G3) were analyzed using the above questionnaire via an iterative process for qualitative research (Creswell, 2003; Denzin & Lincoln, 2000; Heigham & Croker, 2009). Whenever a response matched a different type of design better, it was adjusted. The final stage of the analysis calculated the frequency of each of the identified components.

8.5 Results and Discussion

Results from students' surveys are presented in Table 8.1. The table displays results under each of the three questions corresponding to the three periods distinguished above, the total number of replies per group for each type of design, and the number of mentions each component received in each group. Data showed that the components most remarked upon in the epistemic design were the type of learning activities and the online lessons in the three ERE periods. In the setting design, reference to Moodle scored the highest rate in the three ERE periods, too. Reference to videos (G2, G3) and web pages (G1) followed Moodle in the setting design. Regarding the social design, allusion to what students had enjoyed was the feature most talked about.

8.5.1 Epistemic Design

In the first ERE stage, most students in G1 were unfamiliar with hybrid education. Many had only experienced face-to-face classroom education replaced by synchronic zoom sessions in the first months of the pandemic. Few of them were familiar with Moodle or any other LMS. If familiar, students mainly knew LMSs as assignment repositories, as stated in their answers to the questionnaire.

8 Assessing Instructional Design During Emergency Remote... 157

Table 8.1 Identified components under epistemic, setting, and social designs

	G1 (18 Sts)	G2 (25 Sts)	G3 (19 Sts)
	August–December 2020	January–June 2021	August–December 2021
Q1–Epistemic	72 Replies (100%)	111 Replies (100%)	81 Replies (100%)
Course difficulty	12 (16%)	6 (5%)	12 (14%)
Course organization	8 (11%)	5 (4%)	16 (19%)
Content and topics	10 (13%)	9 (8%)	14 (17%)
Learning activities	24 (33%)	46 (41%)	25 (30%)
Online lessons	18 (25%)	45 (40%)	14 (17%)
Q2–Setting	34 Replies (100%)	53 Replies (100%)	126 Replies (100%)
Web pages	8 (23%)	5 (9%)	18 (14%)
Videos	6 (17%)	15 (28%)	22 (17%)
Zoom sessions	2 (5%)	4 (7%)	16 (12%)
Online forums	1 (2%)	4 (7%)	16 (12%)
Moodle platform	14 (41%)	16 (30%)	38 (30%)
Facebook	2 (5%)	3 (5%)	16 (12%)
Other	1 (2%)	6 (11%)	0
Q3–Social	31 Replies (100%)	44 Replies (100%)	90 Replies (100%)
I enjoyed	19 (61%)	17 (38%)	25 (27%)
I felt comfortable	6 (19%)	11 (25%)	21 (23%)
Interaction w/ classmates	4 (12%)	11 (25%)	19 (21%)
Interaction w/ teacher	2 (6%)	5 (11%)	25 (27%)

S21(G1): 'Moodle was used to store assignments in other classes I have. In this course Moodle was well-exploited: content, multimedia material, forums.'

Despite students' initial complaints were about Moodle, they learned to use this LMS. Above all, students became aware of the advantages of online education. Permanence and flexibility were the most frequent words used to describe online lessons. The convenience of keeping course content and materials in a single place with access flexibility was the benefit most mentioned. Opportunities to revise, reinforce, and even recover missed lessons were remarked on. Access to the whole course after it ended was also acknowledged as being valuable for the future. Assignment

158   M.-E. Solares-Altamirano

submission flexibility and opportunities to learn at their own pace were new experiences for most students.

> S5(G1): 'Hybrid lessons were new for most of us. We learned to use new platforms and identified ways of learning that were worth trying.'

Despite the advantages students found in online lessons, most of them expressed that a combination of synchronic and asynchronic sessions worked best. Students considered the two types of instruction were different but complemented each other.

> S9(G3): 'Both [synchronic and asynchronic lessons] contributed to my learning. Combination allowed me to organize my time better.'

Development of learners' autonomy, unintentionally derived from lesson design, was especially gratifying:

> S6(G1): 'Knowing about the plenty of pedagogical material available on the Internet stimulated my learning autonomy.'
> S15(G2): 'Online lessons developed my learning autonomy as I used to go deeper into each topic.'

Teacher's feedback was appreciated in G1 and G2.

> S2(G1): 'I felt comfortable when the teacher gave us feedback. I felt accompanied at all times.'
> S22(G2): 'Most teachers just give grades. Here we analyzed the mistakes.'

Students' observations in G2 and G3 were prominent on abundant oral practice opportunities.

> S10(G2): 'Having many speaking opportunities was enriching.'
> S6(G3): 'Oral practice was constant.'

8 Assessing Instructional Design During Emergency Remote... 159

Gratitude was expressed for multidisciplinary lessons, too. The designed lessons targeted different majors. Students appreciated not only talking about theirs but also their classmates' majors.

S5(G2): 'I learned things about engineering, business, accounting with much vocabulary in different areas.'

Learning activities were described as practical, motivating, dynamic, and real life in the three groups, *'We did things with language, we created our own enterprise' (S9-G2)*; content and topics as varied, controversial, and fitting the university context, *'Class topics were about every day, major-related topics' (S3-G1)*; course organization as well structured and easy to follow by most students in the three groups. Teamwork and agency were also valued, *'Team projects in each unit were motivating' (S20-G3); 'I felt comfortable when the teacher gave us the freedom to talk about a topic we were interested in' (S12-G3)*. Regarding course difficulty, 25/30 statements described the course as challenging and suitable for their level. Only five comments (3 in G2, 2 in G3) described the course as difficult. Difficulty, however, was expressed as follows *'Difficult for people who are not used to speaking in class. A lot of participation was required' (S9-G3)*.

8.5.2 Setting Design

Despite Moodle being the most widely used LMS in higher education (Bezanilla & Arranz, 2016), students found several flaws in it: unattractive layout, overloaded content, overlapping sections, confusing, difficult to use, no email notifications, and incompatibility with some electronic devices. Students struggled to use Moodle, but finally succeeded. The quality of online lessons and learning activities compensated for Moodle flaws. Moodle lessons became the hub of the course, offering flexible access to course objectives, content, supporting material, submitted assignments, and discussion forums in a single location. Those unfamiliar with online education found this feature useful to organize their learning and time. Online forums (G3) and videos were the most significant components for students in the setting design. Group interaction flowed easily in forums and allowed students to get to know each other. Forums were used for discussions and to share students' work. Task instructions invited participants to comment on at least one of their peers' contributions. Peer observation was longed for and appreciated. Introverted students found forum participation a non-threatening way of interacting with peers. Others indicated forum participation let them plan what they wanted to say. Forums were also perceived as a cohesion tool, an enjoyable way of appreciating their classmates' views and exchanging ideas.

> S4(G3): 'I liked forums because I could practice what I had learned under no pressure.'
> S11(G3): 'Forum participation let me think about ways to communicate myself.'

Multiple positive remarks about videos showed they were central in the design, an *'excellent means to learn, loved them, entertaining, well-explained grammar lessons, English in real life contexts, videos were the best, this is the way I learn, videos were fun, we caught different accents, so instructive, interactive, videos made the class dynamic.'* Links to selected websites were found practical, instructive, and useful to boost exposure to English. *'Websites to learn English independently helped us improve understanding and continue investigating' S4(G2).* Gratitude was also shown when the same topic was approached in reading and audio formats.

The teacher-researcher kept records of students' participation in Moodle activities. Such records were shared periodically with the students. Soon, they understood their contribution to Moodle activities was more important than attending Zoom synchronic sessions. Ungoogleable tasks were also developed to prevent students copying and pasting information. Regarding *synchronic zoom sessions*, students said they were essential to practice speaking, to explain complex matters, and to meet classmates. However, students' comments in G3 suggest participation in synchronic sessions might depend on their personality, *'I felt threatened when asked to speak in zoom sessions' (S15-G3), 'Participating in zoom sessions was intimidating' S2(G3).* Unanimously, students in all groups reported they had enjoyed small group work in breakout rooms. Opinions about the Facebook private group were contradictory. Students expressed that it was good to share personal information beyond academic contexts, though hardly anyone participated. Everybody agreed more participation was necessary. Students in G2 appreciated the availability of printable handouts, especially for interactive exercises on different webpages. Printed versions allowed them to work offline, as they explained.

Regarding the textbook, data revealed students were eventually happy working without a textbook and considered the teacher wise for not requiring one. Yet, students' first impressions revealed their initial reliance on textbooks, *'I panicked when I heard we were not going to use the textbook. As the course continued, I realized I enjoyed the online lessons much more than the ordinary textbook pages' (S15-G2).*

8.5.3 Social Design

Duncan and Young (2009) suggest that OE challenges educators to create a caring virtual classroom that allows students to engage in collaborative learning and interaction. Findings revealed this challenge was met. Students' answers in all groups described their class atmosphere as friendly, harmonic, supportive, and non-punitive. Peers were described as encouraging and caring. To what extent this is cultural or it depends on what Adrian Underhill (as cited in Head & Taylor, 1997) defines as the 'teacher's presence' (the unique psychological climate that a teacher creates in the classroom) requires further investigation. Following Schweizer (1999), however, the teacher-researcher worked toward 'fun, belonging, choice and challenge' aims in course delivery. A unit zero was created to introduce the Moodle platform. Content in that unit approached foreign language learning. Issues such as the affective filter and the negative effect of anxiety were explained in non-technical language. Each class activity and course material were also personalized to make learners the center of the lesson. Several resources were used to raise students' self-confidence. *S11(G3)* said *'The teacher shared things about her, so we gained confidence to talk about ourselves.'* The Facebook group was used to send encouraging messages about students' work. Teamwork projects, whole class discussions, and bonding tasks were signaled as class activities the students enjoyed the most. *'I felt comfortable when we talked about ourselves*

(S7-G2), our lives (S9-G1), our personal experiences' (S8-G3). Some students said they had always felt comfortable and craved their classes.

> S20(G3): 'The pandemic put me down. The English class helped me keep my mind busy and improve my English.'
> S5(G2): 'I attended zoom classes because I enjoyed them. Everything was in the online lesson.'

Building a perfect online course was impossible from one day to the next. Students' suggestions to improve their course were crucial for effective ERE and were addressed before each course implementation. Students requested printable versions of online lessons and class activities, a preplanned course schedule (signaling submission deadlines), pre-established evaluation procedures, exams, and an introductory lesson on Moodle. Teaching the same course for three consecutive terms enabled the teacher-researcher to meet most of the students' demands. By the time G3 took this course, online lessons and course organization were much improved. Despite learners enjoying the combination of synchronic and asynchronic lessons, they manifested a preference for asynchronic sessions, *'Moodle and Zoom sessions were well combined but I would have wanted more Moodle lessons' (S16-G3)*. Students justified this preference, explaining it was difficult to concentrate for longer than one hour. *'Taking several subjects synchronically was physically and mentally exhausting'* they said.

8.6 Post-Pandemic Lessons

This chapter has documented the successful delivery of an instructional design during ERE in a public Mexican university. The emergency made lesson design, website construction, searching for learning sources, and constant cycles of creation-implementation-improvement of lessons a simultaneous endeavor. Doing research in addition to the above responsibilities and within an ongoing unfamiliar crisis explains the methodological limitations and narrative nature of this chapter. Little research exists on how learners perceive and experience learning, design, development, and course implementation in emergency situations. In this period when OE has proven its effectiveness and ERE is under research and assessment (Mae-Toquero, 2021), the author hopes she has made some contribution.

This project ended not because work was complete or the pandemic was over. It ended because the transition period has to end, because it is time to stop improvising and reflect on what has been done. Results show that learners' development of autonomy, awareness of the advantages of online education, familiarization with available learning resources on the Web, and the development of technological and organization skills were some of the learning outcomes. While reporting what people learned from the pandemic, Johnson (cited in Bresnick, 2021) said, 'we learned we had to make decisions when we didn't have the time or the data'. As teachers, we had to decide what LMS to use, how instruction would take place (synchronically, asynchronically), how evaluation would be performed, and how feedback would be provided. Similarly, researchers had to do research when we had no research designs or data collection instruments. When we look back at this ERE period, there are things that all educators might agree we learned. We learned new teaching techniques and tried new digital tools; we changed our attitudes toward OE; but above all, we learned about learning. We learned that quality education (whether hybrid, on-site, or fully online) means engaging 'students in communication, interaction, collaboration, and cooperation, integrating inquiry, discovery, and problem-solving approaches' (Serdyukov, 2021, p. 4). All these are features of TBLT (meaning-focused, goal-oriented, learner-centered, incidental, and reflective learning).

The combination of technology-mediated TBLT and hybrid education proved fruitful. Time, content, and learning experiences were enhanced. Long (2016) remarks that TBLT 'requires expertise [from] course designers and classroom teachers, and a considerable investment of time and effort ... to be successful' (p. 28). Had it not been for the pandemic, the teacher-researcher would never have embarked on this arduous work. She hopes this manuscript will help to refine current approaches to instructional design.

8.7 Conclusion

Despite all the worry and despair, the pandemic also presented an opportunity to learn, create, and experiment. We learned that 'the sole utilization of ICTs does not establish the principles of quality education' (Cabero, 2009, p. 32), as a whole architecture is required. The researcher hopes that after the pandemic, (a) teachers do not return to previous practices nor adopt online or hybrid education for its convenience and (b) that learners have grasped their increased responsibility in online and hybrid education. The way educators incorporate technology into instruction in the post-pandemic world will reveal how close we moved toward Meléndez-Tamayo's (2013) paradigm, one that entails a 'reconciliation between the educational context and society [that] blurs the boundaries between formal, non-formal and informal learning and that supports the distribution and exchange of shared knowledge' (p. 276).

Acknowledgments The author is especially grateful to all her virtual students during the emergency remote education who made this work possible.

Appendix

1. What is your impression about the course you have just finished? Please comment on:

   - course difficulty
   - course organization
   - content and included topics
   - learning activities
   - the online lesson:

   - positive things
   - negative things

   - other: (specify)

2. How did the tools used throughout the course *facilitate /hinder* your learning? Please comment on:

- web pages
- videos
- synchronic sessions via Zoom
- online forums
- the Moodle platform

- positive things
- negative things

- private Facebook group
- other (specify)

3. Complete the sentences below with your own thoughts:

- I enjoyed the course when …
- I felt comfortable when …
- The relationship with my classmates was …
- The relationship with the teacher was …

References

Bezanilla, M. J., & Arranz, S. (2016). Sistema de evaluación de competencias en educación superior utilizando Moodle [Competence evaluation system in higher education using Moodle]. *Opción, 32*(80), 290–310.

Bozkurt, A., Jung, I., Xiao, J., Vladimirschi, V., Schuwer, R., Egorov, G., & Paskevicius, M. (2020). A global outlook to the interruption of education due to COVID-19 pandemic: Navigating in a time of uncertainty and crisis. *Asian Journal of Distance Education, 15*(1), 1–126.

Bresnick, P. (2021, June 10). *Lessons learned from the pandemic will forever shape higher education*. Fierce Education. Retrieved from https://www.fierceeducation.com/best-practices/lessons-learned-from-pandemic-will-forever-shape-higher-education.

Cabero, J. (2009). Educación 2.0. ¿Marca, moda o nueva visión de la educación? In C. Castaño (Coord.), *Web 2.0. El uso de la web en la sociedad del conocimiento. Investigación e implicaciones educativas*, (pp. 13–34). Caracas: Universidad Metropolitana.

Carvalho, L., & Goodyear, P. (2014). Framing the analysis of learning network architectures. In L. Carvalho & P. Goodyear (Eds.), *The architecture of productive learning networks* (pp. 48–70). Routledge.

Creswell, J. (2003). *Research design: Qualitative, quantitative, and mixed methods and approaches*. Sage.

Denzin, N., & Lincoln, Y. (2000). *Handbook of qualitative research*. Sage.

Duncan, H. E., & Young, S. (2009). Online pedagogy and practice: Challenges and strategies. *The Researcher, 22*(1), 17–32. Retrieved from https://www.researchgate.net/publication/282662578.

Ellis, R. (2003). *Task-based language learning and teaching*. OUP.

González-Lloret, M., & Ortega, M. (Eds.). (2014). *Technology-mediated TBLT: Researching technology and tasks*. John Benjamins.

Head, K., & Taylor, P. (1997). *Readings in teacher development*. Australia: Macmillan.

Heigham, J., & Croker, R. A. (2009). *Qualitative research in applied linguistics. A practical introduction*. Palgrave Macmillan.

Long, M. H. (1991). Focus on form: A design feature in language teaching methodology. In K. de Bot, R. Ginsberg, & C. Kramsch (Eds.), *Foreign language research in cross-cultural perspective* (pp. 39–52). John Benjamins.

Long, M. H. (2016). In defense of tasks and TBLT: Nonissues and real issues. *Annual Review of Applied Linguistics, 36*, 5–33.

Mae-Toquero, C. (2021). Emergency remote education experiment amid COVID-19 pandemic in learning institutions in the Philippines. *International Journal of Educational Research and Innovation, 15*, 162–176.

Meléndez-Tamayo, C. F. (2013). *Plataformas virtuales como recurso para la enseñanza en la universidad: Análisis, evaluación y propuesta de integración de Moodle con herramientas de la Web 2.0.* (Unpublished doctoral dissertation). Universidad Computense de Madrid, Madrid. Retrieved from https://eprints.ucm.es/id/eprint/20466/

Nation, I. S. P. (2014). Designing reading tasks to maximize vocabulary learning. *Applied Research on English Language, 3*(5), 1–8.

Paran, A. (2003). Bringing the outside world into the classroom: Ways of making reading lessons less of a tedious task. *ETAS Journal, 20*(2), 26–28.

Patrick, S., & Powell, A. (2009). *A summary of research on the effectiveness of K-12 online learning, effectiveness of online teaching and learning iNACOL.* Retrieved from https://files.eric.ed.gov/fulltext/ED509626.pdf.

Samuda, V., & Bygate, M. (2008). *Tasks in second language learning.* Palgrave.

Schachar, M., & Neumann, Y. (2003). Differences between traditional and distance education academic performances: A meta-analytic approach. *The International Review of Research in Open and Distance Learning, 4*(2). https://doi.org/10.19173/irrodl.v4i2.153

Schweizer, H. (1999). *Designing and teaching an online course. Spinning your web classroom.* Allyn & Bacon.

Serdyukov, P. (2021). A growing formalization of contemporary online education. *Academia Letters,* Article 2601. Retrieved from file:///C:/Users/solar/Downloads/A_Growing_Formalization_of_Contemporary%20(1).pdf.

Sharwood Smith, M. (1993). Input enhancement in instructed SLA: Theoretical bases. *Studies in Second Language Acquisition, 15*(2), 165–179.

Skehan, P. (2003). Focus on form, tasks, and technology. *Computer Assisted Language Learning, 16*(5), 391–411.

Solares-Altamirano, M. E. (2010). Promoting teacher professional development through online task-based instruction. *International Journal of Virtual and Personal Learning Environments, 1*(4), 52–65.

Solares-Altamirano, M. E. (2014). Textbooks, tasks and technology: An action research study in a textbook-bound EFL context. In M. González-Lloret & L. Ortega (Eds.), *Technology-mediated TBLT. Researching technology and tasks* (pp. 79–113). John Benjamins.

Solares-Altamirano, M. E. (2020). Teachers' responses to an online course on task-based language teaching in Mexico. In C. Lambert & R. Oliver (Eds.), *Using tasks in second language teaching. Practice in diverse contexts* (pp. 193–211). Multilingual Matters.

Waters, A. (2009, September). *Tasks in textbooks: Barking up the wrong tree?* Paper presented at the 3rd Biennial Conference on Task-based Language Teaching, Lancaster University, UK.

9

Technology + Pedagogy in EFL Virtual Classrooms: University Teachers' Professional Needs on Technology-Enhanced Pedagogy

Li Li

9.1 Introduction

Due to the outbreak of COVID-19, online learning has become increasingly important as teaching and learning were shifted to online platforms in early 2020 (Hodges et al., 2020; Murphy, 2020). Many studies have documented the effectiveness and efficiency of online and blended learning during this period (e.g., Al-Fraihat et al., 2020; Korkealehto & Leier, 2021; Zou et al., 2021). As evidenced in the literature, many different platforms were utilised by teachers and schools, and varieties of issues also emerged from the new mode of learning due to the combination of synchronous and asynchronous delivery using Tencent Classroom, Google Classrooms, Moodle, Teams and Zoom. Despite the success of moving classes to online swiftly, language teachers have various concerns, particularly in terms of their professional needs and experience. Potential issues include affective aspects of online learning, motivation, autonomy and

---

L. Li (✉)
University of Exeter, Exeter, UK
e-mail: Li.Li@exeter.ac.uk

© The Author(s), under exclusive license to Springer Nature Switzerland AG 2023 **169**
K. Sadeghi, M. Thomas (eds.), *Second Language Teacher Professional Development,*
Digital Education and Learning, https://doi.org/10.1007/978-3-031-12070-1_9

engagement, and teachers' competence and confidence in embracing the new teaching methods (Li & Morris, 2021). One particular challenge for language teachers is developing online interactive and collaborative activities to enable students to use and practise the language. In light of these problems, this study considers the in-service professional development needs and experience of language teachers in China. This line of inquiry is vital for various reasons. First, there is increasing awareness that teachers must be developed professionally throughout their careers to be effective (Burns & Lawrie, 2015; Li & Morris, 2021). Teachers need to be upskilled when innovations are introduced to embrace the changes (Evers et al., 2016; Li, 2017a). Second, teachers as agents for change require an in-depth understanding of the needs, challenges and opportunities for their students and themselves in a given context. Without understanding teachers' professional needs and experiences, it is hard to enable teachers to exercise agency (Li, 2020). Third, insufficient attention has been given to teachers' knowledge, needs and experiences in unexpected situations (Li, 2017a). As indicated earlier, much research has been done to investigate students' learning experiences online during the pandemic, but few studies were carried out to investigate teachers' experiences. Understanding and gaining insights into the success of innovative techniques, methods, learning materials and tests will create a high-quality learning environment and community for the profession.

9.2 Technology-Enhanced Language Education

Technology-enhanced language learning has been an influential research agenda in language education since 2000 (Chapelle, 2003; Li, 2017b; Tu et al., 2020). And there have been numerous research studies investigating the impact of technology on second language learning. Golonka et al. (2014) summarised the effect of technology on (1) improving language learners' learning motivation, efficiency and communication frequency; (2) developing learners' language knowledge and skills (e.g., speaking, listening, vocabulary and grammar), as well as metacognitive and metalinguistic knowledge; (3) enriching input resources; and (4) encouraging peer feedback. Similarly, Li (2017b) discussed "value and usability" of technology in language learning (Chapelle, 2003, p. 67) and proposed six benefits of technology in language learning, claiming that technology can (1) enrich authentic input and provide a context for the language use, primarily through the use of web 2.0 technologies, (2) increase linguistic knowledge through multimedia technologies, (3) enhance shared understanding and facilitate mediation, (4) provide an environment for interaction, (5) offer individualised feedback and (6) enhance motivation and autonomy. Elsewhere, Hubbard (2019) suggested that technology can positively influence learning efficiency, learning effectiveness, access, convenience, motivation, teaching efficiency and teaching effectiveness.

Regarding online and distance learning, the use of a virtual learning environment or synchronous conferencing techniques has been perceived as a critical part of effective learning (Michel & Cappellini, 2019). In particular, online technological tools, such as videos and social media, can offer efficient and convenient ways to achieve learning goals (Pineda et al., 2021). Effective technology-enhanced language teaching requires teachers to have an integrated knowledge about CALL because teachers act as change agents, and they need to be prepared for incorporating technology into teaching. For example, research suggests that students can use computers or electronic devices to access learning resources without the restriction of time and location (Salama et al., 2020); however, to realise the potentials, teachers need to be able to evaluate what materials are compatible with the mobile devices and how to ensure flexibility and accessibility.

9.3 Professional Development and Teacher Need

Day (1999) highlights the importance of professional development for teachers and puts forward a comprehensive definition of professional development.

> Professional development consists of all natural learning experiences and those conscious and planned activities which are intended to be of direct or indirect benefit to the individual, group or school, which contribute through these, to the quality of education in the classroom. It is the process by which, alone and with others, teachers review, renew and extend their commitment as change agents to the moral purposes of teaching; and by which they acquire and develop critically the knowledge, skills and emotional intelligence essential to good professional thinking, planning and practice with children, young people and colleagues throughout each phase of their teaching lives. (Day, 1999, p. 4)

Various research suggests that a positive learning culture is critical, where teachers feel that they are well supported by their colleagues and the management team, provided with time and space to learn from each other and equipped with resources (Hargreaves & O'Connor, 2017; Li, 2017a, 2020; Li & Morris, 2021). However, most professional development programmes rarely consider the issues from teachers' perspectives. Instead, programmes and activities are often well designed and underpinned by educational theories, and teachers do not contribute to the development of the programmes (Gameda et al., 2014). Teachers need to play an active role in learning; thus, the empowerment of individual teachers and support from the critical others are critical (Li, 2017a, 2020; Osmond-Johnson et al., 2019). Therefore, the core elements of teacher development, as Mann (2005) highlights, include the need to address "the insider view rather than the outsider view and its nature of being a continuing process of becoming and a process of articulating an inner world of conscious choices made in response to the outer world of the teaching context" (p. 105). Previous research highlights the value and significance of understanding the teachers' professional needs (Halicioglu, 2015). In a period of ever-greater uncertainty and pressure, as Li and Morris (2021) argued, "the need to take appropriate supportive action has rarely been more significant" (p. 254). Therefore, understanding teachers' professional needs helps teachers cope with difficulties they might encounter. As such, this study focuses on a significant area of inquiry by addressing a research question: what are English as a Foreign Language (EFL) teachers' professional needs when teaching online?

9.4 The Study

This section outlines the context for the study and introduces the mechanism for data collection and analysis.

9.4.1 The Context

The data reported here are a part of an extensive survey. The original project was designed to investigate in-service language teachers' cognition about online teaching in Chinese universities. The participants were recruited through a combination of convenience and snowball sampling strategies. In total, 106 teachers completed the questionnaire, and 12 teachers were selected to be interviewed.

Table 9.1 provides demographic information about the participants. Ethical considerations were adhered to through institutional stipulations and British Educational Research Association (BERA) ethical guidelines (2018), to ensure anonymity, confidentially and participants' well-being.

9.4.2 Data and Analysis

The questionnaire was built upon previous studies and the literature (e.g., Li, 2008; Li & Morris, 2021). It focused on teachers' perceptions and experiences of teaching online to allow the participants to conduct reflection and self-evaluation. The questionnaire consists of five main sections, covering teachers' biographic data, technology-enhanced language learning (TELL) knowledge and skills, TELL practice, professional needs and

Table 9.1 Demographic information

Gender	Male 17% (18)	Female 83% (88)	
Education background	Undergraduate 3.8% (4)	Masters 15.1% (16)	PhD 81.1% (86)
Teaching experience	0–5 years 33.0% (35)	6–10 years 42.5% (45)	11–15 years 11.3% (12)
	16–19 years 13.2% (14)		

contributing factors. This study concerns the professional needs section of the questionnaire, which consists of 13 five-point Likert scale questions. A Cronbach's alpha internal consistency reliability was calculated, and an acceptable Cronbach value was achieved ($\alpha = 0.716$).

The online questionnaire was distributed to teachers, and they were encouraged to pass the link to their fellow teachers. Information about the project was offered at the beginning of the survey, and consent was sought before they completed the questionnaire. Participants were explicitly reminded of the right to withdraw from the study and how their data would be stored, used and destroyed. The questionnaire data was populated to SPSS 28 and analysed by conducting descriptive statistics.

At the end of the survey, participants were asked to volunteer themselves for a follow-up interview, and a scheduled online interview was conducted using Zoom. The interview questions and elicitation techniques used in the study were similar to a reflective dialogue between the researcher and the teacher, focusing on the following:

- The teacher's description of online teaching, including their experience and feelings
- Conducting the interview in a conversational manner and using the teacher's words as the primary data
- Avoiding any evaluative feedback—even if directly asked to on several occasions—the researcher did share some of her thoughts and experiences more constructively
- Seeking clarification and the teacher's interpretation of several key terms used by them

The interview was conducted in participants' first language to allow rich discussion.

Interviews were audio-recorded and transcribed verbatim to provide an in-depth understanding of the themes identified in the questionnaire. The length of the interviews varied from 30 to 80 minutes. Content thematic analysis was conducted to reveal the insights of teachers' professional needs, and the selected extracts were subject to double translation to ensure accuracy. Participants were named under pseudonyms of their choice.

9.5 Findings

The questionnaire and interview data analysis identified four overarching themes regarding teachers' professional needs, namely technology competence, pedagogical design, material evaluation, and assessment and feedback (see Fig. 9.1). In what follows, questionnaire and interview data were integrated to report the results.

9.5.1 Technology Competence

Li (2008, 2014, 2017b) pointed out that technology competence and confidence are important factors in technology integration. Teachers are not prepared to integrate technology into their teaching if they do not feel confident and competent in using technology. Technology competence here can be simply interpreted as knowledge and skills that teachers

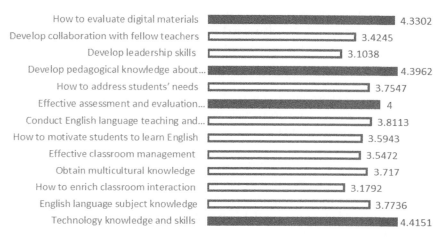

Fig. 9.1 Teachers' needs during the COVID-19 pandemic. SAGE Open. doi:10.1177/21582440211054491

need to integrate technology into teaching, which is well recognised in the literature (Pelgrum, 2001). Figure 9.1 suggests that technology knowledge and skills have the highest mean among all the categories (M = 4.4151; SD = 0.599). When combining *Agree* and *Strongly Agree* categories, 92.5% of the participants (n = 98) suggested that they needed to improve their technology competence, although they all rated themselves as highly skilled technology users. The result is not contradictory as they can be self-perceived as a competent user for social purposes, but not for pedagogical aims. Some of the interview data can further illustrate this point. Linda shares her view:

> I suddenly feel like I need to improve my technology skills. I know how to use some software and applications, but I use them for personal and social reasons. Now I need to use technology to teach, and I would like to learn more tools for teaching. (Linda)

The desire to learn different tools was shared mainly by the interviewees. *Access to technology and resources* was identified as a critical factor for effective technology integration (Li, 2008, 2014; Pelgrum, 2001). Although accessibility is still an important matter, we can see teachers' needs have switched from technology access to technology training. Technology training is not restricted to teachers, as five teachers mentioned that their students also need to be trained to use technology for learning. Sue's comments illustrated this view:

> I want to learn more tools, as currently, I am still using PowerPoint. It is ok to present in a classroom, but when I teach online, I need to find an excellent way to get students to participate. But, of course, students need to learn these tools too. (Sue)

This is in line with Li's (2008) survey of English teachers suggesting that PowerPoint was regarded as the most popular and appropriate technology used by English language teachers in China. However, in a survey of 47 studies, Macaro et al. (2012) pointed out that the most frequently studied technologies were multimedia (22%), computer-mediated communication (CMC) technologies (22%) and the Internet (15%). With

9 Technology + Pedagogy in EFL Virtual Classrooms: University...

the widespread use of social media and web 2.0 tools, teachers are more interested in integrating innovative methods in teaching, as those tools are already part of their daily life. Tina commented on her experience;

> When we just moved to online teaching, I used WeChat every day to ask students to practise English. I asked them to comment on the picture I shared with the group. I think that's a natural way to engage students. (Tina)

9.5.2 Pedagogical Design

Developing pedagogical principles for effective technology-enhanced pedagogy is a second area that teachers identified, as shown in Fig. 9.1 ($M = 4.3962$; $SD = 0.847$). When examining frequency, 89.6% ($n = 95$) of the teachers felt they needed to develop pedagogical knowledge. Li (2017b, p. 99) argued that "teachers adapt technology to fit current teaching patterns rather than making modifications to their instructional ways". Hence, one way that teachers realised in this study was they needed new pedagogical knowledge to enable them to develop appropriate pedagogical design because of the new teaching context they were in. We know that teachers' conception of effective teaching is heavily shaped by the social, cultural and educational contexts. Therefore, what counts as effective teaching will change subsequently when the teaching context changes. Teachers feel less sure about the situation, and they expressed a strong need to develop knowledge to conduct sound pedagogical design. One teacher commented:

> Online teaching is so different because we don't have the actual classroom, the actual blackboard and the actual space where students can meet their friends, so we have to think of a different type of lesson design to give students opportunities to practise English. (Mia)

Teachers felt less confident about transforming their teaching practice. They thought that they needed a framework to help them make critical decisions, such as how to facilitate student-student interaction, organise

178   L. Li

group work and use appropriate materials to engage learners and enhance linguistic knowledge. One teacher expressed:

> I just started to teach online, and I am very frustrated as I don't know how to organise group work, which I used a lot previously. I suddenly feel that I don't have the proper knowledge to do that. (Sam)

This view was widely acknowledged by other participants. One very experienced teacher commented that the challenge was unprecedented. She shared her experience:

> I usually am pretty creative in utilising new materials and approaches, as I've been around for nearly 20 years and have experienced the transformation. However, this time, I feel that I am out of my depth as I don't know how to design an effective, engaging and packed lesson because we are all online, and the technology limits us in terms of what we could do. (Linda)

Such concerns and the need to develop pedagogical knowledge are beyond whether teachers know the advantages of new technology and new methods. It is the lack of technological pedagogical content knowledge (TPACK) (Mishra & Koehler, 2006) that made teachers feel less confident and need to engage with further professional development. TPACK emphasises (1) the dynamic relationships between content, pedagogy and technology for teachers, and (2) successful technology integration in teaching and in developing their knowledge and competence in the technology integration (Koehler et al., 2007; Mishra & Koehler, 2006). Therefore, the core part of TPACK is to know about integrating appropriate pedagogy and CALL technology into English learning materials and teaching. In this case, how to successfully design and deliver a lesson online.

9.5.3 Material Evaluation

The third area that the university teachers identified as a need for further professional development was material evaluation (M = 4.3302; SD = 0.881). The majority of teachers (87, accounting for 82.1%)

9 Technology + Pedagogy in EFL Virtual Classrooms: University... 179

expressed that they need to learn how to evaluate digital materials. Chapelle and Hegelheimer (2004) argue that almost "all teachers need to know how to use the Web as a resource for current authentic language materials in written, audio, and visual formats" (p. 305). However, this study suggests that teachers were not equipped with the skills they needed and they found it challenging to select appropriate materials for the task.

> I know there are many materials on the Internet, but nothing is directly linked to what I need to teach. I don't think there are sufficient resources that I can use to teach those units. (Sara)

When asked for further clarifications, Sara explained that she needed the materials based on the textbook she used. Similarly, Li's 2014 study revealed the same issue, despite the differences in students. Teachers struggled to use existing materials to teach, and they focused on creating customised materials, for example, adding supplementary language materials and constructing tasks using visual and audio materials.

For other teachers, selecting appropriate materials is a critical issue, and they would benefit from upskilling in choosing the materials available to deliver online teaching.

> I have to learn to select some materials because there is too much to choose. I need to know what criteria we can use to evaluate materials. (Laura)

Research suggests that technology can provide authentic input and create a context for language learning, for example, through blogs and videos (e.g., Arndt & Woore, 2018). However, it does require teachers to use them to address their pedagogical purposes. As Li (2017b) notes, the rapid growth of online material makes it difficult for teachers to choose the right resource for their students; teaching in a new environment with a new delivery method made it even more challenging. Apart from learning how to select materials, teachers wanted to see how they became more creative when designing materials and tasks.

> Our university responded very well when we had to switch to online teaching. For example, the unit leader prepared all the sessions with all the tasks

and materials. However, I felt pretty frustrated because I wanted to include more student-oriented tasks. Honestly, I thought it was nice but lack of creativity. (John)

Hubbard (2006) provided a helpful definition for material evaluation regarding technology-enhanced language learning. Material evaluation is

a process of (a) investigating a piece of CALL software to judge its appropriateness for a given language learning setting, (b) identifying ways it may be effectively implemented in that setting, and (c) assessing its degree of success and determining whether to continue use or to make adjustments in implementation for future use. (Hubbard, 2006, p. 1)

It is true that many teachers are novice technology users themselves and do not possess the required knowledge and skills in assessing e-learning materials (Li, 2017b). As it is widely acknowledged in the literature, many teachers have taught from textbooks for years, and moving to online teaching is not simply transferring what they do in a face-to-face classroom to the virtual classroom. Teachers, in general, need to be confident and competent in evaluating and creating digital materials.

9.5.4 Assessment and Feedback

Another highly commented area teachers felt they would benefit from additional in-service professional development resided in assessment and feedback (M = 4.0; SD = 1.014). Among the 106 surveyed participants, 78 teachers (73.6%) claimed that they needed to learn more about technology-enhanced assessment and feedback. With teaching and assessment having to move online, it is understandable that teachers would feel that additional training in evaluation would have been beneficial. This result is also in line with another survey in a Sino-foreign university (Li & Morris, 2021). One teacher reflected on her experience:

I think it's tough to assess students now because everything is online. I tried to find out ways to implement tests, but it's almost impossible. So, we had to replicate what we did in the classroom. That is, every student completes

9 Technology + Pedagogy in EFL Virtual Classrooms: University... 181

the final assessment online with their camera on, and the tutor invigilate online too. This was not efficient and there was technical problems. I suddenly realised that we hadn't learnt much about assessment because usually it is centrally designed and administered, and it is not the individual teacher's responsibility. (Sharon)

It is a moment for some teachers to reassess their knowledge and practice, as assessment was previously not part of teaching and learning. Mark shared his view about technology-enhanced assessment:

I have never thought about using technology for assessment because the expert panel usually designs all the assessments in our unit. However, this time, we realised that this was our weakness. I think every teacher should be trained to carry out a variety of assessment, even if we never use it. (Mark)

When discussing assessment, only one teacher mentioned feedback as part of the assessment. The other 11 teachers all believed assessment meant testing. This teacher shared what she thought.

I would love to learn more about online feedback, especially in class. I usually offer feedback orally and type it quickly in the chatbox in class. I think the students have better uptake. I find it fascinating. (Amy)

9.6 Discussion

By examining teachers' professional needs, we can understand the scope and focus of professional development for teachers, individually and collectively. Professional development is necessary for teachers to develop new skills and expertise (Evers et al., 2016). Teacher education and development becomes even more critical when teachers face unique challenges when using technology to teach. Thus, teacher development needs to focus on providing teachers with competence and confidence "to keep the teacher up-to-date with the continuously changing practices, and student needs" (Badri et al., 2016, p. 1).

In the literature, there is ample evidence to urge for the preparation and education of pre- and in-service language teachers to develop computer-assisted language learning in the twenty-first century (e.g., Liu & Kleinsasser, 2015; Hubbard, 2008; Li, 2017b; Sert & Li, 2017). The current study identified four critical areas for teacher education and development concerning technology-enhanced language teaching. These four areas include technology training, pedagogical knowledge regarding using technology, material development, and assessment.

It is interesting to see technology training become the most crucial area for teachers regarding their professional needs. There are two related issues. Firstly, many teachers are not prepared psychologically and pedagogically for online teaching since the swift move to the new delivery mode as an emergency measure to the global pandemic. Even though they are familiar with some technological tools, they have no knowledge and experience of using them for online delivery. Secondly and more importantly, teachers have had limited experience in using technology for professional purposes. As Li (2014) noted, PowerPoint was the most relevant and frequently used method in English language classrooms for presentation. Online delivery is still in its infancy, so it is hard for teachers to accumulate relevant pedagogical knowledge. As it is widely recognised, technology has advantages in accessibility and flexibility; for example, students can use computers or electronic devices to acquire learning resources instantly without the restriction of location and time (Salama et al., 2020). However, the realisation of technology affordances depends on how teachers adopt technology (Li, 2014) and their technical skills and attitudes towards technology-enhanced pedagogy. Teachers are expected to facilitate interaction through real-time classroom discussions and maximise the flexibility in learning. In that case, they need to master producing appropriate materials and tasks to achieve these pedagogical goals. Without the skills and optimised system platforms, these will not be possible. When a new learning model is expected, technology facilities and training need to be in place. Without training, teachers tend to teach online courses the same way as they would do in traditional classrooms (Kreber & Kanuka, 2013).

Integrating technology successfully into teaching and learning depends on transforming teachers' beliefs and philosophy (Ottenbreit-Leftwicha et al., 2010), requiring teachers to make some pedagogical changes, including their roles in the classrooms. I strongly argue that TPACK needs to be fully incorporated into the teacher education curriculum in terms of teacher training and education. A critical issue emerged here: despite efforts in defining TPACK, there is not an agreed framework or model that captures the critical elements of TPACK. Hampel and Stickler (2005) focused on the knowledge and skills teachers need for online teaching, whereas Healey et al. (2011) proposed a list of skills and standards teachers should acquire to teach with technology. Li (2021) argues that we need to define TPACK from teachers' perspectives and suggests that teachers consider TPACK concerning their professional needs and students' learning needs, which is in line with the previous research (Ottenbreit-Leftwicha et al., 2010; Li, 2014). TPACK is critical for the effective implementation of technology in instruction, and how best to empower teachers to develop this knowledge merits further research, especially concerning online learning.

A related issue is that research suggests that many teachers do not receive sufficient training for incorporating technology, including evaluating materials for teaching purposes (Li, 2017a). There are two crucial points. First, as we know, "(L)anguage teachers who are not accustomed to looking at CALL software may perceive its purpose very differently than those who are more experienced" (Bradin, 1999, p. 159); we need to encourage teachers to critically reflect and analyse the software, application and platforms they use in teaching. Only by doing that can teachers develop integrated knowledge about technology-enhanced pedagogy (Li, 2017a). In that respect, Chen (2022) argues reflective teaching might be a possible approach to applying digital affordances and teacher agency. Second, teachers who have a low level of CALL expertise and experience are less likely to appreciate and understand the range of opportunities and activities that well-designed digital materials and applications might offer (Li, 2008). In this case, developing teachers' knowledge and expertise in technology-enhanced pedagogy is vital, especially in digital material evaluation, as designing authentic attractive, and various resources have always been teachers' focus (e.g., Egbert, 2005; Jung, 2005).

Concerning technology-enhanced assessment, Chapelle and Jamieson (2003) outlined challenges for language teachers. Equally, Li and Morris

(2021) pointed out that conducting the online assessment, especially for group speaking tests, is incredibly challenging, which teachers are not well prepared for. Although every teacher needs to develop "assessment literacy" (Brown & Bailey, 2008), it is hard in reality. Many teachers develop assessment knowledge on the job, resulting in obtaining "fragmented knowledge" (Manning, 2013). Without high assessment literacy, teachers cannot create, administer and interpret language assessments in a new teaching situation. Again, this study points out a critical area for teacher education: developing teachers' digital assessment literacy.

9.7 Conclusion

This study examined university English language teachers' professional needs when teaching online. It identified four significant areas that university teachers need to develop: technology competence, pedagogical knowledge, material evaluation, and assessment. It further revealed that ongoing professional learning has differential influences on effective online teaching. The findings support more significant attention to discipline-specific professional training in helping language teachers to be able to engage in effective online instruction, understand their professional needs and find different approaches to address them. Despite the study's new insights into the field, the study has a few limitations. First, this study cannot be deemed exclusive or exhaustive as it only offers insights into a particular group of in-service teachers. The participants were recruited through a convenient snowball sampling strategy. Therefore, the participant size was relatively small, and participants were predominantly female.

Further research and analysis are required to examine where there are significant differences between professional needs and teachers' teaching experience, gender and age. Second, this study focused on teachers' perceptions of their needs when moving to online teaching to mitigate the impact of COVID-19. A longitudinal study would capture the potential change of teachers' needs over time. Thus, future research with a longitudinal design involving field observations might offer further insights. Nevertheless, the findings reported here establish a ground for us to push our thinking and challenge how we need to address teachers' professional development bearing in mind their level of experience, student cohort and pedagogical purposes. This study carries implications for researchers, teachers and teacher educators in terms of teacher learning.

As noted above, because teachers need to play an active role in their learning processes, understanding their professional needs is critical. Indeed, any professional development activity needs to start with understanding teachers' professional needs. Only by doing that can a professional development programme be successful and effective. As noted in previous research, the process of learning or knowledge building is not straightforward, as individuals' agency or the capacity to act influences the process (Ruohotie-Lyhty, 2011). Individuals are different in interacting with the context, so any programme intended to address a collective need requires a context-specific and flexible approach for individuals to exercise agency. Lai and Jin (2021) reported that professional identity orientations had differential impacts on different types of teacher technology use. Future research needs to focus on how teacher identity interacts with technology use and teachers' pedagogical decision-making process. In addition, further research is required to investigate the other influential factors that affect the development of a teacher's professional knowledge, as pointed out by Cooper et al. (2020).

The study points out that teachers need to develop their knowledge in pedagogy, material evaluation and assessment when teaching online. Various research suggests that teachers, despite contextual differences, prefer engaging in collaborative endeavours (Karlberg & Bezzina, 2020; Li, 2017a, 2020). Thus, from a practical perspective, teachers need to be provided with opportunities to share practical ideas, collectively build a repertoire of teaching resources, understand the process and key elements in student learning, and engage some deliberate practice in assessment and feedback (Li, 2017a). As such, they can engage meaningfully with the pedagogic challenges and demands (Cooper et al., 2020; Mansfield, 2019). Research also suggests that digital technology bears a high potential to create cognitively engaging learning opportunities, and online learning offers flexibility and convenience (e.g., Hillmayr et al., 2020). However, to fully realise the affordances of technology, we need to learn more about teachers' and students' behaviour, experience, and cognition.

Future research might also focus on exploring teachers' motivation and action in addressing their collective needs from an emic perspective. Similarly, an interventional study examining the impact of focused training might also shed light on teachers' professional needs regarding technology-enhanced language teaching.

References

Al-Fraihat, D., Joy, M., Masa'deh, R., & Sinclair, J. (2020). Evaluating E-learning systems success: An empirical study. *Computers in Human Behavior, 102*, 67–86. https://doi.org/10.1016/j.chb.2019.08.004

Arndt, H. L., & Woore, R. (2018). Vocabulary learning from watching YouTube videos and reading blog posts. *Language Learning & Technology, 22*(3), 124–142. 10125/44660.

Badri, M., Alnuaimi, A., Mohaidat, J., Yang, G., & Al-Rashedi, A. (2016). Perception of teachers' professional development needs, impacts, and barriers: The Abu Dhabi case. *SAGE Open, 6*, 215824401666290. https://doi.org/10.1177/2158244016662901

Bradin, C. (1999). CALL issues: Instructional aspects of software evaluation. In J. Egbert & E. Hanson-Smith (Eds.), *CALL environments: Research, practice, and critical issues* (pp. 159–175). TESOL.

Brown, J. D., & Bailey, K. M. (2008). Language testing courses: What are they in 2007? *Language Testing, 25*(3), 349–383. https://doi.org/10.1177/0265532208090157

Burns, M., & Lawrie, J. (2015). *Where it matters most: Quality professional development for all teachers.* InterAgency Network for Education in Emergencies.

Chapelle, C. A. (2003). *English language learning and technology: Lectures on applied linguistics in the age of Information and Communication Technology.* John Benjamins Publishing.

Chapelle, C. A., & Hegelheimer, V. (2004). The language teacher in the twenty-first century. In S. Fotos & C. M. Browne (Eds.), *New perspectives on CALL for second language classrooms* (pp. 299–316). Lawrence Erlbaum.

Chapelle, C. A., & Jamieson, J. (2003). *Three challenges in English language assessment.* Available at http://www.longmanusahome.com/images/stories/monographs/challenges_in_assessment.pdf.

Chen, M. (2022). Digital affordances and teacher agency in the context of teaching Chinese as a second language during COVID-19. *System, 105,* 102710. https://doi.org/10.1016/j.system.2021.102710

Cooper, R., Fitzgerald, A., Loughran, J., Phillips, M., & Smith, K. (2020). Understanding teachers' professional learning needs: What does it mean to teachers and how can it be supported? *Teachers and Teaching, 26*(7–8), 558–576. https://doi.org/10.1080/13540602.2021.1900810

Day, C. (1999). *Developing teachers: The challenges of lifelong learning.* Falmer.

Egbert, J. L. (2005). Conducting research on CALL. In J. Egbert & G. Petrie (Eds.), *CALL research perspectives* (pp. 3–8). Lawrence Erlbaum.

Evers, A., Van der Heijden, B., & Kreijns, K. (2016). Organisational and task factors influencing teachers' professional development at work. *European Journal of Training and Development, 40,* 36–55. https://doi.org/10.1177/1534484310397852

Gameda, F., Fiorucci, M., & Catarci, M. (2014). Teachers' professional development in schools: Rhetoric versus reality. *Professional Development in Education, 40*(1), 71–88. https://doi.org/10.1080/19415257.2012.759988

Golonka, E. M., Bowles, A. R., Frank, V. M., Richardson, D. L., & Freynik, S. (2014). Technologies for foreign language learning: A review of technology types and their effectiveness. *Computer Assisted Language Learning, 27*(1), 70–105. https://doi.org/10.1080/09588221.2012.700315

Halicioglu, M. L. (2015). Challenges facing teachers new to working in schools overseas. *Journal of Research in International Education, 14*(3), 242–257. https://doi.org/10.1177/1475240915611508

Hampel, R., & Stickler, U. (2005). New skills for new classrooms: Training tutors to teach language online. *Computer Assisted Language Learning, 18*(4), 311–326. https://doi.org/10.1080/09588220500335455

Hargreaves, A., & O'Connor, M. T. (2017). Cultures of professional collaboration: Their origins and opponents. *Journal of Professional Capital and Community, 2*(2), 74–85. https://doi.org/10.1108/JPCC-02-2017-0004

Healey, D., Hanson-Smith, E., Hubbard, P., Ioannou-Georgiou, S., Kessler, G., & Ware, P. (2011). *TESOL Technology standards: Description, implementation, integration.* TESOL.

Hillmayr, D., Ziernwald, L., Reinhold, F., Hofer, S. I., & Reiss, K. M. (2020). The potential of digital tools to enhance mathematics and science learning in secondary schools: A context-specific meta-analysis. *Computers & Education, 153,* 103897. https://doi.org/10.1016/j.compedu.2020.103897

Hodges, C., Moore, S., Lockee, B., Trust, T., & Bond, A. (2020, March 27). The difference between emergency remote teaching and online learning. *Educause Review*. Available at https://er.educause.edu/articles/2020/3/the-difference-between-emergency-remote-teaching-and-online-learning

Hubbard, P. (2006). Evaluating CALL software. In L. Ducate & N. Arnold (Eds.), *Calling on CALL: From theory and research to new directions in foreign language teaching*. CALICO.

Hubbard, P. (2008). CALL and the future of language teacher education. *CALICO Journal, 25*(2), 175–188. https://www.jstor.org/stable/calicojournal.25.2.175

Hubbard, P. (2019). Five keys from the past to the future of CALL. *International Journal of Computer-Assisted Language Learning and Teaching, 9*(3), 1–13. https://doi.org/10.4018/IJCALLT.2019070101

Jung, U. O. H. (2005). CALL: Past, present and future—a bibliometric approach. *ReCALL, 17*(1), 4–17. https://doi.org/10.1017/S0958344005000212

Karlberg, M., & Bezzina, C. (2020). The professional development needs of beginning and experienced teachers in four municipalities in Sweden. *Professional Development in Education, 48*(4), 624–641. https://doi.org/10.1080/19415257.2020.1712451

Koehler, M. J., Mishra, P., & Yahya, K. (2007). Tracing the development of teacher knowledge in a design seminar: Integrating content, pedagogy and technology. *Computers & Education, 49*, 740–762. https://doi.org/10.1016/j.compedu.2005.11.012

Korkealehto, K., & Leier, V. (2021). Facebook for engagement: Telecollaboration between Finland and New Zealand in German language learning. *International Journal of Computer-Assisted Language Learning and Teaching, 11*(1), 1–20.

Kreber, C., & Kanuka, H. (2013). The scholarship of teaching and learning and the online classroom. *Canadian Journal of University Continuing Education, 32*(2), 109–131. https://doi.org/10.4018/IJCALLT.2021010101

Lai, C., & Jin, T. (2021). Teacher professional identity and the nature of technology integration. *Computers & Education, 175*, 104314. https://doi.org/10.1016/j.compedu.2021.104314

Li, L. (2008). *EFL teachers' beliefs about ICT integration in Chinese secondary schools*. [Unpublished PhD Thesis, Queen's University Belfast].

Li, L. (2014). Understanding language teachers' practice with educational technology: A case from China. *System, 46*, 105–119. https://doi.org/10.1016/j.system.2014.07.016

Li, L. (2017a). *New technology and language learning*. Palgrave Macmillan.

Li, L. (2017b). *Social interaction and teacher cognition*. Edinburgh University Press.

Li, L. (2020). *Language teacher cognition: A sociocultural perspective*. Palgrave Macmillan.

Li, L. (2021). Learning together online: Insights into knowledge construction of language teachers in a CSCL environment. *Iranian Journal of Language Teaching Research, 9*(3 (Special Issue)), 39–62. https://doi.org/10.30466/ijltr.2021.121075

Li, L., & Morris, G. (2021). Thriving in the new normal: In-service professional development needs and experiences. In C. Xiang (Ed.), *Trends and developments for the future of language education in higher education* (pp. 253–271). IGI Global.

Liu, M.-H., & Kleinsasser, R. C. (2015). Exploring EFL teachers' CALL knowledge and competencies: In-service program perspectives. *Language Learning & Technology, 19*(1), 119–138. http://dx.doi.org/10125/44405

Macaro, E., Handley, Z., & Walter, C. (2012). A systematic review of CALL in English as a second language: Focus on primary and secondary education. *Language Teaching, 45*(1), 1–43. https://doi.org/10.1017/S0261444811000395

Mann, S. (2005). The language teacher's development. *Language Teaching, 38*(3), 103–118. https://doi.org/10.1017/S0261444805002867

Manning, A. (2013). *EAP teacher assessment literacy* [Unpublished PhD Thesis, University of Leicester]. The University of Leicester Figshare Digital Collection. https://leicester.figshare.com/articles/thesis/EAP_Teacher_Assessment_Literacy/10170863

Mansfield, J. (2019). *Pedagogical equilibrium: The development of teachers' professional knowledge* (1st ed.). Routledge. https://doi.org/10.4324/9780429053573

Michel, M., & Cappellini, M. (2019). Alignment during synchronous video versus written chat L2 interactions: A methodological exploration. *Annual Review of Applied Linguistics, 39*, 189–216. https://doi.org/10.1017/S0267190519000072

Mishra, P., & Koehler, M. J. (2006). Technological pedagogical content knowledge: A new framework for teacher knowledge. *Teachers College Record, 108*(6), 1017–1054. https://doi.org/10.1111/j.1467-9620.2006.00684.x

Murphy, M. P. A. (2020). COVID-19 and emergency eLearning: Consequences of the securitisation of higher education for post-pandemic pedagogy. *Contemporary Security Policy, 41*(3), 492–505. https://doi.org/10.1080/13523260.2020.1761749

Osmond-Johnson, P., Campbell, C., & Faubert, B. (2019). Supporting professional learning: The work of Canadian teachers' organisations. *Professional Development in Education, 45*(1), 17–32. https://doi.org/10.1080/1941525 7.2018.1486877

Ottenbreit-Leftwicha, A. T., Glazewskib, K. D., Newbyc, T., & Ertmerc, P. (2010). Teacher value beliefs associated with using technology: Addressing professional and student needs. *Computers and Education, 55*(3), 1321–1335. https://doi.org/10.1016/j.compedu.2010.06.002

Pelgrum, W. (2001). Obstacles to the integration of ICT in education: Results from a worldwide educational assessment. *Computers & Education, 37*, 163–178. https://doi.org/10.1016/S0360-1315(01)00045-8

Pineda, E. J., Tamayo Cano, L. H., & Peralta, A. M. (2021). An inquiry-based framework for teaching English in synchronous environments: Perceptions from teachers and learners learning. *International Journal of Computer-Assisted Language Learning and Teaching, 11*(1), 38–58. https://doi.org/10.4018/ IJCALLT.2021010103

Ruohotie-Lyhty, M. (2011). Constructing practical knowledge of teaching: Eleven newly qualified language teachers' discursive agency. *The Language Learning Journal, 39*(3), 365–379. https://doi.org/10.1080/0957173 6.2010.544750

Salama, R., Uzunboylu, H., & Alkaddah, B. (2020). Distance learning system, learning programming languages by using mobile applications. *New Trends and Issues Proceedings on Humanities and Social Sciences, 7*(2), 23–47. https:// doi.org/10.18844/prosoc.v7i2.5015

Sert, O., & Li, L. (2017). A qualitative study on CALL knowledge and materials design: Insights from pre-service EFL teachers. *International Journal of Computer-Assisted Language Learning and Teaching, 7*(3), 73–86. https://doi. org/10.4018/IJCALLT.2017070105

Tu, Y., Zou, D., & Zhang, R. (2020). A comprehensive framework for designing and evaluating vocabulary learning app. *International Journal of Mobile Learning and Organisation, 14*(3), 370–397.

Zou, B., Huang, L., Ma, W., & Qiu, Y. (2021). Evaluation of the effectiveness of EFL online teaching during the COVID-19 pandemic. *SAGE Open, 11*(4), 1–17. https://doi.org/10.1177/21582440211054491

10

A Pandemic to Remember: Best Practices in an Online Language Acquisition Methods Course

Kristen Carlson and Ramon Serrano

10.1 Introduction

Currently, our institution is a mid-sized, Midwestern public university that prepares teachers who primarily remain within our state to teach after graduation. Our state licensing board requires that graduating teachers are all required to have knowledge of the language acquisition standards and pedagogy prior to obtaining a professional teaching license. With cultural pluralism encouraged within our state's K-12 curriculum, it is crucial that incoming, novice teachers have skills and knowledge to support our young students regardless of their English skills or cultural backgrounds. Bradbury (2021) states that "by 2065, the combined minority populations of the United States will become the majority" (p. 55). As teacher educators, it is

K. Carlson (✉)
Minnesota State University Moorhead, Moorhead, MN, USA
e-mail: kristen.carlson@mnstate.edu

R. Serrano
St. Cloud State University, St. Cloud, MN, USA
e-mail: raserrano@stcloudstate.edu

© The Author(s), under exclusive license to Springer Nature Switzerland AG 2023
K. Sadeghi, M. Thomas (eds.), *Second Language Teacher Professional Development*,
Digital Education and Learning, https://doi.org/10.1007/978-3-031-12070-1_10

our responsibility to prepare and support novice teachers for the future of education, not for what once was or has been.

At the start of 2020, the World Health Organization declared the COVID-19 outbreak a Public Health Emergency Concern. Shortly after that, just before our spring break, on March 11, 2020, the World Health Organization declared COVID-19 a pandemic (Zibaseresht, 2020). This created major changes for teacher educators because we now found ourselves going from teaching face to face to completely online, away from our classroom manipulatives. It was here where we really discovered how limited our knowledge and use of technology as a tool for teaching was at a systemic level across the college of teacher education. With the surge of the COVID pandemic, teacher education courses were forced to move online creating challenges for faculty members and their preservice teachers. Faculty of teacher education were required to teach online, within a matter of two weeks, regardless of if they had any previous online teaching experience. To make the transition from face-to-face teaching to online teaching, the institution's administration worked with experienced online faculty members to support their colleagues who had not taught online previously. Within the college for teacher education, a team of faculty created an online course shell based on the Quality Matters (2021) rubric to maintain consistency between courses offered and to help those faculty who were inexperienced teaching online understand the essential material that should be presented in an online course, such as tutoring support services, university policies, and so on.

Additionally, faculty members were able to support one another in the online transition through co-teaching. Because many faculty members were still struggling to make the transition from face to face to online coursework, co-teaching became essential in allowing our pedagogical practices to be implemented. Throughout this chapter, our goal is to share our experiences with online co-teaching during the COVID-19 pandemic and to share the online learning best practices as we have experienced them during our interactions with our preservice teachers in an online environment. Our main goal throughout the remaining weeks of the semester was to ensure these preservice teachers learned, but also we provided them with the skills necessary to support K-12 English language learners in an online learning environment as these preservice teachers likely now were supporting their own K-12 students during their virtual field experiences.

In spring of 2020, we (Dr. Carlson and Dr. Serrano) were able to co-teach our two classes (ED 462: Teaching English Learners in K-6, and IM 421: Media and Technology for Elementary Teachers) together. The overarching goal of the co-taught courses was to help our preservice teachers integrate technology in the classroom that would be beneficial for teachers to support students who were not native English speakers. After the state shutdown of the university's campus, we began to pivot our face-to-face course into an online course. It became a challenge for us on how we were going to co-plan, co-teach, and co-assess our preservice teachers from a distance. What follows is the story of our experiences through co-teaching during a pandemic in an impromptu, online classroom and how this journey created changes in our teaching today.

10.2 Pedagogical Practices

Our institution has traditionally valued the face-to-face, on-campus experience for our preservice teachers. Our elementary education professional program has been divided into four semesters that we refer to as blocks. Each block has a field experience attached to it. For example, block one consists of two education courses and one media methods course. These courses are Children's Literature, Kindergarten methods, and Information Media. The courses are ten weeks long; then preservice teachers have a five-week field experience. Block two consists of coursework on differentiated learning, curriculum, teaching English language learners, and a Music and Art methods course. Preservice teachers in this block also spend five or six weeks in the K-12 classroom completing field work as well. The final two blocks, three and four, consist of two eight-week segments, where preservice teachers complete eight full weeks of a student teaching in both semesters which provides the preservice teachers opportunity to practice what they have learned in their coursework and to implement their own application of learning into the K-12 classroom. The goal of this pedagogical practice has always been to have preservice teachers learn theory and best practice and then enter the K-12 classroom during field experience to apply what they have learned. Once back in their university courses, there were opportunities to share experiences, receive feedback from peers and their instructors on what worked or did not work, and analyze the experience against the learned theories from the semester.

With the arrival of the pandemic, these practices were required to change due to the university requiring courses be moved to distance learning and K-12 school districts closing their doors to outside visitors (such as our preservice teachers for their field experiences). This brought about challenges that were not expected. Traditionally, ED 462 Teaching English Learners in K-6 has primarily focused on methods of teaching non-native speakers in the classroom, but now the challenge was: how do we effectively teach those methods virtually? Second, during the last eight weeks of the course, preservice teachers were to apply the knowledge they learned within our course in a K-6 English language field experience. We asked ourselves, how would our preservice teachers engage English language learners effectively through technology while making lessons meaningful to their field experience K-6 students based on the experiences we provided them?

10.3 Role-Playing in the Virtual World

In the face-to-face setting, to teach the methods of language acquisition standards, the course was intentionally designed to include student engagement and interaction. For example, within the course, we used a lot of hands-on participation and humor. In an abrupt transition to online and pandemic stressors, we found that the dynamics were not quite the same when we met with the preservice teachers virtually, as when we did previously in person, even though the students were identical and the class community had been created prior to the switch to pandemic distance learning. Within this course, we regularly used role-playing as a means of illustrating what was meant. One of the topics we covered is the importance of vocabulary development. We talked about how important it is to develop and give clear examples of vocabulary to expand K-12 student understanding. As an example, we do a short

10 A Pandemic to Remember: Best Practices in an Online...

role-play in which Dr. Serrano is a young child learning to speak and Dr. Carlson plays the part of the toddler's mother. The scenario goes as follows:

> The child goes up to the refrigerator and says milk. The mother then says, "Here you are Baby, here is some milk". Then the toddler begins to have a tantrum and repeat over and over again "Milk", "Milk", "and Milk". The mother begins to try to calm the toddler down by offering water. Again, the toddler has a tantrum, and the mother calms him down. This time the mother gives him orange juice. To this offer, the toddler has a third tantrum. The mother's frustration grows to the point that she says, "Okay, you want milk, here it is" and hands him a beer, to which the toddler giggles and drinks it.

At this point the class laughs out loud at the absurdity of the role-play. We then tell the preservice teachers it was an exaggerated skit to make a point and ask the preservice teachers, "What happened"? After a debriefing discussion, our preservice teachers came to the conclusion that in the toddler's mind the term "milk" has multiple meanings and as teachers we need to help them sort these meanings out. We then discussed with the preservice teachers what we meant by vocabulary being classified in three tiers. During our discussion, preservice teachers came to the conclusion that Tier one words are words that they encounter daily and in the case of a second language, learner can be explained with visuals. Tier two words are harder to explain. Instruction in Tier two words "can add productively to all students' language abilities" (Soto, 2021). These words can contain words that are cognates and false cognates which can be a support for English language learners. This could also be confusing if they are false cognates, especially if idioms are used. After the definitions are concluded, our methods discussion moved toward application, specifically how we as teachers developed student vocabulary support that is needed to understand the differences between the three tiers and how important they are in learning throughout the different content areas. For example, in the case of the milk, milk is a Tier one word that is a part of everyday speech, meaning that it is a frequency word that can be encountered on a daily basis. Other examples of frequency words are words like water, juice, cereal. Once they come up with other examples, preservice teachers then develop a vocabulary chart with examples of Tier two vocabulary using the Frayer Model Graphic Organizer (as described in Soto, 2021). During this process preservice teachers practice with Tier two words and begin to notice that there were often cognates present that made it easier for English language learners to understand and be transferred across content areas. Finally, Tier three vocabulary contained domain-specific academic vocabulary that are harder to learn for both native and English language learners. As an example, we had our preservice teachers work through the vocabulary tiers demonstrating how they would apply them in teaching a math lesson. Then, again, the preservice teachers practiced teaching a reading lesson for third graders using Tier three vocabulary. Once they completed this activity, they then shared their experiences in small groups and then the class as a whole.

While many educators may not have seen value in the strategy of role-playing and humor, often preservice teachers are amused and engaged in the "milk" scenario. After this skit, the preservice teachers began to see and discuss how as an elementary teacher they needed to integrate not only tiered vocabulary into their lessons, but also integrate the arts and the connections between vocabulary and the arts across their different content areas. Many students saw the arts as something that is taught separately for their own specialist lessons. As a consequence, preservice teachers may miss the opportunity to have engaged students in meaningful learning. In the previous example, we as the faculty members utilized art in the means of performing a skit and the preservice teachers drew vocabulary charts on poster papers. In an upcoming example, preservice teachers utilized hands-on art skills, such as drawing and paper design, to create a written communication project. Within our teacher education courses, media and art integration are vital for modeling learning in today's K-12 classrooms.

As we transitioned to the online classroom because of the pandemic, the role-playing and humor aspects of the course were best delivered during our weekly synchronous meetings. It was difficult to build role-playing and interactive humor into the learning management system especially with limited preparation time. Further, opportunities to

10 A Pandemic to Remember: Best Practices in an Online... 197

role-play and build meaningful connections with our preservice teachers became more strained in the online environment. Our co-planning time became critical to ensure we were building in dialogue and these discussion-based activities. While in the face-to-face classroom, we were able to read cues from one another, play along in scenarios that arose, and ad lib as the preservice teachers' learning needs changed. However, in the online environment, physically apart from one another and the preservice teachers, we found that we needed to be more intentional with our co-planning of each lesson. In our course, we teach that while Reader's Theater is used in the reading courses to explain and support reading fluency and comprehension with K-12 students (Carrick, 2021), Total Physical Response (TPR) is valuable in teaching vocabulary, verbs, and other difficult concepts.

When we made the transition to online classes due to COVID-19, Reader's Theater was an activity that we were able to keep in place. It served us fairly well for synchronous meeting times because our preservice teachers had the opportunity to meet with their small groups to work on their stories and skits in breakout rooms. At first, we skipped the scenes and props but as everyone in the course became more comfortable with at-home learning, we moved to allowing a slideshow and even software such as PowToons to create cartoons to visualize the preservice teachers' stories. This created opportunity for our preservice teachers to experiment with new technologies, collaborate with their peers, and also discuss the language acquisition opportunities that existed during Reader's Theater. While we were not able to fully embed TPR into the online environment, the feedback we received from the preservice teachers and their learning outcomes, the use of the online Reader's Theater provided opportunity that without COVID-19, we may not have recognized. In the future, it would be ideal to experience both modalities (face to face and online) as a preservice teacher. We will likely do one or two skits within the face-to-face class time and then one or two in the online environment so that the preservice teachers have the chance to practice both sets of facilitation skills. This will ensure they are prepared when they teach their own students, regardless of if it is a face-to-face or online class.

10.4 Creativity and Communication

In a world that is constantly shifting, where information is accessible at our fingertips, students need to have the opportunity to be innovative, creative thinkers. Specifically, they also must have the skillset and foundational knowledge to communicate their ideas in a comprehensive manner to children in their classroom and to the broader community. When our preservice teachers were in school, information was not as abundantly accessible; it was still important to learn obscure facts alongside problem-solving skills. Further, school systems have not changed dramatically from when we, as the teacher educators, were in grade school versus our preservice teachers' experiences. The nineteenth-century committee's work that created the structure of curriculum for education can still be found in school buildings today as they reflect the factory model of organization (Hayes-Jacobs, 2010). However, "the year 2020 brought a pandemic that impacted U.S. school structure in a way that has not happened since the 1918 flu. In the 2020–2021 academic year, teachers were required to think outside of the box, be more flexible, and more intentional with the curriculum that was covered" (Carlson, 2022, p. 62). Because our preservice teachers did not experience a large range of creative, authentic experiences in their K-6 classrooms growing up, we work in our courses to help build the growth mindset that fosters designing creative and communicative lessons for their future students.

One activity we used and are trying to integrate in our online courses more frequently is encouraging preservice teachers to use their creativity when designing lessons and engagement opportunities for their future students. One example of modeling this is occurred when we taught about language acquisition through the writing process and comprehension. In this exercise, we had our preservice teachers experience the writing process and how it could be used to develop stronger communication skills for themselves as future teachers. They began by writing a story that described a fantasy island in small groups. We had them be as detailed as possible in their short story, especially with pointing out directions such as using a compass to identify North, South, East, and West. We encouraged them to view the story as if they were creating a written, detailed map of their island which they would then share with the class. Our goal here was to have them experience how important it is to clearly and effectively communicate instructions to others and how a strategy such as the writing process could be used across other content areas.

The activity started with us dividing the preservice teachers into small groups of four. Once in their groups, they wrote a description of their fantasy island to share with other groups. After they had completed their descriptions, the groups were assigned an area in the classroom where one member will stay behind with their island story while the others rotate into another group. The member that stayed behind would take note of the recommendations for improvement made by their peers for their final draft of their paper. After sharing feedback from the notetaker, preservice teachers return to their original group and began working on their final draft. After their drafts were completed, the groups were instructed to exchange their island descriptions with a new group. Each group then read the description of the island and began the second part of this activity. Once group members had discussed the descriptions, their job was to create a three-dimensional model of that fantasy island based on the details of the description. Art supplies such as construction paper, markers, crayons, scissor, string, glue, and foil were available for use and provided to the preservice teachers. The main goal of this written description and then art design was to encourage preservice teacher to think about how they could have students in their own classroom use: (1) the four modes of language arts, (2) use cooperative learning as a key element for communication, and (3) use art in a meaningful and fun way to foster communication.

However, we soon discovered with the pandemic closure that in an online environment, this physical activity of changing papers was more difficult for us as faculty facilitators to plan through. However, with the utilization of collaborative word processing software, such as Google Docs and Word 365, we still attempted the activity with the preservice teachers. We encouraged and provided feedback on technological tools that could be used to design the islands. Some groups creatively sought out to design their islands using visual software such as Canva and Smores, while others chose movie-making software such as Adobe Spark. The online opportunity helped provide the preservice teachers with a chance to critically think about this process for themselves and for their own future students. It also afforded more time in the communication process to cooperatively work with their group members, because in this format, preservice teachers now worked on some of the project asynchronously. The sharing of the island descriptions occurred in breakout rooms via Zoom. These needed to be purposefully designed by us to ensure we had the correct group members in each room with the one designated "left behind group member". We found that with the ample asynchronous time to have written descriptions, there was more editing and descriptiveness in the writing. This is good but did not adequately model what we were intending with the descriptive, communication of an ad libbing teacher in a K-12 classroom or why it was important to practice being descriptive in an impromptu setting. While there were many ways this activity could be implemented within an online course, in the end, this project would remain ideal as an in-person, TPR activity.

10.5   Integration of Online Best Practices

In the online setting, pedagogy is no different from that in a face-to-face setting. Teachers still strive to have students engage with all the three facets of interaction: between teacher and student, between student and the course content, and between student and student. However, what does change in the online classroom is how those interactions and engagements might occur between faculty, students, and the course material. Often, faculty members have the opportunity to spend time designing and developing how those activities might be modified for an online classroom for a semester or year prior to teaching it in a new modality. With COVID-19, faculty, regardless of online teaching experience, did not have that time to transition all of their face-to-face activities for the online classroom. Our approach to this modality modification mid-semester was three-pronged and supported by two of us in a co-teaching scenario which eased the development portion.

First, we discussed how the preservice teachers would continue interacting with our language acquisition content (student to content engagement). Because we had time to build a learning community within the classroom before the pandemic, during our co-planning time we determined that it was important for us to maintain this learning community in the online format. We continued to lean on authentic learning as we had in the classroom as described by some of the activities in the preceding paragraphs. Our preservice teachers had the opportunity to summarize and analyze content readings through one-pager assignments. This choice allowed our preservice teachers to not feel as overwhelmed with a large unit exam and/or final project but provided them the opportunity each week to digest tidbits of information and analyze it to showcase their learning.

Second, our focus turned to faculty to student engagement. In online courses, this can occur in a variety of ways, for example, in the form of faculty feedback on assessments, short announcement videos, and mini lectures via video or podcasts. Because this was an impromptu online course, we chose to maintain connection with the preservice teachers through weekly synchronous meetings on Zoom. In online courses, often there is discussion at the start of a semester regarding proper Internet etiquette for synchronous meeting and/or discussion boards. However, in this case, we were in person one moment and online the next. This immediately showcased that not all preservice teachers are at the same place professionally, even when they are in the same education block and near graduation. Examples of snafus during our live meetings included preservice teachers in bed during class, inappropriately dressed, and, in one case, someone who forgot to mute themselves and fell asleep.

These unexpected occurrences created additional faculty to student engagement opportunities because those scenarios needed to be addressed. Another benefit to co-teaching during the pandemic was the ability to support our preservice teachers through shared and split virtual office hours. There were times when we co-hosted virtual office hours and other times when we each had an hour on different days and times. This provided preservice teachers a larger opportunity to connect with a faculty member, but also allowed them to build purposeful connections with us, if that suited them. As we began to establish the routine of distance office hours, we built a schedule where there was varying availability to accommodate different schedules. On particular days, we offered early and mid-morning zoom meetings, while on other days, we provided late afternoon and evening hours. From our experience, preservice teachers appreciated attending these office hour sessions, especially when we were together synchronously.

Through the collected feedback, our preservice teachers liked being able to bounce ideas off of us for their virtual field experience lessons that they would be teaching to their K-12 English language students. Preservice teachers also appreciated that conversation was laid back, honest, and transparent, in office hours. We thought this was always the case, but from the feedback, our preservice teachers must have felt a community difference between class time and the office hour drop-in sessions. Based on our pandemic, distance learning experience, the virtual Zoom office hours were one of the strongest ways to maintain connection with our classroom community of preservice teachers who had six weeks of face-to-face classroom coursework prior to transitioning to the online modality. However, this evidence of Zoom office hours being a strong connection for building faculty to student engagement may be different for upcoming semesters where the course begins and ends completely online.

The third corner of the engagement triangle is the student-to-student opportunities. "Through active participation and knowledge construction with small groups or networks of other learners, there is opportunity to build relationships with peers in the [online] course, which would lead to increased engagement" (Carlson, 2021, p. 158). Our course utilized active learning strategies in the face-to-face environment so it only made sense to continue that in our online format during the pandemic. Working together to co-teach, we were able to teach brainstorm cooperative learning activities and facilitate small group discussions as they fit within the curriculum. "Examples of learner-learner engagement may include collaboration on assignments, discussion opportunities with varied media (for example video, audio, or text response inputs), and a place within the online course to have conversations about course connection to real-life happenings or current events" (Carlson, 2021, p. 158). Because of the pandemic, there was a short amount of time to transition this course from a face-to-face course to an online modality. It was helpful to have a co-teaching experience to process pedagogical decisions with another faculty member to support preservice teachers together.

10.6 Co-teaching Online

Similar to the learning engagement triangle, the theory of co-teaching is three-pronged to include planning, teaching, and assessing. Authentic co-teaching does not happen from simply showing up to teach at a given day and time with another faculty. True co-teaching first involves co-planning. We developed a regular meeting time and place, that eventually moved to Zoom. During our planning time, we shared our content knowledge with one another since we have different backgrounds (English language learners and technology integration) and had discussions about how to cover specific learning outcomes in effective ways. With the pandemic, we were forced to be even more intentional in our discussions and planning. It was more difficult to be on the same page online versus in the classroom. This extra layer of intentionality probably improved the synchronous sessions with our preservice teachers; we were able to support one another and lean toward our skillsets as well. For example, Dr. Carlson's strong suit is designing and facilitating online asynchronous courses, so she designed the bulk of the asynchronous activities and uploaded the content. While Dr. Serrano is a strong in-person facilitator, so he took the lead in designing the activities for our synchronous, Zoom meetings.

After co-planning, we then implemented our plan and co-taught. There are several strategies for co-teaching such as parallel teaching, differentiated opportunities, one leads while one assists, and one leads while one observes (St. Cloud State University, 2011). We followed the recommended strategies for co-teaching and applied them during our weekly asynchronous content creation and in our Zoom sessions. Our weekly asynchronous recordings featured one faculty member, while the other one assisted or in some scenarios, we both shared the recording time.

Finally, co-assessing in the online environment was really not different from when we were in the face-to-face classroom on campus. We would determine during our planning sessions who would grade what assessments and the key elements of each unit that aligned specifically with our student learning outcomes for the course. In the online environment, assessing felt likely took more time compared to the face-to-face classroom because we were no longer able to observe all of the discussions and roam from table to table answering questions as they arose.

Overall, it was important for us to be intentional with our co-teaching practices as this was a rare opportunity for our preservice teachers to see co-teaching modeled in ways that are often found in elementary education classrooms. As teacher educators, we were often modeling pedagogical theories and strategies that we hoped preservice teachers would do with their own future students.

10.7 Lessons to Carry Forward, Post-Pandemic

While the experience of pandemic, crisis teaching occurred during the spring semester of 2020, there is much to be said about the flexibility and opportunities that were learned and implemented from the occurrence. Moving forward, in our experience, there is room for teacher education to be more flexible in its modalities, meaning that teacher education does not need to be a one-size-fits-all, face-to-face experience. Purposeful selection of a hybrid and/or online approach provides the opportunity to model pedagogical practices for tomorrow's K-12 learners who likely will not take all of their K-12 schooling in a face-to-face-only environment. Further, allowing for a more flexible modality within teacher education will provide opportunity for more teachers of color and of indigenous background to complete these programs.

Purposeful course design should remain a requirement in a flexible classroom because some activities are best supported in the face-to-face environment while other activities and content delivery work well in an online format. Utilization of the best of both worlds could create a very robust and engaging methods course for supporting English language acquisition. For example, to maintain continuity, a schedule could be created where preservice teachers were online for four hours a week and in the classroom for a hands-on activity for two hours a week during the semester. Likewise, using the online classroom for connecting with classmates and the instructor during field experience weeks provides an added feedback opportunity.

Specifically, within our own course transition caused by COVID-19, we found that Reader's Theater was a learning activity that was well suited in both environments: online and in the face-to-face classroom. This TPR strategy in the classroom provided students with opportunity to physically move about the room and engaged their emotions as they performed skits for their classmates. In the online setting, the preservice teachers still utilized creativity to design the set and perform the Reader's Theater skit but they had to present the story in a different format than what they were likely used to from their own educational experience. This remarkable finding of how a seemingly small adaption created different learning benefits for our preservice teachers would be a strategy that we continue to utilize in upcoming semesters. It would be valuable to have our preservice teachers practice Reader's Theater in the face-to-face and online classroom settings. Reader's Theater is a method that is often utilized within the K-6 classroom by elementary teachers. As teacher educators, we would want to ensure that our preservice teachers have the ability to facilitate TPR activities, such as Reader's Theater, in both modalities if possible.

10.8 Conclusion

General education and language acquisition teachers underwent transformative changes due to the COVID-19 pandemic that began in March 2020. This challenge was seen by many educators and teacher educators as a chance for change in the way the system of education is ran. Post-pandemic, it will be crucial to continue advocating for the transformative changes that benefited the K-12 students and the preservice teachers. Teacher educators had the opportunity to experience online enough to learn that it is not scary, but enough to know they (as a whole) may need further training. Regardless, it is evident that our preservice teachers will need to "understand how to utilize technology within the context of teaching and learning" (Bradbury, 2021, p. 28) and fully grasp pedagogical resilience and cultural competence to ensure we are supporting all students within the classroom.

References

Bradbury, B. (2021). *The nexus of teaching and demographics: Context and connections from colonial times to today.* The Rowman and Littlefield Publishing Group.

Carlson, K. (2021). Supporting students through online learning. In L. Kyei-Blankson, J. Blankson, & E. Ntuli (Eds.), *Handbook of research on inequities in online education during global crises* (pp. 148–162). IGI Global. https://doi.org/10.4018/978-1-7998-6533-9.ch008

Carlson, K. (2022). Upgrading classroom environments for tomorrow's learners. In T. Driscoll III (Ed.), *Designing effective distance and blended learning environments in K-12* (pp. 61–72). IGI Global. https://doi.org/10.4018/978-1-7998-6829-3.ch005

Carrick, L. U. (2021). Readers theatre strategy guide. Read write think. https://www.readwritethink.org/professional-development/strategy-guides/readers-theatre

Hayes-Jacobs, H. (2010). *Curriculum 21: Essential education for a changing world.* ASCD.

Quality Matters, Inc. (2021). *Quality Matters rubric and standards.* https://www.qualitymatters.org/research

Soto, I. (2021). *Shadowing multilingual learners.* Corwin.

St. Cloud State University. (2011). *Co-teaching strategies & examples.* Teacher Quality Enhancement Center. https://www.stcloudstate.edu/soe/coteaching

Zibaresht, R. (2020). How to respond to the ongoing pandemic outbreak of the coronavirus disease (COVID-19). *European Journal of Biomedical and Pharmaceutical Sciences, 7*(6), 1–6.

Part III

Emergency Integration of Technology into Tecaher Education Programmes

11

Enhancing Professional Learning of Primary Student Teachers of L1 and L2 Through a Hybrid Learning Environment

Mirja Tarnanen, Merja Kauppinen, Johanna Kainulainen, Mari Hankala, and Eija Aalto

11.1 Introduction

Over the past two decades, teachers have faced numerous changes in both in-school and out-of-school contexts as a consequence of digitalization, mobility, the global economy, climate change, and, most recently, the COVID-19 pandemic, that challenge their professional learning and development. Amid these changes in contemporary society, schools are expected to provide pupils with competencies that they will need in life, such as technology literacy and multiliteracy, collaboration, and critical thinking (Lavonen, 2020; Zhao, 2010). At the same time, teachers are considered to have a critical influence on the learning

---

M. Tarnanen (✉) • M. Kauppinen • J. Kainulainen • M. Hankala • E. Aalto
University of Jyväskylä, Jyväskylä, Finland
e-mail: mirja.tarnanen@jyu.fi

© The Author(s), under exclusive license to Springer Nature Switzerland AG 2023
K. Sadeghi, M. Thomas (eds.), *Second Language Teacher Professional Development*,
Digital Education and Learning, https://doi.org/10.1007/978-3-031-12070-1_11

of pupils with diverse backgrounds and are expected to be able to carry out educational reforms successfully, help diminish inequality and construct sustainable living (Fullan & Hargreaves, 2016; OECD, 2020), and, particularly lately, to engage productively in distance learning as well as blended and hybrid learning models (Darling-Hammond & Hyler, 2020). Thus, because of these changes, possibilities to support teachers' learning-to-learn skills should be reconsidered to promote teachers' career-long professional learning more systematically and proactively (Korthagen, 2016).

In this chapter, we explore and discuss the development of a technology-enriched learning environment to prepare student teachers to teach Finnish as a first and second language, and literature in primary schools (grades 1–6, age 7–13). The aim of designing this type of hybrid learning environment is twofold; firstly, to enhance student teachers' pedagogical content knowledge (Shulman, 2004), that is, the combination of specific subject knowledge – such as (multi)literacy, communication, literature, and grammar—and pedagogical knowledge, including information and communication technology (ICT) skills, and, secondly, to support their professional learning through digital assessment and reflection. As working as a teacher in school requires an elaborate understanding of learning and its prerequisites, it is essential that learning in teacher education is guided by the self-same practices of development and renewal such as student-centred learning activities, assessment for learning and use of appropriate technologies which teachers are expected to develop and pupils are taught in school. To us as teacher educators and researchers, action research plays an essential, natural role in the preparation and professional development of student teachers as it helps us in developing new knowledge related to teacher education, promotes reflective teaching and learning, reinforces the link between practice and student achievement, and enables the development of research-based teacher education (Hine, 2013).

11.2 Conceptual Framework for a Hybrid Learning Environment

11.2.1 Professional Development Through a Personal Learning Environment for Reflection and Digital Assessment

In this chapter, we draw on the concept of professional development (PD), which can be considered as processes of learning, growth and development of teachers' expertise (social and personal skills and content knowledge including subject knowledge and pedagogical, instructional, and classroom management skills) leading to changes in their practice to support their pupils' learning (Avalos, 2011). PD is also about a process of extending teachers' self-knowledge, including reflecting on professional identity and agency (Eteläpelto et al., 2013). Thus, in addition to acquiring content knowledge, student teachers should learn to learn professionally during their studies. This requires raising awareness of their mental models, i.e. their prior knowledge, existing ideas and assumptions and past experiences of learning and teaching language, as they observe, select, explain and interpret new information through their existing mental models (Tarnanen et al., 2021). Consequently, as they have spent years in school, their teachers and teaching materials used in school have shaped their mental models. Therefore, instead of single knowledge-loaded lectures, teacher education should be able to support student teachers' professional learning with bottom-up approaches that are context-specific and emanate from identified needs for each student teacher's professional learning (Opfer & Pedder, 2011).

At the same time, there has been a debate around digital learning environments and technology-assisted learning that the most typical and most used learning environments, such as learning management systems (LMS), do not support learner learning per se. In addition, the design of most LMS environments (or VLS, virtual learning environments) has been instructor- or course-centric and not designed for students to build their own pathways to construct their PD and awareness as lifelong learners (Loureiro et al., 2013). In contrast, the personal learning environment

(PLE) concept approaches learning from the learner's perspective, emphasizing the learner's autonomy, agency, and responsibility for their own learning (Dabbagh & Kitsantas, 2012). PLEs are platforms for integrating formal, informal and nonformal learning and fostering self-regulated learning in education (Dabbagh & Kitsantas, 2012) where the learner has an active role as a manager of their learning environment and as a planner and owner of the learning process. The open and learner-centred PLE concept was developed to complement other e-learning systems as early as the mid-2000s but, according to Weller (2018), its development and modification of practices have progressed quite slowly. One reason for this is that there has been a lack of good practices in teacher education to model the possibilities of PLEs in learning processes and developing PD.

The accelerating digitalization of teaching and education also calls for the development and digitalization of assessment practices (Timmis et al., 2015), which in turn also places new developmental pressures on teacher and learner assessment literacy (Xu & Brown, 2016). By supporting the development of assessment literacy in teacher studies, assessment can also be developed in the field to better respond to the prevailing perceptions of learning and the demands of current changing learning environments (Atjonen et al., 2019).

The development of digital assessment has largely focused on the efficiency-enhancing features of technology and the efficient transfer and publication of assessment data, rather than considering the role of assessment as a supporting and promoting factor in learning (Timmis et al., 2015). However, digital assessment brings entirely new possibilities to support learning: competence and its development can be modelled in more diverse ways and demonstrated in completely new ways, such as e-portfolios, vlogs, and blogs. Digital assessment can, among other things, increase assessment flexibility (no traditional time and place linkage), help integrate formative and summative assessment, and support collaborative skills development, for example by allowing more flexibility in peer feedback and peer assessment practices (Timmis et al., 2015). With the help of digital assessment, it is also possible to assess more complex meta-skills, such as problem-solving skills (Ahonen et al., 2018). This brings flexibility to feedback practices and enables the utilization of learning analytics locally and internationally (Timmis et al., 2015).

11.2.2 Pedagogical Content Knowledge: Focus on Multiliteracies and Language

Traditionally, L1 and L2 teaching and learning have been disconnected both as research fields and as pedagogical approaches in Finland. However, increasing mobility and diversity in societies together with the concept of *multiliteracies* in the current Finnish core curriculum for basic education (FNBE, 2014) have highlighted the diversity of languages as well as language and literacy skills needed in all classrooms, also among L1 learners. Multiliteracies have a transversal role in all school subjects and learning environments (traditional and digital) (New London Group, 1996). As a notion, multiliteracies cover *multimodal* representations of knowledge and communication, be they verbal, visual, auditive, numeric or kinaesthetic symbols or their combinations (New London Group, 1996). Multiliteracies also refer to a *multicultural* aspect that concerns different cultural and social contexts of meaning-making modes and the way language is constructed and how meanings vary across these contexts (Cope & Kalantzis, 2000).

In line with sociocultural premises, the current research promotes the idea of inclusive pedagogy and developing mainstream education to engage all learners, hold high cognitive expectations, and provide support for the learning of all students regardless of their skill profile or background (Spratt & Florian, 2015). Furthermore, instead of focusing on disconnected language or even on one grammatical category at a time, language is perceived as action present in each learning environment in unique ways and connected to learning of meaningful content knowledge (Walqui & van Lier, 2010). It is therefore essential to establish objectives that integrate language and content learning and that perceive subject learning from a wider perspective than the memorization of content knowledge. Content knowledge is constructed through various multimodal meaning-making tools, including named languages and language varieties as well as other semiotic tools ranging from graphs and visuals to mathematical patterns and different modalities in various environments of use. These are treated as a unity of tools, complementing each other in a flexible and situationally effective way.

Moreover, from sociocultural premises, language acquisition is not primarily seen as an individual endeavour but as a social process of apprenticeship that enables individuals to socialize to become members of a community of practice and accomplish demanding actions with the assistance of more capable others (Heritage et al., 2015; Vygotsky, 1978). When learning is regarded as a social endeavour focusing both on language and content, L1 and L2 learners learn in interaction and scaffold each other's learning (Heritage et al., 2015). In teacher education, student teachers are encouraged to develop pedagogical practices that enable dynamic and creative use of different multimodal and multilingual tools in making meaning and shaping experiences, understandings, and knowledge. This approach is often referred to as *translanguaging* (Li, 2018). Learning content knowledge in multilingual groups provides a natural environment for utilizing all available cognitive, semiotic, sensory, and modal resources in learning and communication. Li (2018) claims that people have an innate translanguaging instinct, and thus a tendency to solve challenging communicative and learning tasks by utilizing various linguistic and multimodal resources in a flexible and situationally efficient way. L1 and L2 are not seen as separate and separately developed skills, but as resources complementing each other in the student's linguistic repertoire.

In the Finnish National Core Curriculum for Basic Education (FNBE, 2014), the syllabuses of all language subjects (including L1, L2 and foreign languages) approach multiliteracies from the viewpoint of students' text-related competencies, whereas originally the concept was perceived primarily from a pedagogical point of view (Palsa & Ruokamo, 2015). The language syllabuses recognize 'interpreting texts' and 'producing texts' as main content areas of teaching and learning. The wide concept of *text* in the syllabus covers practically all kinds of genres and text forms from non-fiction to fiction and from printed to various multimodal hybrid texts. Moreover, language awareness is included in the core content of language subjects as part of 'understanding language, literature and culture'. Literature education is connected in the language syllabus to cultural aspects of human development through a socio-emotional development perspective. Literature is approached through experiential reading, canon-based teaching, and literature analysis (Kauppinen,

2010). Furthermore, aspects of vocabulary growth, reading rate, motivation to read and reading for pleasure are treated as crucial objects of learning (Aerila & Kauppinen, 2020). In all, the phenomena of languages, texts and cultures are explored simultaneously from diverse perspectives. Finally, the content area of 'acting in interactive situations' includes communication both in face-to-face encounters and in multimedia environments. The core curriculum also specifies the pedagogical content knowledge for pre-service teacher education and sets guidelines for teacher development for all of the above content areas.

In teacher education, future teachers should be prepared to encounter school as a multilingual and multimodal learning environment with students of different backgrounds and varying skills. Future teachers need to learn to recognize the multiple ways knowledge and relations are constructed and assist learners in using all of their linguistic and multimodal resources for problem solving and constructing their understandings of new knowledge. It is essential to recognize the diversity among all learners (not just L2 learners) and promote their abilities to learn language and content in parallel. This requires cooperation in learning (sharing ideas, discussing the phenomena of education using diverse texts including media texts as well as professional literature), discussion of hands-on experiences in school, and classroom interventions during teacher training periods. These all form a valuable resource of language learning pedagogy.

11.3 Description of a Hybrid Learning Environment for L1 and L2 Student Teachers

In this chapter, we present a hybrid learning environment (HLE) created for teaching Finnish as a L1 and L2, and literature syllabus to primary student teachers who will teach pupils from 1st to 6th grade (age 7–13). In Finland, primary teachers hold an MA degree in education and can teach most subjects across the primary school curriculum. Thus, besides a major in education, the educational foundation of primary teachers includes the multidisciplinary school subjects taught in primary school. Subsidiary subject studies address the pedagogy of the primary school subjects along with cross-curricular themes to be implemented in various subjects at the primary level. In this teacher education programme, the goals of the L1 and L2 and literature syllabus (5 credit points) are to enable students to: (1) understand the social and situated nature of language and the meaning of language in identity construction; (2) support and promote the learning of language and literacy skills of diverse pupils; and (3) actively self-assess and develop their own expertise in promoting the literacy and language learning of diverse pupils. In turn, the aim of developing the HLE was to have the necessary technological, social, educational, and cultural affordances to provide opportunities for the student teachers to learn the wide-ranging pedagogical content knowledge within a limited timeframe. The developed learning environment can be considered a hybrid learning environment as it provides both a physical and digital setting in which learners can carry out their work and have access to the tools, documents, and other artefacts needed (Goodyear, 2001).

In the hybrid learning environment, assessment—diagnostic, formative, and summative—plays a guiding role in learning, including self-assessment and teacher assessment, forming a continuum throughout the learning phases and learning processes (see Fig. 11.1). Formative assessment is understood as assessment that supports learning at all stages of the process, guiding student teachers to advance their skills and helping

Fig. 11.1 Phases of the hybrid learning environment for L1 and L2 and multiliteracy learning

the teacher to assess and support learning processes appropriately (Wiliam, 2011). Thus, high-quality formative assessment also tells the learner how they should continue in the learning process in order to achieve the goals set for learning, and teaches the learner to take responsibility for their own learning (Wanner & Palmer, 2018). In the development work described here, assessment is also considered to support learning and reflection skills and, thus, is not only about assessment *of* and *for* learning, but also assessment *beyond* learning (Wanner & Palmer, 2018).

The hybrid learning environment consists of four phases: (1) Diagnostic phase, carried out online, in which students complete a digitalized diagnostic test and self-assess their pedagogical content knowledge competences on a five-level scale; (2) Elaborating phase, in which pedagogical content knowledge is studied following the ideas of both informative and transformative learning to enhance engagement of the student teachers in the transformative processes of critical self-reflection and reflective judgement through face-to-face group discourse (Mezirov, 2018). This phase also includes complementary online tasks on teaching literacy and language, which are reflected on in face-to-face groups; (3) Summative phase, in which students take an applied exam online. Students prepare a plan for an exam to reflect on their strengths and challenges regarding their pedagogical content knowledge, also taking into consideration the self-assessment and diagnostic test; and (4) Final reflection phase, in which each student reflects on their own expertise in language education and sets goals for their professional learning in the future. Furthermore, the learning environment provides a platform for student teachers' collaboration and development of mutual material projects and teaching interventions. The assessment practices and the learning environment in its entirety enable the student teachers to see and plan their individual path of professional development from pre-service education to continuous development throughout their career, and they are also able to access the platform after their basic studies.

11.4 Empirical Insight into Development of a Hybrid Learning Environment

11.4.1 Data and Analysis

Development of the hybrid learning environment was carried out within the framework of action research, as we worked in the capacity of teacher educator, researcher, and pedagogical developer. In this context, we consider action research as a process of studying teacher education to understand and improve the quality of the educative process in order to acquire new research-based and practical knowledge and understanding about how to improve pedagogical practices (Hine, 2013). We followed an iterative cycle comprising the following phases: (1) identifying pedagogical issues and resources and collecting and analysing the baseline data, such as feedback and learning tasks, to reformulate the pedagogical challenge; (2) making an action plan, designing learning and assessment, and collecting and analysing the data; (3) reflecting on and assessing the new learning environment and practices in the light of data analysis; and (4) reconsidering the original plan and revising the learning environment with its content and pedagogical practices (Kitchen & Stevens, 2008). In the following, we discuss one such data collection cycle carried out during the action research process.

The qualitative data were collected using convenience sampling from the student teachers participating in the course. The average age of the selected 27 participants (19 female and 8 male) was 23 years. A few participants had approximately five years of work experience but most did not have any at all. The data consist of student teachers' digital reflections and digital self-evaluations written (1) at the beginning of the course immediately after making preliminary self-evaluations and self-assessments, (2) after getting the results of the diagnostic test in the elaborative phase, and (3) at the end of the course during the summative and final reflection phase. In total, the qualitative data comprised approximately 98 pages of written material. The students were asked to specify and discuss the results of the diagnostic assessment (self-assessment and the results of the diagnostic test) in their reflections. They were also asked to reflect on their pedagogical competencies in relation to the national core curriculum and children's developmental needs. The data were analysed using data-driven thematic analysis to capture both explicit and underlying meanings of professional learning in HLE (Braun & Clarke, 2013). First, the main themes of pedagogical development in each reflection were identified. Next, the reflections of each student were analysed as a continuum to clarify which phases were experienced as most meaningful and what themes they addressed. As a result, the key themes of pedagogical development and the most meaningful phases of HLE were extracted.

11.4.2 Student Teachers' Reflections on Their Professional Learning

In this section, we present some key findings concerning the student teachers' reflections on their professional learning. First, we illustrate the findings in more general terms, describing typical characteristics of each phase (diagnostic, elaborative, summative, and final reflection phase). Thereafter, we illustrate the findings using the case examples of two different reflection profiles.

In the student teachers' reflections, the diagnostic phase of the model was considered meaningful to their goal setting for L1 and L2 and multiliteracy learning. The self-assessment and the skill-based diagnostic test guided the students to consider both their own literacy and language skills and their pedagogical content knowledge and helped them to orientate towards the course in several ways. The students perceived the extent and the diversity of the contents of the Finnish as an L1 and L2, and literature syllabus. The richness of the contents, for instance the multilingual and multicultural nature of the syllabus, inspired many of the student teachers to orientate positively towards their learning, although it also raised questions concerning their competence to cope with everything they should learn to teach their future pupils. However, the diagnostic phase helped the students to specify what competencies and pedagogical content knowledge they should learn. In addition, it allowed them to look back and make visible their own school experiences, emotions, and attitudes related to literacy skills, e.g. writing or grammar, and then to set their goals for learning in the course and as a language teacher in the future.

Based on the students' reflections, the structure of the HLE enabled the student teachers to make meaningful choices regarding their individual learning. For example, in the summative phase some students found it meaningful to choose an exam task that deepened their learning in the independent tasks of the elaborative phase. In turn, some students considered it more useful to choose an exam task on a completely different topic. In the different phases of the HLE, sharing ideas and developing them further in the learning tasks was considered meaningful and fruitful by the students. According to the students, possibilities to collaborate with peers brought forth new topics concerning both the content and pedagogical understanding of language learning.

In the final reflection phase, the students' reflections revealed difficulties in using the PLE environment as a resource for learning as they were not familiar with it as a tool for learning. They also acknowledged that they should have utilized the PLE in a more goal-oriented way. Few students understood the potential of the PLE. This clearly implies that students should be guided step-by-step in using the PLE at the beginning of their studies. Despite the challenges of pedagogical use of the PLE, it enables student teachers to reflect on their own professional learning in a way that is individually specific or relevant to them. The following examples of Maria and Julia illustrate how learning in the HLE was experienced and reflected on.

The Case of Maria

Maria referred to all of the phases of the HLE in her reflection and showed concretely how the phases benefitted her in terms of language and literature pedagogy. She also experienced that some contents of the course contributed to other studies. Maria raised digital skills as a target for development in the initial mapping and selected independent learning tasks that dealt with digital texts and learning platforms. After completing these tasks, Maria realized that her digital skills had developed, and that the digitalization permeated many areas of linguistic interaction:

> *Independent learning tasks helped me develop and learn. Especially diving into the world of Minecraft, TikTok and vlogging was instructive.*

In her reflections on the exam tasks, she was convinced of the importance of maintaining and re-developing her digital skills.

The article on literature education read in the small group helped Maria to discover her own literature education practices and provided further pedagogical ideas. In addition, Maria found small group discussions on the characteristics of the Finnish language and language awareness rewarding. For her, students' acting as linguistic detectives was an idea worth experimenting with as a part of functional language teaching. The visiting lecturer, in turn, opened Maria's eyes to children's multilingual everyday life in Finland and led her to choose the exam task focusing on this topic. Literature also provided ideas for teaching multilingual children. In terms of writing pedagogy, Maria found discussions about feedback practices and the role of handwriting, in particular, pedagogically inspiring.

Maria selected her exam tasks with the practical aim of being able to put them into future use in her own class. Through the exam literature she felt she gained perspective, faith, and confidence in her linguistic skills and pedagogical competences. Furthermore, she stated in the self-assessment that she learned most from the exam:

> *Out of everything, I got the most from taking the exam. Fortunately I dared to choose tasks where I wasn't in my comfort zone. I will return to the exam literature and learn more. What an instructive and varied course!*

Maria finds the PLE suitable for monitoring her own development and enhancing pedagogical thinking if it is actively updated.

The case of Julia

Julia reflected on her learning and developmental needs in a very holistic way throughout the phases of the HLE. Julia found the diagnostic phase very meaningful as she drew on the criterion-referenced self-assessment and diagnostic test results in all phases of the HLE, particularly when setting individual learning goals for the course. Julia also reflected on her assessment literacy as a student and as a teacher, which reinforces the importance of assessment practices when developing assessment literacy in teacher education.

Julia felt that her pedagogical content knowledge increased remarkably during the course. When reflecting on her learning she relied on criterion-referenced self-assessment of pedagogical knowledge, such as learner orientation and the development of language awareness, and she also referred to the key aspects of the national core curriculum for basic education. By focusing on these aspects she appeared to approach her professional learning from a holistic point of view, i.e. being a teacher in practice. Her holistic view of the pedagogy of Finnish language and literature and her expertise as a teacher were also visible in the final reflection phase:

> *I feel that I have developed a lot as a teacher and as a language and communication expert during the course. I realize, though, that I'm still really just at the beginning, but then again this is one of those things that I don't think you can ever finish. Self-development is constantly required. For example, supporting and building students' own language identity is something I would like to further deepen my knowledge of. Another area that needs to be deepened is how to support students when they have different learning challenges. I would also like to pay more attention to the equality of teaching in the future. However, I feel that I have gained a lot more confidence in these areas as well as good foundations on which to start building and developing competence.*

As Julia's and Maria's cases show, the HLE helped the students to discover which skills and pedagogical content knowledge they should focus on in their learning of L1, L2, and multiliteracy pedagogy. Additionally, the structure of the HLE and the students' autonomy enabled them to make individual choices and take responsibility for their learning. Thus, the HLE as a learning environment can support and make visible individual learning needs and paths in a flexible way and, most importantly, enhance the meaningfulness of their learning.

11.5 Discussion

In this chapter, we explored a hybrid learning environment developed for primary student teachers for an L1, L2, and literature syllabus. As we work as both teacher educators and researchers, we have adopted an action research approach in the development of our teaching and learning environments to prepare student teachers for their work in changing environments and to enhance their professional learning. The experiences of teaching, feedback from students, and the analysed data show that learning in the HLE was experienced as both challenging and rewarding by the student teachers. As a whole, the HLE serves as a supportive learning environment in terms of pedagogical content knowledge, and it also provides a concrete way to practise digital skills in practice. However, this bottom-up approach to enhancing professional learning (Opfer & Pedder, 2011) was not only about a different style of teaching or a new learning environment, it was also about the mental models of the student teachers (Tarnanen et al., 2021). As the data showed, according to the students, this type of learning, particularly the PLE, challenges traditional ways of learning because it demands taking responsibility for one's own learning in diverse ways that they are perhaps not used to through, e.g. self-regulation, critical reflection, and discussing pedagogical content knowledge, including viewing language and literacy from new perspectives (see also Dabbagh & Kitsantas, 2012; Mezirov, 2018).

According to the student teachers' experiences, the self-assessment and the diagnostic test at the beginning of the studies significantly oriented their further studies, e.g. task selection and group discussions, and focused their reflections. The HLE appeared to be so flexible that it permitted individual learning paths as well as increased efficiency of pedagogical resources and enhanced experiences of professional learning.

For us as teacher educators, this process has taught that meta-talk about ways of learning and ways of thinking plays a significant role in professional learning, and that it should be timed wisely according to the needs of the students and supported by guiding the students and giving them feedback. This process has also given us an opportunity to learn at the same time as developing the HLE and has thus enhanced our own professional development, including acquiring new skills and knowledge about digital applications, designing, and doing assessment and iterative and research-based teamwork. The HLE development process will be continued with the goal of advancing primary student teachers' and our own professional learning in order to promote learner-centred language and literature pedagogy for all pupils with diverse backgrounds.

11.6 Lessons for Post-COVID-19 Period

The COVID-19 pandemic forced a rapid transition of the infrastructure of teacher education over to fully remote teaching and learning environments. For teacher education, which is centred on in-person teaching and where face-to-face interaction is considered a core element of professional learning, this transition can be considered to have been more impactful than in many other fields. These new circumstances based on distance teaching require student teachers to develop their metacognitive skills and learning-to-learn abilities and to take more independent responsibility for their learning without daily social, academic, and structural support from teacher educators and peer students. The pandemic has therefore not only affected the infrastructure but also the socio-emotional and cognitive aspects of academic and professional learning. This situation has brought new challenges to teacher educators, particularly those less technology-oriented, although, due to the widespread use of digital learning platforms, in teacher education in Finland sharing materials and assigning tasks has been paperless for years prior to the COVID-19 pandemic. In addition, as our teaching already made use of digital platforms—for taking diagnostic tests and applied exams, making self-assessments, sharing materials, signing learning tasks, and holding peer feedback chats—the changes brought by the pandemic have not, in this sense, been dramatic. Arranging distance group teaching through Zoom has, in terms of remote technology use, been the only visible change. After the pandemic, assumingly, traditional in-person teaching will make use of the practices familiar from the distance teaching setting and, valuable face-to-face interaction on site will be used resource-wisely and in pedagogically meaningful ways. Therefore, in-person teaching and distance teaching will in future not be competitive modes, but complementary, and will be developed as such. Accordingly, teacher education could better prepare student teachers to face future challenges of digitalization, pandemics, or any other unexpected events that may impact existing ways of organizing teaching and supporting learning.

References

Aerila, J.-A., & Kauppinen, M. (2020). Stories make readers: Enhancing the use of fictional literature with multilingual students. In G. Neokleous, A. Krulatz, & R. Farrelly (Eds.), *Handbook of research on cultivating literacy in diverse and multilingual classrooms* (pp. 368–392). IGI Global.

Ahonen, A., Häkkinen, P., & Pöysä-Tarhonen, J. (2018). Collaborative problem solving in Finnish pre-service teacher education: A case study. In E. Care, P. Griffin, & M. Wilson (Eds.), *Assessment and teaching of 21st century skills: Research and applications* (pp. 119–130). Springer International Publishing.

Atjonen, P., Laivamaa, H., Levonen, A., Orell, S., Saari, M., Sulonen, K., Tamm, M., Kamppi, P., Rumpu, N., Hietala, R., & Immonen, J. (2019). *Että tietää missä on menossa. Oppimisen ja osaamisen arviointi perusopetuksessa ja lukiokoulutuksessa.* The Finnish Education Evaluation Centre.

Avalos, B. (2011). Teacher professional development in teaching and teacher education over ten years. *Teaching and Teacher Education, 27*(1), 10–20. https://doi.org/10.1016/j.tate.2010.08.007

Braun, V., & Clarke, V. (2013). *Successful qualitative research: A practical guide for beginners.* Sage.

Cope, B., & Kalantzis, M. (2000). *Multiliteracies: Literacy learning and the design of social futures.* Routledge.

Dabbagh, N., & Kitsantas, A. (2012). Personal learning environments, social media, and self-regulated learning: A natural formula for connecting formal and informal learning. *Internet and Higher Education, 15*, 3–8. https://doi.org/10.1016/j.iheduc.2011.06.002

Darling-Hammond, L., & Hyler, M. E. (2020). Preparing educators for the time of COVID … and beyond. *European Journal of Teacher Education, 43*(4), 457–465. https://doi.org/10.1080/02619768.2020.1816961

Eteläpelto, A., Vähäsantanen, K., Hökkä, P., & Paloniemi, S. (2013). What is agency? Conceptualizing professional agency at work. *Educational Research Review, 10*, 445–465. https://doi.org/10.1016/j.edurev.2013.05.001

FNBE. (2014). *National core curriculum for basic education 2014.* National Board of Education.

Fullan, M., & Hargreaves, A. (2016). *Bringing the profession back call to action.* Learning Forward.

Goodyear, P. (2001). *Learning and digital environments: Lessons from European research. In education and the information age: Current progress and future strategies* (pp. 1–25). Bradshaw Books.

Heritage, M., Walqui, A., & Linquanti, R. (2015). *English language learners and the new standards. Developing language, content knowledge, and analytical practices in the classroom.* Harvard Education Press.

Hine, G. S. (2013). The importance of action research in teacher education programs. *Issues in Educational Research, 23*(2), 151–163.

Kauppinen, M. (2010). *Literacy delineated – Reading literacy and its instruction in the curricula for the mother tongue in the basic education* (Doctoral dissertation, University of Jyväskylä). Retrieved from https://jyx.jyu.fi/handle/123456789/24964

Kitchen, J., & Stevens, D. (2008). Action research in teacher education. Two teacher-educators practice action research as they introduce action research to preservice teachers. *Action Research, 6*(1), 7–28. https://doi.org/10.1080/09650790701833105

Korthagen, F. A. J. (2016). Pedagogy of teacher education. In J. Loughran & M. L. Hamilton (Eds.), *International handbook of teacher education* (Vol. 1, pp. 311–346). Springer Science.

Lavonen, J. (2020). Curriculum and teacher education reforms in Finland that support the development of competences for the twenty-first century. In F. Reimers (Ed.), *Audacious education purposes* (pp. 65–80). Springer. https://doi.org/10.1007/978-3-030-41882-3_3

Li, W. (2018). Translanguaging as a practical theory of language. *Applied Linguistics, 39*(1), 9–30. https://doi.org/10.1093/applin/amx039

Loureiro, A., Messias, I., & Barbas, M. (2013). Learning in knowledge society: The different roles of VLEs & PLEs. Springer e-learning and knowledge management for human capital development, 277. https://www.researchgate.net/publication/257615958_Learning_in_Knowledge_Society_the_different_roles_of_VLEs_PLEs

Mezirov, J. (2018). Transformative learning theory. In K. Illeris (Ed.), *Contemporary theories of learning* (pp. 114–128). Routledge. https://doi.org/10.4324/9781315147277

OECD. (2020). *TALIS 2018 results (volume II): Teachers and school leaders as valued professionals.* TALIS, OECD Publishing.

Opfer, V. D., & Pedder, D. (2011). Conceptualizing teacher professional learning. *Review of Educational Research, 81*(3), 376–407. https://doi.org/10.3102/0034654311413609

Palsa, L., & Ruokamo, H. (2015). Behind the concepts of multiliteracies and media literacy in the renewed Finnish core curriculum: A systematic literature review of peer-reviewed research Seminar.net – International Journal of Media. *Technology and Lifelong Learning, 11*(2), 101–118. https://doi.org/10.7577/seminar.2354

Shulman, L. S. (2004). *Knowledge and teaching: Foundations of the new reform.* Jossey Bass.

Spratt, J., & Florian, L. (2015). Inclusive pedagogy: From learning to action. Supporting each individual in the context of 'everybody'. *Teaching and Teacher Education, 49*, 89–96. https://doi.org/10.1016/j.tate.2015.03.006

Tarnanen, M., Kostiainen, E., Kaukonen, V., Martin, A., & Toikka, T. (2021). Towards a learning community: Understanding teachers' mental models to support their professional development and learning. *Professional Development in Education.* https://doi.org/10.1080/19415257.2021.1959383

The New London Group. (1996). A pedagogy of multiliteracies: Designing social futures. *Harvard Educational Review, 66*(1), 60–92.

Timmis, S., Broadfoot, P., Sutherland, R., & Oldfield, A. (2015). Rethinking assessment in a digital age: Opportunities, challenges and risks. *British Educational Research Journal, 42*(3), 454–476. https://doi.org/10.1002/berj.3215

Vygotsky, L. S. (1978). *Mind in society: The development of higher psychological functions.* Harvard University Press.

Walqui, A., & van Lier, L. (2010). *Scaffolding the academic success of adolescent English language learners.* WestEd.

Wanner, T., & Palmer, E. (2018). Formative self- and peer assessment for improved student learning: The crucial factors of design, teacher participation and feedback. *Assessment & Evaluation in Higher Education, 43*(7), 1032–1047. https://doi.org/10.1080/02602938.2018.1427698

Weller, M. (2018). Twenty years of Edtech. *Educause Review Online, 53*(4), 34–48. https://er.educause.edu/-/media/files/articles/2018/7/er184101.pdf

Wiliam, D. (2011). What is assessment for learning? *Studies in Educational Evaluation, 37*, 3–14. https://doi.org/10.1016/j.stueduc.2011.03.001

Xu, Y., & Brown, G. T. L. (2016). Teacher assessment literacy in practice: A reconceptualization. *Teaching and Teacher Education, 58*, 149–162. https://doi.org/10.1016/j.tate.2016.05.010

Zhao, Y. (2010). Preparing globally competent teachers: A new imperative for teacher education. *Journal of Teacher Education, 61*(5), 422–431. https://doi.org/10.1177/0022487110375802

12

CALL for Global Learning: Using *World 101* for Teacher Training in an Online TESOL Methods Course

Estela Ene

12.1 Introduction

Preparing English language teachers in the areas of both Computer-Assisted Language Learning (CALL) and global learning has never been more important. The need for proficiency with both CALL and global-mindedness and cultural sensitivity is a reality of our technologized, globalized world. This chapter illustrates a way to combine the focus on CALL and global-mindedness in the preparation of pre- and in-service teachers, in the hope that the students of the student-teachers thus exposed will eventually benefit further down the line.

12.1.1 The Importance of CALL Training

The COVID-19 crisis made the need for CALL competence sharply evident. When teaching had to shift rapidly from the face-to-face to the

E. Ene (✉)
Indiana University—Purdue University Indianapolis, Indianapolis, IN, USA
e-mail: eene@iu.edu

© The Author(s), under exclusive license to Springer Nature Switzerland AG 2023
K. Sadeghi, M. Thomas (eds.), *Second Language Teacher Professional Development*, Digital Education and Learning, https://doi.org/10.1007/978-3-031-12070-1_12

online medium worldwide, the largely inadequate preparation of teachers for online instruction as well as access inequities everywhere came to light. Overall, teachers heroically adapted to the new demands for teaching with technology online. As the COVID-19 emergency online teaching scenarios become a thing of the past, the need for CALL preparation remains. Technology was with us before COVID-19 and will stay with us after the pandemic. If anything, after increased exposure, teachers' and students' expectations for more competent use of technology and online resources have likely increased. CALL teacher education and professional development are paramount.

At the same time, CALL does not need to be practiced at an extreme level of technological integration to be successful. Among other things, the COVID-19 crisis has revealed stark differences in access to technology worldwide (Karatay & Hegelheimer, 2021). Against the backdrop of a still relatively low preparedness of CALL, comparatively less involved uses of CALL present an attractive, attainable option (Alexandre et al., 2021, p. 31). Not everyone is going to know how to game and not everyone is going to have access to virtual reality for learning purposes, but it is likely that many or most will be able to access a website. The allure of CALL still rests, to a large extent, in its affordances, which include the authenticity of materials and participants to interact with, the learners' empowerment through choice and agency, and the embedded opportunities to develop multimodal literacies (Thorne & Smith, 2011).

It has been apparent for a while that, when it comes to CALL and teacher education, as Hubbard and Levy (2006) also point out, several needs are important, including:

- The need for both technical and pedagogical training in CALL, ideally integrated with one another;
- The idea of using CALL to learn about CALL—experiencing educational applications of technology firsthand as a student to learn how to use technology as a teacher;
- The value of having CALL permeate the language teacher education curriculum rather than appear solely in a standalone course. (p. ix)

The idea that experiencing the teaching that one will apply as a teacher is rooted in the area of social psychology known as role theory (Biddle, 1986), which posits that professionals, including teachers, define themselves and the knowledge they need to possess based on the roles they will need to fulfill. It follows then that teachers in training need to acquire the technical and pedagogical knowledge and skills to apply CALL, as their role will entail both teaching the target content and teaching with technology to some extent. Moreover, based on the aforementioned experientialist framework, teachers can and should acquire that knowledge through practice, as also advocated by Bauer-Ramazani (2006) and Warschauer's (2002) discussion of electronic literacies.

12.1.2 The Importance of Global Learning and Intercultural Competence

The pursuit of global learning goals—in which the development of intercultural competence is included—has become a priority in many institutions of higher education. This includes the institution where this research took place and where the aspiration is to supply all students with at least a single meaningful global learning experience that takes place either locally or internationally (IUPUI Office of International Affairs [IUPUI OIA], 2020, 2022). In fact, today, it is common for institutional strategic plans to envision the infusion of the entire curriculum with global realities and ways of thinking that cultivate students' curiosity and respect for cultural difference in a variety of ways (IUPUI OIA, 2020).

Global learning is vital for effectively educating students to live, operate, and solve problems in an increasingly interconnected world (Hovland, 2005). It is now considered a significant component of a complete education that provides learning opportunities for university students to understand vital information about the issues in their world today and how these impact various peoples or environments around the globe. Beyond gaining knowledge, students must think critically about the role, place, and influence that their communities, their countries, and themselves have had in the world (Hovland, 2014).

There is a close relationship between global learning and intercultural competence, with the latter being often subsumed to the former. Global learning aims to give students the chance to develop a skill set that will allow them to navigate interactions with others who do not share the same cultural background as individual students themselves to solve these problems (Hovland, 2005, 2014; Landorf et al., 2018). Without this ability to successfully and respectfully navigate intercultural interactions, students will not be ready to adequately meet the world's demands today in a responsible manner.

Intercultural competence is defined as the "complex abilities that are required to perform effectively and appropriately when interacting with others who are different from oneself" (Fantini, 2009, p. 458). In language teaching and TESOL, Canale (1983) established a model of communicative competence that included four interrelated competencies: grammatical, sociocultural, discourse, and strategic. This model signaled the importance of teaching culture in its various forms to prepare communicatively competent language learners. Models and definitions of intercultural competence have evolved from emphasizing the communicative aspect to a more complex representation in which a variety of ways of achieving and demonstrating intercultural competence at various levels are taken into account. Thus, Deardorff's (2006, 2009) model emphasizes the interaction between the levels of knowledge and comprehension of oneself and others, attitudes, and the internal and external outcomes that represent intercultural competence (from empathy and flexibility to actual effective and appropriate communication). This is the model that has been at the basis of models that guide internationalization and globalization efforts at higher education institutions today, such as AAC&U's Intercultural Knowledge and Effectiveness VALUE Rubric (2009).

Importantly, the development of interculturally competent and globally minded students hinges on faculty. In order to teach culture and develop their students' intercultural competence and wide global outlook, language teachers need to be interculturally competent themselves (Senyshyn & Smith, 2019). Thus, during their training, they have to be exposed to content and materials that facilitate their own intercultural development while giving them tools and strategies to later use with their own students. In Howard's (2016) words, "we [teachers] can't teach what we don't know." Of course, teachers' training can be done through professional development on the job, but it is likely that it will be more comprehensive and deep-reaching if it begins while those teachers are still in training in semester-long courses or longer degree programs. This is the premise at the basis of the intervention described in this chapter, which explores how pre- and in-service teachers can be guided to work with materials that expose them, first and foremost, to global topics and perspectives, so that they can do the same in their own classrooms.

This chapter links the importance of CALL, on the one hand, and of global learning/intercultural competence, on the other hand, by providing an example of how an online TESOL Methods course facilitated through the Learning Management System known as Canvas was supplemented with an external online material—*World 101,* from the Council of Foreign Relations. By doing so, the course supported the development of pre- and in-service ESL teachers by modeling a low-tech CALL implementation and focusing them on intercultural competence/global learning development. The students experienced an online course and a globally minded online resource embedded in it as students themselves. At the same time, by fulfilling the course requirements that required them to use *World 101,* they were challenged to be prepared to enhance their own students' CALL and intercultural competence.

12.2 Research Questions

Despite the abundance of research performed on ESL pre- and in-service teacher training, global learning outcomes, and CALL, there remains a need to evaluate the potential *World 101* materials have within the context of an online university-level teacher education course. As a way to explore the use of these global-minded materials within this specific institution and population, the teacher-researcher sought to answer these research questions:

1. What *World 101* topics would the pre- and in-service teachers in this course gravitate toward to make a lesson about?
2. What rationale would the pre- and in-service teachers use to justify their choice in lesson topic?
3. What level of proficiency and age/grade would the pre- and in-service teachers design the lesson plan for using *World 101* materials?

So that the answers to these question may be sufficiently explored, this chapter provides an example of how pre-service and in-service ESL teachers were focused on global learning instruction in a TESOL Methods course in which they were asked to design ESL lessons using online materials from *World 101*—a multi-module website by the Council on Foreign Relations (CFR, 2022).

12.3 Context

This implementation took place at a midsized midwestern university in the United States. A group of eight faculty and advisors from across the institution, which has included global learning goals in its strategic plan (IUPUI, 2021), participated in a community of practice that piloted the integration of *World 101* in their courses and advising activity. The author of this chapter participated in the pilot as a representative of the School of Liberal Arts. She already had a history of involvement in faculty professional development and curriculum design that focuses on intercultural competence, teaching, and learning (Allen et al., 2022; Ene, 2021).

As TESOL faculty, the author regularly teaches a TESOL Methods course for pre-service and in-service teachers. The course is a requirement for graduate students in the MA in TESOL Program and an elective for upper-level undergraduate majors in English, linguistics, and education. In addition to providing an overview of TESOL methods, the course engages the students in curriculum creation and lesson planning. The course requirements include designing several ESL lessons solidly grounded in language-learning theory and research and targeting the development of both language skills and intercultural competence.

In the spring 2020 semester, the course was offered online independently of the COVID-19 crisis, meaning it was not converted into an online course due to the pandemic. Before that, it had been offered face-to-face and gradually transitioned by the instructor-researcher into Canvas modules that supplemented the face-to-face modality. The online platform was never used as a transcript of the face-to-face content. "[T]he major course components—goals, content interaction, assessment, outcome, and overall quality [of an online course]—should remain intact" when such a transition is made (Bauer-Ramazani, 2006, p. 186). The goal to prepare technology- and culture-aware TESOL professionals was pursued through the implementation of a flipped, interactive, and technologically enhanced design in which the course content was explored through readings that the students perused on their own and then explored interactively through discussions with their peers and instructor, supplementary audio-video materials, and applied assignments that were frequently workshopped/peer reviewed and revised based on feedback. While CALL training was not the sole objective of the course, the instructor blended it in, based on the philosophy explained above—that CALL training is a necessity and it is best achieved experientially through modeling and practice.

In Spring 2020, the course had 23 students—16 undergraduate (12 female and 4 male) and 7 graduate (6 female and 1 male) students. All the undergraduate students were from the United States; one male and one female student were naturalized citizens and relatively recent refugees from the Middle East and South-East Asia and three other female students were children of immigrants from Spanish- and Chinese-speaking backgrounds. In the graduate student group, there were a male and a female student from Central and South America, respectively; the other five students were native speakers of English from the United States. The undergraduate students' ages ranged between 20 and 22 years, except for the male refugee who was in his forties. The graduate students were in their mid and late twenties, except for one who was in her mid-sixties. Three undergraduate students and three graduate students were in-service teachers of English Language Arts or ESL in K-12 (2), university programs (2), and refugee-support programs (2). *World 101* was presented to them as a source they could use in their lesson design assignments to fulfill two purposes: (1) to incorporate technology-enhanced learning, since the material was exclusively online, and/or (2) to develop intercultural competence.

World 101 is a multi-module online material created by the Council on Foreign Relations. It consists of information-based modules about various topics, including "Global Era Issues," "Regions of the World," "How the World Works … and Sometimes Doesn't," "Historical Context," "Foreign Policy," and "COVID-19" (CFR, 2022). The website also includes a page that offers instructor resources such as syllabi, instructions for embedding *World 101* into learning management systems (LMSs), and other teaching resources. Modules are frequently updated, in synch with important world events. For example, the unit on COVID-19 was added some time during the pandemic.

The TESOL Methods course uses two required texts—Kumaravadivelu (2003) and Brown and Lee (2015)—and a multitude of recent research articles and book chapters to expose the students to TESOL methodology and related Second Language Acquisition theories. The course unfolds over 15 weeks of effective instruction over a semester. A new topic is introduced each week or two, building upon the previous ones and scaffolding the next. Sample topics include an overview of TESOL methods, Kumaravadivelu's (2003) microstrategies, teaching each language skill and integrating skills, feedback, interaction, assessment, technology, and culture in the classroom. The course assignments provide the pre-service and in-service teachers the opportunity to observe and develop TESOL lessons which apply their knowledge. In the online course, class observations and teaching demonstrations had to be completed online. This was one of the major differences between the face-to-face and online course. Once the pre- and in-service teachers identified a context, either online or in person, in which to conduct observations of teaching, the process unfolded without issues. For teaching demonstrations, they were grouped with four to five other peers and took turns teaching the rest of the group an ESL lesson over a recorded Zoom session. This too occurred uneventfully.

The course always incorporates a unit on culture and technology, respectively. Usually, the students are given the option to design lessons that purposely use or target these. In the Spring 2020 semester, however, they were required to include these elements in a lesson plan. The professor based this decision on a couple of factors. First, in previous semesters she noticed that few students chose to develop lessons for intercultural development, and when they did so they tended to approach culture superficially, through the lens of commonly known cultural traditions. Secondly, the rise of diversity, equity, and inclusion conversations on campuses across the United States underscored the increased need for higher intercultural competence among students and teachers. Pre- and in-service TESOL professionals, who need to be prepared to work with diverse domestic and international populations, fall into the category of present and future teachers whose intercultural competence should be high so that they can guide their own students on to the path to high intercultural competence for the classroom and the real world. *World 101,* with its online materials about both United States and worldwide issues, emerged as a promising material to use in the lesson design assignments.

The teacher-researcher's goal was to assess the potential of *World 101* as an instructional material to use with and by the TESOL Methods students. The questions of interest were: What topics would the pre- and in-service teachers gravitate toward and based on what rationale? For what level of proficiency and age/grade would they design using *World 101*?

The assignment in which the TESOL Methods students were asked to implement *World 101* (as can be seen in the Appendix) occurred in the ninth week of the semester. It was the sixth in a series of assignments for which the students practiced designing lessons that focused on each language skill, as well as technology. The option to use *World 101* was open all along but not required until week nine.

At the time that the author began designing assignments for the Spring 2020 online TESOL Methods course, her institution's stated international learning goals, fashioned on the model of AAC&U's VALUE Rubric (2009), stated that students at the institution should:

1. Have a good working knowledge of the broader world, its natural systems and nations, their characteristics, and their relationship with each other.
2. Are able to analyze and evaluate the forces shaping international events, both now and in the past.

3. Have detailed knowledge of the cultures, languages, history, and/ or current condition of at least one country beyond the United States.
4. Recognize the many ways "the global is reflected in the local" within the United States and beyond.
5. Have reflected upon the distinctive position of the United States on the international stage, and have a good, working knowledge of American history and cultural systems.
6. Appreciate the complexity of contemporary cultural systems and know the fundamental principles of intercultural understanding and communication.
7. Are skilled at interacting and collaborating with individuals and organizations from other countries.
8. Use diverse frames of reference and international dialogue to think critically and solve problems.
9. Are humble in the face of difference, tolerant of ambiguity and unfamiliarity, and are willing to be in the position of a learner when encountering others.
10. Understand the global context of their chosen profession and have blended international perspectives into their professional learning.
11. Have developed a sense of responsibility and involvement with pressing global issues concerning health, poverty, the environment, conflict, inequality, human rights, civil society, and sustainable economic development.
12. Can apply their international learning to diversity in the communities in which they live. (IUPUI, 2020)

The sections that follow provide an analysis of the lessons designed by the TESOL Methods students from the point of view of the soundness of the lesson plan goals and structure, as well as based on how they used *World 101* to promote the abovementioned international learning dimensions.

12.4 Lesson Analysis

12.4.1 Pedagogical Structure, Populations Targeted, and Skills

Of the 23 students in the course, 16 fulfilled the assignment. The students used the lesson plan structure presented in Echevarria et al. (2017). The author-instructor catalogued the intended population age, grade, and English proficiency level of the students targeted; the language and content goals targeted by the lesson plans; and the intercultural competence/international or global learning goals they corresponded to.

The lessons designed by the TESOL Methods pre- and in-service teachers were for a wide variety of populations of English language learners in both ESL (12) and English as a Foreign Language (EFL) contexts (4); across the elementary (3), middle (5), high school (5), university (1), and adult community (2) contexts; and for the low and high intermediate levels. All lesson plans integrated skills, but the most targeted skills were writing such as reading, speaking, and listening. The language goals of the lessons were for the students to be able to:

- Understand the structure of genres or text types such as opinion article, argument, exposition, or fictional short story (genre)
- Master the vocabulary needed to express an opinion, an argument, exposition, or fictional short story
- Structure a debate
- Develop a thesis
- Develop a researched argument
- Develop a sense of voice as a writer/narrator
- Use new vocabulary related to a chosen globally minded topic and genre

The activities meant to support the achievement of such goals included reading and answering comprehension questions as pre-writing, free-writing, and other brainstorming and planning in pairs or groups, discussing topics in pairs or groups to generate ideas and practice topic-related or genre-related vocabulary, reflective journaling, peer review, and listening to a presentation by the teacher or other peers to learn about a topic.

240   E. Ene

12.4.2   Topics

The topics chosen for lesson design were based on the modules about *Global Health* (5), *Regions of the World* (5), *Climate Change* (4), and *Migration* (1). One lesson was about international agricultural commerce but did not use *World 101* due to the student misunderstanding the assignment; this lesson was not included in the analysis here. With their choices, the pre- and in-service teachers in the TESOL Methods course demonstrated interest in current global events and social concerns with local ramifications, knowledge about the world in relation to historical and current US realities, and the identity of their English language learning students as transnational individuals that bring complex knowledge, experience, and emotions to their life and learning experience in the United States.

Working with the *Global Health* module, one student focused her lesson on "The Rising Tide of Diabetes in Mexico" from the module on *Global Era Issues*. As one would have predicted, four students chose the pandemics topic, focusing specifically on the relevant and timely topic of COVID-19. One of the students reflected as follows:

> The program I work for has many elderly students who are high risk and unsure about how to navigate the [COVID] situation. In a time of rapidly developing news related to global health, it is essential that all people understand the news and are comfortable reading, discussing, and writing about it. Writing can help students share the feelings of anxiety and fear they may not be addressing otherwise. (Grace, teacher for adult refugees, city-based ESL program)

As the quote above shows, the in-service teacher took into account how her students related to the pandemic both through the lens of news from their home countries and from their current location in the United States—in other words, at the intersection of the local with the global. She considered the students' feelings and state of mind as a portal into developing information literacy and writing skills.

Another student eloquently explained his choice to explore the pandemic not only as a global health phenomenon with local consequences, but also as a global social phenomenon that unveiled inequities locally and globally.

The lesson I prepared fully encompasses our current social climate, as we all have been affected by the pandemic. The content objectives established in this lesson are met through the reading and further analysis of the article, as students delve deeper into the consequences of systematic racism. Given that a large majority of my hypothetical students fall into one of the demographic categories discussed in the article [ethnically or racially], this lesson is not only meaningful to them, but is also relevant to their daily lives. The lesson follows the social relevance and cultural consciousness micro strategies established by B. Kumaravadivelu (2003). (Cody, education major, pre-service teacher)

Similarly, the motivation for four TESOL Methods students to select materials from the module on migration was also rooted in their desire to offer English language learners opportunities to share their own experiences and delve into the sociopolitical complexities of their own stories. While apparently more neutral, the *Regions of the World* module first opened opportunities to learn factual, geopolitical, and historical information about the Middle East and North Africa, South-East Asia, and the target students' own countries of origin. From the geopolitical and historical information, the lessons branched into discussion of foreign relations, colonization, and national identity. Jack, a pre-service teacher, considered that "Understanding how the United States has interacted with other regions of the world gives those just coming to the United States a sense of history for the country they are now a part of as well." Adam envisioned that "The students will explore the colonization that shaped the region [of South and Central Asia]. Students will be able to chronologically document points of history that influenced the way the region functions today."

The four lesson plans based on the *Climate Change* module were geared toward understanding the causes, solutions, and participants in climate change. Frank, who designed for elementary-school English language learners, reflected:

I believe the choice of 'climate change' is appropriate for elementary-aged students because educating younger audiences about the impact we have on our planet is of utmost importance in building a more sustainable

242   E. Ene

future. Of the topics listed on *World 101*, climate change seemed to be the most relevant to my selected student demographic, where students can more directly see their impact/contributions.

12.5   Discussion

The lesson descriptions and reflections above demonstrate that the online materials available through *World 101* can be useful in a number of ways in online teacher training. The student-teachers in the online course described here experienced CALL, both through the online course and the *World 101* website, as well as global-mindedness through the *World 101* applications they were asked to develop. This type of support provided in teacher education programs, combined with the provision of early career supports and further exposure, increases teachers' self-perceived sense of preparedness (Deng et al., 2020).

The design presented proved fit from a TESOL pedagogical perspective: the pre- and in-service teachers were able to identify modules and submodules on a variety of topics of interest to themselves and their students. The materials lent themselves to a rigorous lesson design that followed best practices in TESOL, as illustrated by the use of the Sheltered Instruction Observation Protocol (SIOP) (Echevarría et al., 2000) lesson plan model by the teachers in training and other models offered in the course. The lessons designed targeted a variety of student populations and contexts, testifying to the versatility of the materials. Frequently, the lesson designers were able to find a way to activate prior knowledge by asking the students to link their personal experiences and feelings to the topics discussed. This is in accord with the macrostrategies for language learning that were being taught in the TESOL Methods course (Kumaravadivelu, 2003, p. 39).

With respect to exposure to and practice with CALL, in the process of designing with *World 101*, the pre- and in-service teachers were themselves exposed to the online material, in addition to receiving instruction through an overall online TESOL Methods course that already contained posted texts, hyperlinks, and other audio-visual materials. Thus, *World 101* not only added to the diversity of materials embedded in the online course, but it added value to the course through its global-minded orientation. The first tier of individuals who benefitted from this were the students in the TESOL Methods course who were pre- and in-service ESL teachers. The second tier of learners who have benefitted or will benefit from this orientation in the future are the real and hypothetical students of those enrolled in the TESOL Methods course. Pedagogically, the assignment provided opportunities to experience both technology and global-minded materials in an experience-based approach based on role theory (Bauer-Ramazani, 2006; Biddle, 1986).

As far as global-mindedness is concerned, *World 101* materials supported several international/global learning goals included in IUPUI's rubric (IUPUI OIA, 2020). Though future research should confirm this with student testimonials and an assessment of their intercultural development, the above lesson analysis revealed uses of *World 101* that take steps in the direction of the following IUPUI global learning goals:

- Have a good working knowledge of the broader world, its natural systems and nations, their characteristics, and their relationship with each other.
- Are able to analyze and evaluate the forces shaping international events, both now and in the past.
- Recognize the many ways "the global is reflected in the local" within the United States and beyond.
- Have reflected upon the distinctive position of the United States on the international stage and have a good, working knowledge of American history and cultural systems.
- Are humble in the face of difference, tolerant of ambiguity and unfamiliarity, and are willing to be in the position of a learner when encountering others.
- Have developed a sense of responsibility and involvement with pressing global issues concerning health, poverty, the environment, conflict, inequality, human rights, civil society, and sustainable economic development.
- Can apply their international learning to diversity in the communities in which they live. (IUPUI, 2020)

As shown above, *World 101*-based lessons introduced the student-designers and the target student populations to regions of the world in factual and critical ways. They highlighted for the students that the local and the global are in interaction with one another in a variety of ways, through historical as well as contemporary geopolitical, environmental, and health-related topics.

12.6 Conclusion

After having success with teaching this course in Spring 2020 online using *World 101*, the author taught the TESOL Methods course online again in Spring 2021 with similar outcomes and feedback from the students. By Spring 2021, the frenzy induced by the debut of the COVID-19 pandemic had subsided somewhat. Regardless, the students' choices from *World 101* were almost identical. The author's institution featured the implementation described in this chapter and several student-designed lesson plans using *World 101* on a university website dedicated to global learning: https://sites.google.com/iu.edu/iupui-global-learning/world-101?authuser=0. Judging by the experience presented in this chapter, the combined exposure of pre- and in-service teachers to CALL and global learning is well worthwhile. The participants in this study engaged with a free online resource with global outlook, benefitting from both its availability—an affordance of CALL—and its focus—which, much like CALL, democratizes education through the representation of diverse global realities and views. In particular, this chapter illustrates the value of blending a global learning focus into an online teacher training course. Teacher training focused on global learning and geopolitical awareness, and global citizenship builds a conceptual basis in global social justice and learner-centered, participatory methods that set teachers up to recognize their role as developmental actors of change (Bourn, 2021, p. 70; Walkington, 2000). Engaging with such material means developing an understanding of global forces, and equipping learners, both directly and those who will benefit in turn from their teachers' instruction, with the means to promote lasting, positive global change (Bourn, 2021, p. 71).

As illustrated by the success this teacher-researcher found when using these materials and the promising global learning outcomes associated with *World 101*, TESOL programs would likely benefit similarly from offering online TESOL Methods courses that introduce pre- and in-service TESOL teachers to both technology and intercultural competence in a similar manner. With the COVID-19 pandemic still continuing, it is important to understand that good quality online teacher education courses, of the likes in which teachers have the opportunity to design lessons, are paramount (Morell, 2020). In those contexts where courses will return to the face-to-face modality post-pandemic, we recommend utilizing *World 101,* or other free resources with global focus, for the horizons they open onto the world.

Appendix

Assignment Prompt

Create a lesson plan focused on writing that uses materials from https://world101.cfr.org/. Review the website and consider what lesson you can create from the information available on a topic of your own choosing. You will need to justify your choice of chapter and topic. Why do you think what you chose is the best fit for the population for which you are designing? Also include a short summary of why the lesson you prepared should meet your language and content goals. Be sure to follow the SIOP lesson plan model or another model provided in the course. Specifying the intended audience, SIOP features included, language and content objectives, materials, targeted skill, topic, materials, and procedural breakdown.

Please cite any external sources used at the end of your assignment.

References

Alexandre, D. H., Junior, E. M., Piurcosky, F. P., & Frogeri, R. F. (2021). Virtualization of internationalization: Inclusion for global learning? In T. DeLaquil, M. Gelashvili, & R. Schendel (Eds.), *Innovative and Inclusive Internationalization: Proceedings of the 2021 WES-CIHE Summer Institute Boston College, WES-CIHE Perspectives, 19* (pp. 31–33). Boston College.

Allen, M., Ene, E., McIntosh, K., & (Eds.). (2022). *Building internationalized spaces: Second language perspectives on developing language and cultural exchange programs in higher education*. University of Michigan Press.

Association of American Colleges and Universities (AAC&U). (2009). *Intercultural knowledge and effectiveness VALUE rubric*. Retrieved from https://www.aacu.org/value/rubrics/intercultural-knowledge

Bauer-Ramazani, C. (2006). Training CALL teachers online. In P. Hubbard & M. Levy (Eds.), *Teacher education in CALL* (pp. 183–200). John Benjamins.

Biddle, B. J. (1986). Recent developments in role theory. *Annual Review of Sociology, 12*, 67–92.

Bourn, D. (2021). Pedagogy of hope: Global learning and the future of education. *International Journal of Development Education and Global Learning, 13*(2), 65–78. https://doi.org/10.14324/ijdegl.13.2.01

Brown, H. D., & Lee, H. (2015). *Teaching by principles: An interactive approach to language pedagogy* (4th ed.). Pearson Education.

Canale, M. (1983). From communicative competence to communicative language pedagogy. In J. C. Richard & R. W. Schmidt (Eds.), *Language and communication* (pp. 2–14). Longman.

Council on Foreign Relations. (2022, October 8). *World101*. https://world101.cfr.org/

Deardorff, D. K. (2006). The identification and assessment of intercultural competence as a student outcome of internationalization at institutions of higher education in the United States. *Journal of Studies in International Education, 10*, 241–266.

Deardorff, D. K. (2009). Implementing intercultural competence assessment. In D. K. Deardorff (Ed.), *The SAGE handbook of intercultural competence* (pp. 477–491). Sage.

Deng, C. H., Wang, J. Q., Zhu, L. M., Liu, H. W., Guo, Y., Peng, X. H., Shao, J. B., & Xia, W. (2020). Association of Web-Based physical education with mental health of college students in Wuhan during the COVID-19 outbreak: Cross-Sectional survey study. *Journal of Medical Internet Research, 22*(10), e21301. https://doi.org/10.2196/21301

Echevarría, J., Vogt, M. E., & Short, D. (2000). *Making content comprehensible for English language learners: The SIOP model*. Allyn and Bacon.

Echevarria, J., Vogt, M., & Short, D. (2017). *Making content comprehensible for secondary English learners: The SIOP model* (3rd ed.). Pearson.

Ene, E. (2021). *Setting the stage for intercultural engagement via professional development.* The TESOL Intercultural Communication Interest Section Newsletter. http://newsmanager.commpartners.com/tesolicis/issues/2021-03-11/2.html.

Fantini, A. E. (2009). Assessing intercultural competence: Issues and tools. In D. Deardoff (Ed.), *Intercultural competence* (pp. 456–476). Sage.

Global Learning @ IUPUI. (2021). https://sites.google.com/iu.edu/iupui-global-learning/world-101?authuser=0

Hovland, K. (2005). Shared futures: Global learning and social responsibility. *Diversity Digest, 8*(3), 1.

Hovland, K. (2014). *Global learning: Defining, designing, demonstrating.* American Association of Colleges and Universities. https://www.aacu.org/GlobalLearning.

Howard, G. R. (2016). *We can't teach what we don't know: White teachers, multiracial schools.* Teachers College Press.

Hubbard, P., & Levy, M. (Eds.). (2006). *Teacher education in CALL.* John Benjamins.

IUPUI Office of International Affairs. (2020, April 6). *IUPUI dimensions of global learning developing global mindsets for all IUPUI students.* Office of International Affairs: Curriculum Internationalization. https://international.iupui.edu/global-learning/curriculum-internationalization/global-dimensions.html

IUPUI Office of International Affairs. (2022, May 23). *International planning efforts are expanding IUPUI's strong foundation of global engagement.* Office of International Affairs: Strategic Planning. https://international.iupui.edu/about/planning.html

Karatay, Y., & Hegelheimer, V. (2021). CALL teacher training - Considerations for low-resource environments: Overview of CALL teacher training. *CALICO Journal, 38*(3), 271–295. https://doi.org/10.1558/cj.20159

Kumaravadivelu, B. (2003). *Beyond methods: Macrostrategies for language teaching.* Yale University Press.

Landorf, H., Doscher, S. P. & Hardrick, J. (2018). *Making global learning universal.* VA: Stylus Publishing.

Morell, T. (2020). EMI teacher training with a multimodal and interactive approach: A new horizon for LSP specialists. *Language Value, 12*(1), 56–87. https://doi.org/10.6035/languagev.2020.12.4

Senyshyn, R. M., & Smith, P. (2019). Global awareness dialogue project: Exploring potential for faculty transformation through a professional development series. *Journal of Transformative Education, 17*(4), 318–336.

Thorne, S. L., & Smith, B. (2011). Second language development theories and technology-mediated language learning. *CALICO Journal, 28*(2), 268–277.

Walkington, H. (2000). The educational methodology of Paulo Freire: To what extent is it reflected in development education in the UK classroom? *The Development Education Journal, 7*(1), 15–17.

Warschauer, M. (2002). A developmental perspective on technology in language education. *TESOL Quarterly, 36*(3), 453–475.

13

Learning to Collaborate Through Telecollaboration: Key Knowledge for Novice Teachers in Today's World

Melinda Dooly

13.1 Introduction

Even before the current pandemic, it had been argued that the current state of globalization poses entirely new empirical challenges (OECD, 2020) for society, and subsequently, for teacher education. These last few decades of technological, social, political, economic and cultural changes demand that teachers rethink the content of what they are teaching, beginning at the core of what comprises distributive knowledge within a framework of continuous interconnectivity (Ulferts, 2021). There have been visible recognition and attempts to integrate the on-offline ecosystem that makes up everyday lives in the field of education (Egan, 2020), and in particular in language teaching and learning (Giannikas et al., 2019). This development was hastened significantly more by the school shutdowns precipitated by the COVID-19 pandemic. However, there had been advances in areas of distanced and telecollaborative teaching in

---

M. Dooly (✉)
Universitat Autònoma de Barcelona, Bellaterra, Spain
e-mail: melindaann.dooly@uab.cat

© The Author(s), under exclusive license to Springer Nature Switzerland AG 2023
K. Sadeghi, M. Thomas (eds.), *Second Language Teacher Professional Development*, Digital Education and Learning, https://doi.org/10.1007/978-3-031-12070-1_13

250   M. Dooly

the decades before the pandemic, in a large part concomitant to greater relative ease of access to technology and improvement in and access to communication technology (Smith, 2017; Thomas & Reinders, 2010). These developments in technology have helped drive learning opportunities for collaborative work between distanced partners and teachers, in particular language learners (Dooly & Vinagre, 2021); much of which is currently being drawn on as 'forced' online teaching continues.

Nonetheless, educational innovation is often decades behind innovation in other areas of society (Glennan et al., 2004) and perhaps more so when it comes to efficiently adopting and adapting to technology used in everyday lives (Ulferts, 2021). Since the 1970s, there has been a call for more student-centred collaborative learning (see Johnson & Johnson, 1975/1999). Collaborative learning is now commonly listed as a key characteristic for pupils of the twenty-first century (Ulferts, 2021) and it is also a commonly cited feature for Virtual Exchange (Dooly & Vinagre, 2021), indicative of a growing general recognition of its applicability and usefulness for teaching and learning languages and cultures. As research, and more significantly, telecollaborative language teaching practice extends to wider berths of educational circles, it is imperative that we have more insight into the ways in which technology-rich environments promote (or not) collaborative learning; both in-person as well as online. Taking a close look at learner interaction in situations designed to promote collaborative learning—without teacher presence, this study aims to identify discursive strategies that support collaborative orientation (Watanabe & Swain, 2007) versus discursive patterns that lead to lower levels of collaboration (Parks et al., 2003).

13.2   Collaborative Learning and Telecollaboration

Optimal integration of telecollaboration into language teaching requires an understanding of how to organize distanced-partner collaboration. There has been considerable research on essential features for collaborative learning in general (Dooly, 2018), as well as studies on telecollaborative learning between distanced student-teachers (O'Dowd & Dooly, 2021). The technology-mediated aspect of geographically distanced collaboration has been a cornerstone for telecollaboration in language education for some time now (Dooly, 2017). This type of teaching and learning exchange is understood as a technology-mediated exchange that is incorporated into teaching to involve students in social interaction and collaboration with distanced partners. Perhaps most importantly, this type of teaching approach is *not* the same as online teaching (as was witnessed *en masse* during the Covid-19 pandemic) because it involves a co-designed and mutually guided learning process between distanced classes; 'it is not a one teacher per class set up' (Dooly & Vinagre, 2021, p. 3) and therefore requires joint collaboration from students as well as between teachers. However, there has also been considerable debate on the correct terminology for these types of exchanges and how to best define these exchanges (Colpaert, 2020); for this chapter, we will use telecollaboration and Virtual Exchange synonymously.

According to Watanabe and Swain (2007), one of the most significant factors in collaborative learning is that the interactants have a collaborative orientation towards the activity. Parks et al. (2003) identify four types or levels of collaboration: joint collaboration with equal responsibility distributed among participants (although contributions to the final output may vary); parallel, yet unequal collaboration with varied contribution to the final product; incidental collaboration made up of brief, sporadic requests for help with the task; and covert collaboration related to looking for resources that may or may not be used in the final output. The first type, joint collaboration, requires a positive interdependence that is considered the most difficult to achieve, yet it is the optimal level of collaborative learning. It is also the type of collaboration that most mimics situations pupils will confront in the near future (OECD, 2020; Ulferts, 2021).

13.3 Data Compilation and Data Management

The video exchanges between preservice language teachers come from weekly online meetings held during a four-month course. There was a total of 36 students enrolled in both classes studying a course on technology-infused language teaching (TILT). Ten were studying in a university in the USA and 26 were studying in Spain. All of the students were minimally B2 level of English, several were C1 level and there was one L1 speaker of English in one of the groups included in this study.

The students were divided into five working groups, with members from both universities, and a weekly meeting time was arranged for each group. Each meeting was guided with specific instructions aimed to help the groups assimilate the theoretical foundations and practical know-how to design telecollaboration for project-based language learning in primary and secondary schools. At the end of the term, the telecollaborative projects were then presented to other teachers in local professional education associations.

The teachers were not present at the meetings and the participants were expected to self-organize their weekly sessions. Students self-recorded the meetings and shared them with the teachers. Written consent was given for anonymized use of the recording (transcripts) and their developed materials.

All the recordings were viewed before selecting the video fragments to be transcribed. Following Du Bois (1991), we have adopted a transcription system based on widely used notional conventions to make them as accessible to the reader as possible. The key for the notations is included in the annex.

For our analysis, video-recorded data came from two working groups. Group 1 (G1) consisted of two students in the USA (one from Brazil, the other from Germany, both with C2 levels of English) and five from Spain, with B2-C1 English level. The second group (G2), was made up of six students in Spain; five of whom had C1 level English. One student was an exchange student from Russia, with a B2 level. From the USA, one of the member's L1 was English while the second student was proficient in both English and Spanish. The analysis looks at fragments from detailed transcriptions of two synchronous online meetings, one at the beginning of the term, the other at the last. All names have been changed to keep participants anonymous.

13.4 Analysis

For the first meeting, the groups were asked to look over sample telecollaborative projects that had been created by students from earlier iterations of the same course and following an ice-breaking activity, the groups discussed the projects. A group leader had been assigned for the meeting before it began. Guiding discussion points were provided to help them consider the projects from both teacher and student perspectives, ponder potential challenges in implementation, identify main language learning goals and reflect on how well these goals were supported.

We begin with G1. Elisa takes the leader role. At the beginning of the meeting, Elisa suggests how the group can proceed (lines 2–4) and then opens the discussion by providing her own example (lines 10–22), which, notably, focuses on how the telecollaborative project can support language learning (Fragment 13.1).

Fragment 13.1 It's recording now

	Participants: USA: Helena, Elisa; Spain: Clara, Joana, Elisabet, Rocio, Luisa	
	Mins:	00:00–02:29
1	???	ok\ it's recording now\
2	ELI	((smiles)) ok (.) then i'll repeat what i just said:\ ((inhales)) maybe we can just go through
3		and: tell each other what paper we read: and what we liked/ and what we **did**n't like and
4		what we would improve if we like- rewrote the paper\
5		((Clara, Júlia, Hana and Àngela nod their heads. Ana is quite distant from the screen.
6		Raquel is facing a different direction from the screen))
7	ELI	ehm: i wrote the one- i **read** the one about: wrote the one hee hee (.) i didn't wrote- i
8		didn't write it hee hee
9		((giggles))
10	ELI	I **read** the one about gender stereotypes/ (.) ((Hana nods her head)) I really liked it\ (.)
11		em that's also what i like to do with my students in German\ because- i don't know how it
12		is in Spanish but in German we have clearly feminine and clearly masculine forms/ and

(continued)

254   M. Dooly

Fragment 13.1 (continued)

		Participants: USA: Helena, Elisa; Spain: Clara, Joana, Elisabet, Rocio, Luisa
	Mins:	00:00–02:29
13		now this term of gendering/ everything comes up/ so: that marking that it's neither nor
14		feminine nor masculine (.) and lot of people write about that and say this is not what we
15		want with our language etcetera it's not good what is happening etcetera here and then i
16		like to tell the ok let's draw i don't know an italian and i give them five minutes to draw
17		an italian and they all draw a man\ (.) and then i get that's why we @need to@
18		change the terms in the language because women are also there and non-binary
19		people are ALSO there but we think of the male terms if we use the male terms uhm and
20		i think they did something similar/ they just let people drew-draw fireworkers or i don't
21		know\ (.) like specific jobs that are either male or female/ ehm:: which i really liked
22		ehm:: so the idea was really nice ehm:: the only thing i didn't like about the paper is i
23		searched for like a conclusion part/ which i couldn't find so where was there like insight
24		from this lesson which i think maybe lacked\ but (.) **yeah** otherwise i think it's a cool
25		lesson or a cool research\ ((inhales)) what about you/ what did you read and what did you
26		like/ or (.) do you agree with me or do you not agree with me/ hee hee
27		(5)
28	LUI	well: i can talk if you want:
29	ELI	**yeah** ((smiles))
30	LUI	uhm yeah\ (.) i totally agree with you\
31	ELI	((nods)) uh huhm
32	LUI	and well i read another one which was let's exchange our legends (.) i don't know if you have read it/
33	ELI	uh huhm
34	Chorus	uh huhm ((several nod their heads))
		(meeting continues in this fashion; each member explaining and supporting each other's answers))

13 Learning to Collaborate Through Telecollaboration: Key...   255

Elisa is careful to ensure that others are encouraged to take part in the interactional moves by opening the floor to others. For instance, in line 25 she says: what about you/ what did you read and what did you like. In parallel, she remarks that she is open to contradictory opinions: do you agree with me or do you not agree with me/ hee hee (line 26). When Luisa indicates that she is willing to take the floor, Elisa is supportive of her intervention (lines 29, 31, 32). Throughout the transcription there is very little overlap or interruptions during other turns and Elisa nods, smiles and provides encouraging tokens such as 'uh huhm' and 'yeah' frequently. Despite Elisa's quite long first intervention (lines 10–26), the rest of the meeting interaction is evenly distributed among the different participants. She also allows long pauses during the interactional unfolding (line 27).

In G2's first meeting, the discussion leader, Rosa, is the predominant speaker throughout the meeting. In a tightly controlled discussion that follows the instructions very closely (versus the more open interpretation that Elisa had adopted for her group), Rosa introduces the projects through a round of short-answer questions ('who saw this project?'; lines 7 and 8). The discursive style of the meeting is more like a teacher-pupil interaction than a collaborative peer discussion as it resembles the well-established teacher interactional pattern of IRE (Initiation-Response-Evaluate; Mehan, 1979). There is little encouragement for expansion on the other participants' answers and most of them answer either with gestures (lines 12, 13, 16, 21) or very short responses (lines 12–16; 19, 23, 25). The IRE-type interaction lasts nearly five minutes, with extremely short pauses (Fragment 13.2).

Fragment 13.2 Let's start talking about the collaborative projects ...

		Participants: USA: Rosa, Ethan; Spain: Alicia, Lorena, Mila, Susana, Sasha, Lila
	Mins:	00:12–02:39
1	ROS	ehm::: so: now/ let's start talking about the collaborative projects/ ((shares screen to
2		show meeting instructions)) ok/
3		((Screen recording shows participants on side of screen. At one point Lorena

(continued)

256   M. Dooly

Fragment 13.2 (continued)

	Participants: USA: Rosa, Ethan; Spain: Alicia, Lorena, Mila, Susana, Sasha, Lila	
	Mins:	00:12–02:39
4		yawns. Everyone is looking at the camera except Ethan.))
5	???	°ok°
6	ROS	so just to get acquainted with it (.) let's see which one did we choose/ (.) for
7		example how many people chose ((scrolls through projects titles on screen)) °let's
8		see\ (.) is there a way I can see people here/ how many people chose the: uh- water
9		we doing to our planet/ (.) >did anyone chose that one< ((raises her hand)) did
10		so just to get acquainted with it (.) let's see which one did we choose/ (.) for
11		anyone choose that one/
12	ALI	no\ ((shakes her head))
13		((Lorena shakes her head))
14	???	no\
15	ROS	no/ (.) **how**: about\ gender stereotypes in writing\
16	LIL	me\ ((raises her hand with a finger pointed upwards))
17	ROS	great\ lila\ (.) susana\ (.) anyone else/ no one/ ok\ how about tales of tomorrow/ (.)
18		[no/]
19	ALI	[me\]
20	ROS	ok alicia\ (.) good\wa-wat (.) waster- yes - waster fighters/no: (.) how can we make
21		positive changes towards climate change/ (.) no: (.) small steps can change the
22		world/ me\ ((raises hand))
23	SUS	me\
24	ROS	susana too/(.) anyone else/
25	ALI	me\
26	ROS	ahh\ you too alicia\ great:
27	02:39–03:20 ((went through the entire list of projects in this manner for 2 minutes))	

Rosa had asked each member to explain why they had chosen the projects. She closely follows the order of the guiding questions provided for the discussion leader rather than allowing a more naturally flowing discussion to develop between the participants. Mila had attempted to

13 Learning to Collaborate Through Telecollaboration: Key... 257

expand a bit more on the positive features of the project she had chosen to present (she focused on linguistic and intercultural exchange as positive aspects; not included in the transcription for brevity). However, at one point she struggles with a specific word. This prompts Rosa to interrupt and then to synthesize what she appears to understand regarding the point Mila was trying to make (lines 1, 3, 5. Her overlap (and interpretation) of Mila's explanation is eventually accepted by Mila, although somewhat faintly (a quiet yes in line 6) (Fragment 13.3).

Fragment 13.3 The opportunity to know other cultures

	Participants: USA: Rosa, Ethan; Spain: Alicia, Lorena, Mila, Susana, Sasha, Lila	
	Mins:	15:26–15:32
1	ROS	oh yeah/ so it was very centred on this intercultural component right/
2	MIL	yes-
3	ROS	[of getting to XXX]
4	MIL	[and the final-] sorry sorry\
5	ROS	and to get to know each others as cultures\ right/
6	MIL	°yes\°
7	(…)	
	Mins:	16:03–17:06
8	ROS	/ok\ so: how about [lorena:/] you have many ideas/
9	LOR	[well-]
10	LOR	((laughs)) yes\ i @had too much@ but i had that one as mila too and- and i wanted to
11		add that ehm:: i think that working collaboratively with ah- kids from other parts of the
12		world is really motivating: for the students because they are making friends ((uses scare
13		quotes)) or saying- and in this- in this ah: age i think it's really important for them and
14		well- bueno i wanted to add that\ and:: one of my: many: ((laughs))
15	ROS	don't forget to- excuse me lorena before you continue \ >don't forget to tell us briefly
16		what the project was about/ what you like and don't like from the teacher's perspective
17		and the students' perspective and what was the final product and the activities and the

(continued)

258   M. Dooly

Fragment 13.3 (continued)

		Participants: USA: Rosa, Ethan; Spain: Alicia, Lorena, Mila, Susana, Sasha, Lila
	Mins:	15:26–15:32
18		overall sequencing of the project contributes to uh the final product to making the final
19		product\<
20	(…)	
	Mins:	18:39–19:10
21	ROS	ok/ that's fantastic\ (.) did you mention the final product/
22	LOR	it's like a game (.) you don't have to= ((makes a slashing gesture with her hand))
23	ROS	=[so yeah yeah there's no final product]
24	LOR	[you don't have to achieve-]
25	ROS	so what about a reflection at the end/ maybe a reflection at the end of the game/ what
26		they have learnt with it/
27	LOR	there are like different missions and °you have to achieve different levels and go up to
28		win the game\°
29	(…)	
	Mins:	19:10–19:42
30	ALI	((briefly explains the project she liked))
	Mins:	19:47–19:52
31	ROS	>ok:::< so does anyone want to add anything about the projects before we wrap up/ >no
32		one/<
33		((several people shake their heads))

In line 8, Rosa then invites Lorena to continue, although her comment could be interpreted as a teacher-type mechanism (she implies that Lorena has intervened more than most). Lorena, who is the most outspoken of the Spanish university participants, seems to jokingly accept that she has self-allocated a lot of turns (line 10). Lorena then elaborates on Mila's turn regarding the project Mila has chosen before offering another one for discussion. However at this point, Rosa interrupts again in line 15 to remind Lorena that she should follow the points set in the instructions and then provides her a long list of features that she should include in her comments (lines 15–19). Lorena then finishes her turn rather quickly, without covering all these points, as Rosa mentions in line 21. Lorena provides a short answer and then Alicia gives a brief outline of her

13 Learning to Collaborate Through Telecollaboration: Key... 259

project. Following this, no one appears to be willing to discuss their chosen projects in much detail (lines 32 and 33).

In this group's meeting, there are frequent interruptions by the leader, extremely short pauses and latching of comments by Rosa during turn-relevance places (natural lags in conversations where a participant can initiate a turn). By the end of the meeting, the discussion is mostly between Rosa and Lorena. The rest of the participants contribute very little verbally and there is also very little non-verbal interaction.

In contrast, in G1, the discussion of the chosen projects was much more open and participative and continues to focus on aspects of language teaching (lines 1–3, 5, 10–11; 24–25) (Fragment 13.4).

Fragment 13.4 Our main goal is to learn

		Participants: USA: Helena, Elisa; Spain: Clara, Joana, Elisabet, Rocio, Luisa
		08.49 to 10:42
1	CLA	(…) i think that if we are carrying out a project in which our main goal is to learn (.) a
2		foreign language/ maybe we can provide some kinds of support in order to ensure that
3		children can acquire this language (.) and for sure that they can be able use it in a
4		discussion (.) so there is no need to think that they cannot do it/ (.) but that if we: >as
5		teachers< provide them with the necessary support they for sure that can do it\
6		((Elisa and Joana both nod their heads vigorously when Clara mentions support. Luisa
7		nods slightly less empathically. Hana is looking at the camera but does not do anything.
8		Rocio and Elisabet are turned away from the camera.))
9	ELI	yeah:(.) that's a very good point (.) i wanted to raise the exact same point hee hee hee (.)
10		providing them with sentence starters or phrases (.) you can do so much to like let them
11		speak in the language learnt in the classroom\ (.) yeah- i agree with you clara\ (.) any
12		other points or criticisms you would have/
13		((Clara nods vigorously while Elisa is talking. Joana nods less noticeably. Clara smiles

(continued)

260   M. Dooly

Fragment 13.4 (continued)

		Participants: USA: Helena, Elisa; Spain: Clara, Joana, Elisabet, Rocio, Luisa
14		broadly when Elisa giggles.))
15		(5)
16	???	°hmmm°
17		(1)
18	LUI	((eyes scanning, seems to be towards bottom of the screen. Perhaps looking to unmute
19		mic))
20	LUI	well i: i have also seen that there are a few projects ((gestures with her hands downward))
21		in which they work through a theatre/ (.) ((pushes her hair behind her ears)) like theatre
22		performance ((gestures again)) and i don't know what you think about it ((slightly covers
23		her face with hand then moves hair again then begins gesturing with hands all the way till
24		the end of her utterance)) but i think it's a good way to know how to express yourself in
25		english in front of a public and it's a great way to to work with it/ (.) and: yeah i find it
26		quite interesting/
27	ELI	[uh huhm] ((nods))
28	CLA	[uh huhm] ((nods))
29		((Helena and Joana both nod))
30		(10)
31	ELI	anything else you want to comment on/ (.) i think this is our main goal isn't it/ (.) we are
32		to write such a paper/ ha ha ha
33		((laughter))
34	ELI	((smiling)) seems like a bit of work: (.) but ok/
35		((laughter))
36	(…)	
	Mins:	11:40–12:00
37	ELI	yeah:: (.) anything other further comments (.) ru- we **did a great job** hee hee what?
38		we finished our last point after a half an **hour**/ hee hee \ that's crazy (.)
39		((laughter. Everyone smiles))
40	ELI	i mean that's great\ but if anyone wants to raise another point (.) i'm fine with that\

13 Learning to Collaborate Through Telecollaboration: Key... 261

Elisa allows for much longer turns by the other participants, followed by supportive comments, for example in line 9, yeah:(.) that's a very good point (.) i wanted to raise the exact same point and also affirmative interjections (line 27). Elisa allows very long moments of silence (5 seconds, line 15; 10 seconds, line 30); a wait time which may actually contribute to more contributions and participation (Rowe, 1974).

Rosa appears to be focused principally on the organizational aspects of the online group work and in her focus on task, adopts a 'teacher-centred' discursive style. In contrast, Elisa works to create a collaborative atmosphere in which she presents a supportive response to the other contributions and elicits trust by providing examples while listening to and encouraging other points of view, and building up a sense of a team (in line 40, she exclaims 'we did a great job').

We now look briefly at the last required meetings of the two groups (both groups arranged for an extra-official meeting to finalize their projects). For this meeting, students were given instructions to revise their project drafts in light of observations made by other peers and teachers from the previous week.

In the G1's meeting, the person who had been assigned to be discussion leader (Helena) was absent (Fragment 13.5).

Fragment 13.5 We can all be the leader

	Participants: USA: Elisa; Spain: Clara, Joana, Elisabet, Rocio, Luisa	
	Mins:	00:00–00:21
1	ELI	°ok° ((holds a thumb up)) @right@
2		((everyone smiles))
3	CHORUS	((giggles))
4	JOA	well:: (.) now we are only missing a leader (.) right/
5	ELI	°yes::° (.) i mean we can all be the leader (.) it's our final meeting\
6		((shrugs shoulder))
7	JOA	yes\
8	CLA	[yes\]
9	LUI	[yes\]
10	ELI	°we're good at [group work hee hee\]

262   M. Dooly

As with the first meeting, we see that Elisa continues in the role of group 'cheerleader', (we're all capable of leading, line 5; we're good at group work; line 10). The participants effectively share responsibility of deciding how to proceed, although in the end, Elisa appears to take more of the leader role (line 4). This can be seen as a natural unfolding of the progression of the interaction since it has been Clara who has pointed out that Elisa had facilitated some prior work in a whatsapp text to advance their progress (Fragment 13.6, line 2).

During the rest of the meeting (which lasted an hour longer than had been allocated), the participants systematically worked through each of the comments made by their peers and teachers, contributing equally and in similar patterns to the way in which they had interacted in meeting 1. At the end of the meeting, the participants assigned tasks to each member to be completed, after having arranged an extra meeting. As we can see in lines 1 and 5, Elisa continues with her positive assessment of the group effort, reinforcing the image of the collective over individualistic work, to which Joana concurs (line 6), adding that 'it was worth it' (Fragment 13.7).

Fragment 13.6 Maybe we can look at …

		Participants: USA: Elisa; Spain: Clara, Joana, Elisabet, Rocio, Luisa
		Mins: 01:23–01:50
1	CLA	maybe we can take a look at the ehm: (.) final project criteria/ that i have seen that you
2		have sent something through whatsapp/
3	ELI	((nodding head))
4	ELI	uh huhm ((nods head, smiles)) (.) we could also just walk through the paper ((gestures
5		with hands as if moving through
6		points downwards)) cause i've think some had questions and we can just walk through
7		the document and then see where questions arise and then split up more work if we
8		have more work\ yeah/
9		((Clara, Elisabet and Luisa nod their heads))
10	CLA	yes
11	JOA	°yes°
12	ELI	perfect\ (.) let me open it (.) hee hee ((clicking sounds, Clara smiles)) ehm:

13 Learning to Collaborate Through Telecollaboration: Key... 263

Fragment 13.7 Perfect

		Participants: USA: Elisa; Spain: Clara, Joana, Elisabet, Rocio, Luisa
	Mins:	01:43:48–01:44:08
1	ELI	ok **perfect**/ ((she types in the names for the last assignment, stretches
2		her arms)) oh::: ((yawning))
3	JOA	[((laughs))]
4	ELI	[((laughs))]
5	ELI	i'm proud of us hee hee\
6	JOA	this was hard work but worth it because if not/
7	ELI	yeah\
8	JOA	after we started taking out things and it was nonsense it was like: (.) @oh
9		my go::d@
10	ELI	@yeah@ (.) i agree\ (.) hee hee

This collaborative, dialogic interaction stands in sharp contrast to the G2's final meeting. Coincidentally, this group's appointed leader was also absent so Rosa took the lead (there is no evidence in the recording that this was negotiated although it may have taken place before the recording started).

Rosa begins with a problem-posing statement (line 1, 'we were attempting to do too much') and then after outlining more specific problems (lines 10–14) she proceeds to elaborate a proposal that completely changes the project focus that the group had been working on since the beginning of the term (lines 24–28). Significantly, Rosa's proposal is far less didactically focused on language learning than the original plan. This change in orientation seems to confuse and annoy the other members (line 15). In presenting her ideas, Rosa speaks very quickly, with few pauses, even at times speeding up her speech at transition-relevant places where a change of speaker might occur (lines 16–17, Alicia appears to be preparing for a turn) (Fragment 13.8).

Rosa holds the floor, almost completely un-interrupted for the first eight minutes of the 43-minute, 15-second meeting. She facilitates few moments for others to take the floor and performs far fewer discursive strategies to encourage and support other contributions.

264   M. Dooly

Fragment 13.8   We were attempting to do too much

	Participants: USA: Rosa, Ethan; Spain: Alicia, Lorena, Mila, Susana, Sasha	
	Mins:	00:26–08:02

1	ROS	ok everyone\ so i think this project/ (.) yea:h we were attempting to do too much\ right:/
2	ALI	°eh hem°=
3	ROS	=so i think it would be a good idea to- can you see my screen/
4	ALI	no
5	MIL	not yet
6	ROS	ok\ ehm: (.) give me a moment please\ (.) >ok yes< can you see it now/ ((screen
7		shows))
8	ALI	[yes]
9	MIL	[yes]
10	ROS	>oh so:< i think it would be a good idea to do it as na:rrow as possible i think you saw
11		this/ that i made the final outcome right/ that it was supposed to be: *how* social how
12		ehm social media promotes consumerism right/ and then i put the *consequence* of
13		consumerism and the *environment* and the *consumers* and a call to action and i think
14		that's too much\ right/ because we have to teach every single we are saying\ right/
15		((Mila looks confused; Susana looks annoyed; Ethan is looking away from the screen))
16	ALI	[eh hem] ((moves closer to the camera; shifts position; opens mouth slightly))
17	ROS	[((takes quick breath)) another thing] is that maybe: or at least i was thinking about
18		digital marketing\ digital strategies\ and maybe we don't know much about it and we
19		need to know the content we are teaching right/ ((takes quick breath)) so:: ehm: it's
20		something very specific for markers right/ like how markers target eh: teams\ and i was
21		looking for that type of content ((screen shows her quickly clicking through a EU
22		working document on promoting lifelong skills; two example project)) and it's not like
23		there is a specific you know like eh: *topics* that you can look somewhere around and

(continued)

Fragment 13.8 (continued)

	Participants: USA: Rosa, Ethan; Spain: Alicia, Lorena, Mila, Susana, Sasha
	Mins: 00:26–08:02
24	then teach\> you know/< so i was thinking about maybe just decide >to do ehm:
25	rhetorical appeals\< i don't know if you have heard about that/ ethos pathos and
26	logos/it- it's something very useful in life and it's something is relatively simple to
27	teach right >ok< so in commercials there are usually three appeals ethos which is an
28	appeal to character (...)
29	((Rosa continues talking uninterrupted until 08:02))

13.5 Synthesis of the Findings

At the end of the term, G1 turned in one project that received very positive feedback from both teachers and an external examiner whereas G2 requested special permission to split into two groups—the USA members and the Spanish members and produced separate projects. Both of the projects were scored low by the teachers and external examiner for lack of specific focus on language teaching.

One of the most noticeable differences in interaction between the two groups is the distribution of talking time. In the first group, the leader takes a guiding role and is careful to make sure the group stays on task and stays focused on the didactic issues of the project. She also ensures that others are encouraged to take a turn in the talking and does not usually interrupt the others when they are speaking. Contributions are evenly distributed among the participants through the meetings and while Elisa does take some longer turns to exemplify points, the others do so as well. As leader, she takes very long pauses, providing key moments for others to initiate a turn and is a positive supporter of the contributions. It is proposed that Elisa's discursive strategies contribute to a collaborative orientation (Watanabe & Swain, 2007) towards varied, but parallel contributions towards the final project.

In contrast Rosa tends to dominate the talk while taking extremely long turns with few pauses. She displays far fewer discursive strategies to encourage and support other contributions. Elisa's intervention seems to lead to a higher level of dialogic discussion than attained in Rosa's group. The second group exhibits incidental collaboration with brief, sporadic requests for contributions to the task (Parks et al., 2003) and in the final meeting, Rosa presents an entirely new idea for the project with little dialogic space for negotiation regarding these changes.

13.6 Conclusion

While it is not within the scope of this brief analysis to venture conjectures on why the collaborations in the groups were so dissimilar, it is of interest for teacher educators to bear in mind how differently the two exchanges developed and ended. As the pandemic has made painfully clear, online collaborative learning is here to stay and this will inevitably impact individual academic achievement. Ensuring that technology-rich environments such as these are effective is imperative for teacher education, especially given that 'joint collaborations' (Parks et al., 2003) both in-person and increasingly online are becoming essential skills for learners (OECD, 2020; Ulferts, 2021). One way forward is to harness the lessons learnt from previous work done on telecollaboration, combined with the abundant findings that are emerging from research on online teaching during the pandemic. Learning to collaborate through telecollaboration has been advocated as paramount for the digital citizen (Ulferts, 2021), while, unfortunately, the technopedagogical skills to introduce these competences to students (in particular younger pupils) remain elusive for many novice and experienced teachers in today's world, despite the abundant experience of online teaching brought about by the pandemic (OECD, 2021).

Looking forward, post-pandemic, it will remain crucial that teacher educators continue to integrate telecollaborative elements into their classes. However they cannot assume that assignments for groups will instinctively translate into collaborative learning, nor that the didactic elements of language teaching will automatically emerge. The use of recorded data for student work that is not teacher oriented can help teacher educators identify key language teaching principles that emerge for positive reinforcement or require further scrutiny.

Finally, encouraging student-teachers to analyse their online interactions can assist them in identifying discursive strategies that help achieve (or not) collaboration and thus deepen their understanding of how to support collaborative learning. Thus they will then be better prepared to orient online exchanges that promote effective telecollaboration with their future pupils.

Transcript key

text:	elongation of syllable
((text))	transcriber notes
(...)	transcribed text left out
>text<	faster utterance
text-	truncated utterance
[text]	overlapping utterances
[text]	
text/	rising pitch
text\	falling pitch
text==text	latching utterances
(.)	short pause of less than 0.5 seconds
(1)	pause of 1 second (number given)
@text@	laughing voice
°text°	uttered quietly
text	uttered more loudly for emphasis

References

Colpaert, J. (2020). Editorial position paper: How virtual is your research? *Computer Assisted Language Learning, 33*(7), 653–664. https://doi.org/10.1080/09588221.2020.1824059

Dooly, M. (2017). Telecollaboration. In C. Chapelle & S. Sauro (Eds.), *The handbook of technology in second language teaching and learning* (pp. 169–183). Wiley-Blackwell.

Dooly, M. (2018). Collaborative learning. In J. I. Liontas & M. DelliCarpini (Eds.), *The TESOL encyclopedia of English language teaching* (pp. 1–7). John Wiley & Sons.

Dooly, M., & Vinagre, M. (2021). Research into practice: Virtual exchange in language teaching and learning. *Language Teaching, 55*(3), 392–406. https://doi.org/10.1017/S0261444821000069

Du Bois, J. W. (1991). Transcription design principles for spoken discourse research. *Pragmatics, 1*(1), 71–106. https://doi.org/10.1075/prag.1.1.04boi

Egan, A. (2020). *A review of technology in teaching and learning.* Education International. https://issuu.com/educationinternational/docs/2020_ei_research_technologyteaching_eng_final.

Giannikas, C. N., Constantinou, E. K., & Papadima-Sophocleous, S. (Eds.). (2019). *Professional development in CALL: A selection of papers.* Research-publishing.net. https://doi.org/10.14705/rpnet.2019.28.9782490057283

Glennan, T. K., Jr., Bodily, S. J., Galegher, J. R., & Kerr, K. A. (2004). *Expanding the reach of education reforms: Perspectives from leaders in the scale-up of educational interventions.* Rand.

Johnson, D. W., & Johnson, R. T. (1999 [1975]). *Learning together and alone: Cooperative, competitive and individualistic learning* (5th ed.). Allyn & Bacon.

Mehan, H. (1979). *Learning lesson.* Harvard University Press.

O'Dowd, R., & Dooly, M. (2021). Exploring teachers' professional development through participation in virtual exchange. *ReCALL, 34*(1), 21–36. https://doi.org/10.1017/S0958344021000215

OECD. (2020). *PISA 2018 results (volume VI): Are students ready to thrive in an interconnected world?* PISA, OECD Publishing. https://doi.org/10.1787/d5f68679-en

OECD. (2021). *Using digital technologies for early education during COVID-19: OECD report for the G20 2020 education working group.* OECD Publishing. https://doi.org/10.1787/fe8d68ad-en

Parks, S., Huot, D., Hamers, J., & Huot-Lemonnier, F. (2003). Crossing boundaries: Multimedia technology and pedagogical innovation in a high school class. *Language Learning & Technology, 7*(1), 28–4. 10125/25186.

Rowe, M. B. (1974). Pausing phenomena: Influence on the quality of instruction. *Journal of Psycholinguistic Research, 3*(3), 203–224. https://doi.org/10.1007/BF01069238

Smith, B. (2017). *Technology in language learning: An overview.* Routledge.

Thomas, M., & Reinders, H. (2010). *Task-based language learning and teaching with technology.* Continuum.

Ulferts, H. (Ed.). (2021). *Teaching as a knowledge profession: Studying pedagogical knowledge across education systems.* Educational Research and Innovation, OECD Publishing. https://doi.org/10.1787/e823ef6e-en

Watanabe, Y., & Swain, M. (2007). Effects of proficiency differences and patterns of pair interaction on second language learning: Collaborative dialogue between adult ESL learners. *Language Teaching Research, 11*(2), 121–142. https://doi.org/10.1177/136216880607074599

14

Opportunities for Pre-Service Teacher Learning in Video-Mediated Peer Interactions: Focus on Classroom Interactional Competence

Ufuk Balaman

14.1 Introduction

The language teacher education (henceforth LTE) approach in this chapter has recently been conceptualized as Conversation Analytic Language Teacher Education (CALTE; Balaman, 2023). CALTE aims to maintain an evidence-based, data-led, reflective approach to LTE based on previously uncharted knowledge and praxis bases. While the knowledge base comprises an ever-growing theoretical infrastructure drawing on Conversation Analysis (CA) research mainly on L2 classroom interactional settings (cf. Sert, 2015 for an overview), the praxis base includes preparation (e.g., lesson planning conferences, task design conversations; cf. Ekin et al., 2021; Badem-Korkmaz et al., 2022), implementation (e.g., practicum teaching), and revision (e.g., post-observation conferences after

U. Balaman (✉)
Department of English Language Teaching, Hacettepe University, Çankaya/Ankara, Turkey

© The Author(s), under exclusive license to Springer Nature Switzerland AG 2023
K. Sadeghi, M. Thomas (eds.), *Second Language Teacher Professional Development*, Digital Education and Learning, https://doi.org/10.1007/978-3-031-12070-1_14

practicum) procedures. Overall, the perspective requires increasing pre-service teachers' awareness of the CALTE knowledge base for the purpose of eliciting pre-service teacher learning outcomes across the diverse phases of the praxis base. Relatedly, the research-oriented stance of CALTE calls for the generation of natural data during the operationalization of the knowledge and praxis bases for the sustainable development of this LTE approach and the examination of such data using multimodal CA as the research methodology. While the praxis base has been enriched to some extent, the operationalization of the knowledge base, which refers to the teaching of the CA findings on L2 instructional settings as actionable knowledge for pre-service teachers (cf. Huth, 2021; Waring & Creider, 2021), remains to be an LTE challenge. Nevertheless, there have been diverse attempts to tackle this challenge by utilizing research findings and actual classroom recordings as LTE materials in dedicated CALTE models (e.g., IMDAT, Sert, 2015, 2021; SETT, Walsh, 2006; SWEAR, Waring, 2021). However, the affordances of digital spaces for this purpose have remained unexplored to date despite the huge potential.

To further elaborate, within the scope of his influential model, IMDAT, Sert (2021) argued for the positive impact of CA findings on L2 classrooms on teacher development in the first step (i.e., introducing Classroom Interactional Competence; CIC) of the model claiming that the impact would be maximized if such training resources include video recordings (and their transcripts in fine-grained detail) of experienced teachers. Another contribution to this perspective is Waring's (2021) SWEAR model which dedicates a major space to language teachers' active engagement with the recordings of actual language classrooms. In this LTE perspective, the recordings can come from open video repositories (e.g., TalkBank, Youtube) or from subject-specific ones such as Corpus of English for Academic and Professional Purposes (CEAPP) upon consent and the researchers' earlier projects of relevance. Therefore, access to target-specific videos and viewing them along with detailed transcripts play a prominent role in CALTE and commonly require setting up technology-rich LTE environments to deliver pedagogically sound LTE activities.

Regarding pedagogical soundness, in an earlier work, Seedhouse (2008) noted that the affordances of transcribed videos are maximized when they are critically examined by practitioners. Accordingly, despite their rich implications for teacher learning, showing videos and transcripts would be limited in scope if pre-service teachers are not provided with opportunities to critically examine the interactional practices of (preferably) experienced teachers, which aligns with diverse perspectives toward video use in teacher education (Baecher et al., 2018; Christ et al., 2017; Mann et al., 2019; Seidel et al., 2013). Among these perspectives are video clubs and videography activities that take place in digital spaces and aim to enable teacher collaboration through the critical examination of the recordings of other teachers' classroom teaching, and in return create teacher learning opportunities (e.g., Blell & von Bremen, 2020; Blume & Schmidt, 2020; Dobie & Anderson, 2015; van Es, 2012).

Therefore, the operationalization of the CALTE knowledge base to ensure an awareness of L2 classroom interactional realities in pre-service LTE and expecting transferrable teacher learning outcomes are increasingly becoming an integral part of LTE. To these ends, this chapter sets out to bring evidence for the affordances of digital spaces and presents a case study showcasing the emergent pre-service teacher learning opportunities in and through video-mediated peer interactions. The following research questions describe the coverage of the present study:

1. What are the interactional resources deployed by the pre-service teachers while collaboratively analyzing short video clips in video-mediated peer interactions?
2. What kinds of teacher learning opportunities emerge during the pre-service teachers' video-mediated interactions?

14.2 Data and Context

The data for current study comes from an LTE project that took place during the pandemic. As part of a fully online (due to COVID-19 pandemic) course module (i.e., Analysis of Discourse and Language Teaching) at the third year (sixth semester) of a four-year undergraduate English language teacher education program in Turkey, the data were collected from diverse teacher education activities. The course contents and delivery modes were restructured for a complete compatibility with online education means. Accordingly, the course pursued a three-part structure combining asynchronous and synchronous modes of delivery. In Part 1, the teacher trainer posted lecture captures on the course management system, and the pre-service teachers based in the department of English Language Teaching delivered their lecture-related questions on an asynchronous discussion forum after watching the lectures. In Part 2, the pre-service teachers were given some reading tasks and submitted their reflective summaries of the shared articles on another asynchronous forum. In Part 3, pre-service teachers met with their peers in groups of four (without the presence of the lecturer or a moderator) using Microsoft Teams for so-called Analysis and Discussion meetings via synchronous video-mediated interactions.

In line with the CALTE perspective, the lecturer identified an exclusive focus on multimodal CA as an approach to analyzing naturally occurring discourse and its impact on language teaching. Accordingly, the three-part structure was repeated for the main constructs of CA, namely turn taking (Weeks 3–5), sequence and preference organization (Weeks 5–7), repair (Weeks 8–11), and embodiment (Weeks 12–14). The 14-week course started with an introduction to course contents (Week 1) and to the construct, Classroom Interactional Competence (Walsh, 2006, 2013; also see; Sert, 2015; Can Daşkın, 2015) (Week 2), and the three-part structure for each construct followed. To better establish the link between CA and language teaching, the lecturer shared an additional lecture capture (i.e., in Part 1) including a sample classroom video analysis and selected all course materials based on their relevance to L2 classroom interaction. Therefore, the course aimed to equip pre-service teachers with (a) the actionable disciplinary knowledge required for a discursive understanding of language classrooms in lecture and sample analysis formats (Part 1), (b) the means for critically analyzing published work on the constructs and improving their familiarity with L2 classroom discourse (Part 2), (c) ways for putting their emerging knowledge on these constructs into practice while collaboratively analyzing a short video clip taken from an actual language classroom (Part 3), and overall reflective lessons for their future practices mainly with reference to the affordances of L2 teacher talk. In doing so, the course provided opportunities for the operationalization of the CALTE knowledge base— that is, by increasing the pre-service teachers' knowledge about Classroom Interactional Competence.

14 Opportunities for Pre-Service Teacher Learning... 273

This chapter primarily deals with Part 3 (video-mediated peer interactions during Analysis and Discussion meetings) and presents one instance showing how the course structure created pre-service teacher learning opportunities in and through the pre-service teachers' critical analyses of teacher interactional practices based on a short video clip from an actual language classroom. The short clip also included the transcript of the classroom interaction and the pre-service teachers examined the recordings collaboratively in response to two guiding questions: "What do you observe in the recording in terms of sequence and preference organization? What do you think about the role of sequence and preference organization practices in this language classroom?" Although the same procedure was repeated for the four constructs, this chapter presents a snapshot (three minutes) from the second cycle (i.e., sequence and preference organization).

Against this background and drawing on the methodological underpinnings of multimodal CA (cf. Sidnell & Stivers, 2013; Mondada, 2018), the following section showcases a single case analysis (cf. Balaman & Sert, 2017; Kardaş İşler et al., 2019; Waring, 2009).

14.3 Single Case Analysis: Opportunities for Pre-Service Teacher Learning in Video-Mediated Peer Interactions

The extract comes from the seventh week of the semester while the pre-service teachers were analyzing a short clip regarding the sequence and preference organization in an actual language classroom. The extract is presented in four segments to increase the readability and showcases an episode during which the group members deal with one turn only with reference to the teacher's sequential practice and the underlying preference organization. The focal turn includes a teacher question that is produced in response to a student contribution and the subsequent 1.1 s of silence. The transcript of the short clip will not be shared in this chapter because the consent to use the clip only covers pedagogical purposes but not research purposes. However, clarifications will be provided when needed to better understand the references of the pre-service teachers. In the focal group, there are four participants, CAR, HAN, BUR, and NAT

274 U. Balaman

(pseudonyms). BUR shares her screen on Microsoft Teams and the group members discuss and analyze one turn and its sequential environment for almost three minutes presented across four consecutive segments.

Extract 1 Segment 1 Setting up the scene (04:12–05:04)

```
 1   CAR:  um this is (0.3) actually a good point to point out that
 2         the teacher immediately learns +from her mistake+ *%(0.5)*%
     nat                                 +----nat nods----+
     han* bur%                                                   *%nods*%
 3         so she's doing marginally better than the last one
 4         $↑right now AH HAH$ (0.3)
 5         because you know um $↑ah hahhhh$ *(0.6)*
     han                                   *smiles*
 6         uhm the video before this↓ (.)
 7         the teacher +was very um (0.3) static
     nat               +multiple brief nods--->
 8         and (0.3) she waited all the ↑time+ (0.4)
     nat                                --->+
 9         +this one (0.8)+ in line one hundred (0.3) uhmm %(0.3) thirty six
     nat   +looks down tow+ards her desk
     bur                                                   %--->
10         %and [one hundred
11   BUR:       [huh huh%
     bur   %-----🖥-----%
              🖥: bur moves the cursor on lines 136 and 137 repeatedly
12   CAR:  thirty seven after waiting for you know% %four point two
     bur                 gets closer to the screen--->% %nods
13         mill-% seh- seconds .hhh ↑uhm and not getting an ↑answer (0.5)
     bur   --->%
14         uhm she learns (0.5) she understands↓ (.)
15         not learns >+she understands+<
     nat               +-----nods-----+
16         right at that time that she needs to e↑la: elaborate (0.5)
17         +um ↑for the students, for the students to continue, (0.6)+
     nat   +--------------looks down towards her desk--------------+
18         um adding to the discussion so like (0.7)
19         uh >what would< (.) >what would< this be↑ what did you *(0.4)*
     nat                                                          *nods*
20         [uhhh
21   BUR:  [huh huh
22   CAR:  the (0.7)
```

The first segment of the extract starts with CAR's evaluation of the teacher's social action in the short clip. After referring to the suitability (a good point to point out) of the focal social action for delivering her evaluation, CAR, in line 2, analyzes the teacher's action as *learning from her mistake*. The co-participants align with CAR's evaluation by nodding. Following the 0.5 s of pause in the turn-final position, CAR continues her analysis by providing a *so*-initiated reasoning for her evaluative analysis of the teacher's action. CAR compares the action in the focal clip with

14 Opportunities for Pre-Service Teacher Learning... 275

the previous teacher from the earlier Discussion and Analysis meeting and delivers an explicit positive evaluation (she's doing marginally better) in line 3. Her positive evaluation is also accompanied with laughter (lines 4 and 5) which is oriented with smile by HAN in line 5. CAR maintains providing her reasoning in lines 5 and 6, re-addresses the comparative nature of her positive evaluation, and in line 7, continues the comparison by negatively evaluating the teacher in the earlier video clip (the teacher was very um (0.3) static).

In line 8, CAR's justification for the negative evaluation includes a teacher interactional practice, namely wait time. We see that CAR treats extended wait time as a negative practice and uses this practice as the basis for her comparison. Also note that NAT aligns with CAR's evaluative stance with multiple brief nods. In what follows, CAR continues analyzing the current teacher's interactional practices with reference to the line number visible on the shared screen (and in the short clip). Her reference to the line number leads NAT to look down toward her desk, which remains outside the camera coverage. CAR's reference also prompts a screen-based activity on the shared screen and BUR moves the cursor next to the lines that CAR refers to (see line 11). BUR also produces an acknowledgment token in coordination with her screen-based activity and displays her understanding of the extent of CAR's ongoing analysis. In line 12, CAR completes referring to the lines of talk and starts describing the talk primarily by uttering the pause in the transcript of the short clip (4.2 s). I should also note that CAR treats this pause as wait time (after waiting for), which establishes the link (i.e., the use of wait time) between the two teachers that CAR compares in this extended turn.

In line 13, CAR argues for the negative outcome of the extended wait time, that is *not getting an answer* from the students. From this point onward, CAR describes what she identifies as the main difference between the two teachers and makes it clear for the co-participants what she meant earlier with her negative evaluation by using *static*. In lines 14 and 15, CAR shares her analysis in a self-repair turn (not learns >she understands<). BUR and NAT bodily align with CAR's analysis so far. In what follows, CAR continues analyzing the teacher talk and explains what the teacher does after not being able to elicit a response from the students. She refers to the teacher's deployment of an interactional resource to maximize participation (she needs to e↑la: elaborate) and to the potential

276   U. Balaman

interactional accomplishment in a next turn in line 17 (for the students to continue) and 18 (adding to the discussion).

By the end of line 18, CAR completes her analysis and comparison with the teacher from a previous clip. Her analysis shows that CAR positively evaluates the interactional practices to resolve non-participation if wait time does not work and compares this to another teacher by referring to her use of extended wait time as being static. She carefully refers to the line numbers on the short clip, draws the co-participants' attention to these lines of talk, elicits embodied alignment from the co-participants, and completes the delivery of her comparative analysis. It can be observed that she is not interrupted at all but only oriented minimally with acknowledgment tokens and embodied actions. From line 19 onward, she initiates an epistemic search (>what would< this be) to find the term that would define the action in her analysis:

Extract 1 Segment 2 Epistemic Search (05:04–05:41)

```
23  CAR   >i'm trying to remember< the technical term but i'm not (0.5)
24        uh it's on the tip of my tongue, (0.3) the um
25        (1.2)
26        ↑you called it ↑pre:: something (0.) pre: something (0.4)
27        what was it (0.8)
28        [like
29  BUR:  [%uhhmm
30  HAN:  [*hmm
31  NAT:  [+hmm
          %*+bur han and nat nod
32  CAR:  pre: *(0.5)*
    han       *lateral headshake*
33  CAR:  ↑geh (0.7) [>okay i-<
34  BUR:              [.hh (0.2) i can't remember it
35  NAT:  [yeahh same
36  CAR:  [yeshhh >i (haven't-) $hah$<
37  NAT:  me too=
38  CAR:  =$like it was$ right on the tip of my tongue
39        but you understand what i mean
40  NAT:  yeah
41  HAN:  [yes
42  BUR:  [yes
43  CAR:  [the teacher learns from her  [mistake
44  BUR:                                [huhm
45  CAR:  and she (0.3) uhmmm elaborates for the students (.)
46        before the discussion can go on
47        #(0.7)
    ?     #mouse click
48  HAN:  yea:hh↓
```

14 Opportunities for Pre-Service Teacher Learning... 277

CAR explicates trouble in remembering a term in lines 23 and 24 (it's on the tip of my tongue) that would define the teacher's action in the focal part of the short clip. She also uses a past reference (you called it) to hint at a previously used utterance (Balaman, 2019; Can Daşkın & Hatipoğlu, 2019; Kardaş İşler & Can Daşkın, 2020). After telling a candidate/incomplete term (pre:: something), CAR designs a question that includes past tense with reference to the earlier use of the co-participants and invites candidate resolutions to her ongoing epistemic search (what was it). Following 0.8 s of pause, CAR's similarity marker overlaps with all co-participants' verbal and embodied acknowledgments in lines 29 to 31. Their acknowledgments show the receipt of the epistemic search; however they do not necessarily resolve it, which leads CAR to repeat the hint in lines 32 (pre:) and 33 (geh). In response, HAN deploys a lateral headshake displaying her failure to help resolve the search in line 32 while BUR in line 34 (i can't remember it) and NAT (yeahh same) in lines 35 and 37 (me too) do the same verbally. Therefore, by the end of line 37, we see that epistemic trouble is not only due to CAR's individual search but it is the whole group that fails to remember a relevant term to describe what CAR proffers as an analysis of the teacher's action. CAR orients to this with laughter in line 36 and reiterates her remembering status in line 38 (on the tip of my tongue).

Subsequently, CAR changes the target of the epistemic search from an exact term to understanding the reference of the searched-for term with an understanding check (but you understand what i mean) in line 39. All co-participants respond to CAR with claims of understanding. The sequential structure here is quite similar to the epistemic search sequence initiated in line 27. Although the co-participants could not resolve the epistemic search, they acknowledged the receipt of the search. Similarly, they do not display any evidence for their understanding but simply claim understanding with their confirmatory responses in lines 40 to 42. Their claims of understanding lead CAR to continue her analysis. Therefore, the searched-for term is not searched for any more and CAR returns to her analysis. This is a complete return to the earlier analysis because her turn in line 43 is a repetition of her earlier turn in line 2 (Segment 1 above) and her turn in lines 45 and 46 is a reformulation of her earlier turn in lines 16 and 17 (Segment 1 above).

278   U. Balaman

Therefore, the interim epistemic search is terminated after the group failure to resolve it and the participants recalibrate their orientation to the main task of the video-mediated meeting, that is to analyze the teacher interactional practices in the short video clip. This shows that the progressivity of the analysis is preferred over the terminological vocabulary use by all group members. In CAR's reformulated turn, she refers to a teacher interactional practice in line 45 (elaborates for the students) and specifies the pedagogical plan in doing so in line 46 (before the discussion can go on). Subsequently, a mouse click sound is heard in the meeting room followed by HAN's short response (yea:hh↓) in line 48 which leads us to the next segment:

Extract 1 Segment 3 Disagreement with Peer Analysis (05:41–06:11)

```
49  CAR:  that was what i had to  [say
50  HAN:                         [>uh uh> (.) ↓uh-
51        actually i thought *a little (1.0)* bit differently
    🖵               *--video plays--*
52        about this +statement+ because
    nat           +---nods--+
53  BUR:  huh huh=
54  HAN:  =er: >uh- i< thought that (0.4)
55        she ↑disagrees with the student [&and
56  BUR:                                  [&huh huh
    car                                   &raises eyebrows and-->
57  HAN:  she delays this disagreement (.)
58        wha- by er: asking a question↓& so:
    car           keeps them raised--->&
59  BUR:  [huh huh
60  HAN:  [uh:::=
61  NAT:  =yeah (0.6) i think [so too
62  HAN:                      [>uh uh< i thought in (.) that way
63  BUR:  [huh huh
64  HAN:  [errr >instead of< (.) you know elaborating their sentence
65  BUR:  °uh huh°
66  HAN:  uh:: (0.4) she is just (0.3)
67        ↑she ↑she instead of seh- sah- simply saying no:: she's just,
68  BUR:  [>huh huh<
69  HAN   [you know asking a question
```

Following HAN's *yeah* in line 48 that is marked with falling intonation, CAR closes her analysis in line 49. In turn-final position, HAN enters the turn by overlapping CAR in line 50 and delivers her disagreement with CAR's analysis (actually i thought *a little (1.0)* bit differently about this statement). Note that HAN carefully designs her disagreement by using an epistemic stance marker (i thought) and mitigation markers (a little bit) in line 51. Her reference to the teacher's turn in line 52 shows that the analysis so far has been oriented to one statement (about this statement) in particular. Although all co-participants including HAN primarily acknowledged the receipt of CAR's epistemic search and claimed understanding for the target of the search, they seemed to have waited until the completion of CAR's analysis to share their stances toward the analysis. When they do so, the disagreement stance is carefully delivered with a mitigated turn format. NAT bodily aligns with HAN's disagreement by nodding in line 52 although BUR simply deploys an acknowledgment token in line 53. After signaling an expansion for her disagreement (because) in line 52, HAN starts providing further grounds from line 54 onward.

HAN analyzes the teacher's social action in the focal part of the short video clip initially as disagreement (she ↑disagrees with the student) in line 55 and later extends this by analyzing the teacher's question design as delaying disagreement (she delays this disagreement by asking a question) in lines 57 and 58. CAR, whose analysis has been oriented with disagreement by a peer, bodily orients to HAN's analysis by holding her eyebrows raised until this part of the analysis is completed by HAN in line 58. On the other hand, BUR delivers repetitive acknowledgment tokens in lines 56 and 59, while NAT agrees with HAN's analysis more explicitly (yeah (0.6) i think so too) in line 61. In what follows, HAN first signals the closing of her analysis in line 62 and continues providing additional accounts from line 64 onward. Initially, she upgrades (>instead of<) her disagreement with CAR's analysis (elaborating their sentence). Subsequently, she delivers an alternative analysis in line with her earlier one and describes the teacher's social action as avoiding a direct disagreement (instead of simply saying no) by delaying disagreement with a question.

At this point, I should note that this is a practice that was part of a lecture in an earlier round of the LTE activity related to sequence and preference organization and here we see that HAN brings this to her analysis. Therefore, HAN does not only disagree with her peer's analysis but she also does so by citing an interactional practice that was part of their training within this cycle of the teacher education course. The final segment shows how HAN's disagreement plays out in the group meeting.

280 U. Balaman

Extract 1 Segment 4 From Disagreement to Group Agreement (06:11–07:13)

```
70 CAR:  [↑yeah i know she leads them to
71 HAN:  [she understands (the meaning)
72 CAR:  the correct answer (.) i think=
73 NAT:  =and actual[ly
74 HAN:             [yeah
75 NAT:  ermm (0.3) before she: (0.4) asks anything (0.3)
76       <the student> +(0.2)
   nat                 +looks down towards her table--->
77       ahmm (0.5) in the *>one hundred+ and forty six&%< actually
   nat                     --->+
   han* car& bur%          *get closer to the screen    &%
78       self selects himself or herself
79 BUR:  huh huh (.) yes
80       (1.0)
81 NAT:  he states his opinion *(0.4)*
   han                         *nods*
82       and then like HAN said in my opinion too
83       (0.3) the teacher (0.3) actually %(0.5)% uhm (0.6)
   bur                                    %nods%
84       disagrees with the (0.4) *answer* (.)
   han                            *two quick nods*
85       and rather than just (0.4) saying
86       >↑no it's not like that< *(0.2)* and
   han                            *nods*
87       (0.5)
88 CAR:  yeah (i saw it=)
89 NAT:  =gives an (0.3) %gives an (0.2) opportunity to% (.) you know (0.3)
   bur                  %---------nods---------------%
90       elaborate and (0.6)
91 BUR:  [huh huh
92 NAT:  [giving ↑mo:re *(0.5) correct answer (.) by delaying it*
   han                  *--------nods and smiles------------*
93       (0.7)
94 HAN:  yeah
95 CAR:  yeah-
96 HAN:  maybe changing the answer
97 NAT:  ↑yeshh
98 CAR:  >it's it's it's< it's a way for these students to lead themselves
99       +to the correct answer+ (.) *by you know* (.) %erghh
   nat   +---two quick nods---+
   han                             *---nods---*
   bur                                         %nods--->
100 CAR  basically% you know >following the teachers questions< so
   bur          --->%
101 NAT:  yeah
102 CAR:  you know it's still a disagreement
103      but yeah it's a delayed disagreement
104      (0.5)
105 NAT:  yeah (0.5)
106 HAN:  yeah (0.6)
107 CAR:  huh huh
108 BUR:  °yeah° (0.4) so- so we can continue::
```

14 Opportunities for Pre-Service Teacher Learning... 281

HAN completes her analysis in line 71 in overlap with CAR's turn in line 70. Despite HAN's disagreement with CAR's earlier analysis, we see that CAR does sanction this or not even treat it as a disagreement and designs an affiliative turn claiming knowledge about HAN's analysis (yeah i know). Interestingly, neither CAR's initial analysis nor HAN's counter-analysis includes a reference to leading the students to the correct answer. Therefore, by not showing an explicit orientation to HAN's disagreement, CAR moves the collaborative analysis forward by topicalizing another teacher interactional practice—that is, leading the students to the correct answer. CAR ends her turn with an epistemic stance marker (i think), which is latched by NAT's turn entry in line 74. NAT takes the turn with a continuation marker (and) and contributes to the analysis by addressing the sequential organization (before she: (0.4) asks anything) that leads to the part which caused disagreement between HAN and CAR. After looking down toward her desk in line 76, NAT refers to a line number which is bodily oriented by all co-participants through getting visibly closer to the screen. NAT grammatically completes the part of her analysis with reference to a focal line in the short video clip by using a technical term related to turn taking (self selects himself or herself).

Also note that self-selection as a turn taking resource has not been proffered as part of the analyses so far, which shows the rationale behind her earlier continuation marker use. It becomes clearer that NAT takes the turn to add to the analysis, addresses a turn taking method, and returns to the main topic that defines the scope of the analysis. BUR acknowledges NAT's addition in line 79 and following 1 s of silence, NAT identifies the student's action in the clip as opinion statement in line 81. Subsequently, NAT maintains her earlier agreement with HAN's analysis (like HAN said in my opinion too) in line 82. After a second round of explicit agreement with HAN, NAT delivers an analysis similar to HAN's in-between lines 83 and 86. Before NAT can continue, CAR displays alignment with NAT's analysis and claims an earlier noticing of NAT's (and indirectly HAN's) observation (yeah (i saw it=)) in line 88. Similar to her earlier action in response to HAN's analysis and despite the divergences in their analytic stances, CAR does not sanction NAT's divergent analysis but claims knowledge about it for a second time in the extract. In what follows, NAT continues her analysis and after a brief word search (you know (0.3)), refers to the teacher's social action as *elaboration* in line 90. Her reference to elaboration marks an interesting moment in the meeting. Although NAT explicitly agreed with HAN in two consecutive instances, here we see a divergence from HAN as HAN displayed disagreement earlier (line 64 Segment 3) with CAR's analysis of the teacher's social action as elaboration.

Subsequently, NAT upgrades her analysis (giving ↑mo:re (0.5) correct answer (.) by delaying it) in line 92 and maintains her agreement with HAN regarding delaying an action. Therefore, despite the explicit agreement with HAN, NAT manages incorporating different analytic observations both from HAN and CAR. In the meantime, HAN does not sanction this divergence but nods and smiles first and then displays alignment with NAT's analysis (yeah) in the next relevant position in line 94. CAR does the same in line 95 which is followed by HAN's candidate addition to the analysis (maybe changing the answer). HAN's addition is in line with NAT's analysis (giving ↑mo:re correct answer) and NAT shows that with her aligning response in line 97. In what follows, CAR takes the turn in line 98 and ties her turn with NAT's (it's a way) and recirculates her analysis regarding leading the students to the correct answer. However, CAR reformulates the agent of the action from *teacher doing leading* to *students leading themselves* in response to the teacher's question and this becomes the first of an extended summary turn. All co-participants bodily acknowledge CAR's analysis and NAT also verbally aligns with CAR. Toward the end of the extract, CAR continues summarizing the analysis so far. In line 102, she describes the teacher's action as disagreement (it's still a disagreement) and adds that *it is a delayed disagreement* in line 103.

Although CAR's analysis has been oriented to the teacher's resolution of non-participation with elaboration (Segment 1 and 2) and leading the students to the correct answer (Segment 4), by the end of the extract, CAR has fully embraced the unfolding group analysis after HAN's disagreement. Therefore, HAN's disagreement has been the main point shaping up the collaborative analysis of the group as seen in the alignment markers and the transition into another episode by the end of the extract.

14.4 Concluding Discussion: Lessons for Post-Emergency LTE

The earlier section of the chapter demonstrated the implementation of the CALTE perspective in a video-mediated interactional setting based on a CA analysis of pre-service teachers who engaged in doing CA analysis with peers and described the pre-service teacher learning opportunities that emerge in due course. The pedagogical objective of the course module was to operationalize the knowledge base of CALTE by teaching CA and CIC in digital spaces (cf. Balaman, 2023). The close analysis of the single case indicated evidence for diverse learning opportunities: The first example was the evaluation of a teacher interactional practice, namely *wait time*. We observed that *extended wait time* was treated as a problematic teacher action and the potential resolutions were proposed. Accordingly, delivering further *elaborations* to *maximize student participation* rather than waiting for longer periods of time was marked as a good practice. Another moment showing increased awareness of CIC was oriented to the teacher's *elicitation practices*. The pre-service teachers extensively discussed the interactional consequences of the teacher's interactional behaviors and referred to the teacher's pedagogical aim as leading to a preferred answer or eliciting it from the students by sequentially organizing her talk, specifically her disagreement. Other examples of skillful use of CA and CIC related constructs in pedagogically relevant moments included references to line numbers to competently reflect their analytic stances; *self-selection* as a turn taking method; sequential impact of *teacher questions*; and the interactional nuances between *disagreement* and *delayed disagreement*. Therefore, the course structure and the strategic use of the digital spaces in asynchronous and synchronous modes created opportunities for an increased familiarity with CA and CIC.

What is more, the pre-service teachers engaged in critical analysis, which would be the ideal way of learning truly reflective lessons that can be transferred to their future teaching practices. The evidence for their critical perspectives went beyond evaluating teacher practices and covered carefully disagreeing with one another's analysis. We saw that HAN's disagreement with CAR was very carefully designed, thus implicating an effort to maintain the affiliation among group members while also properly analyzing the teacher practices. The fact that HAN cited course materials also had a prominent impact on the entire discussion, which is further evidence for the learning opportunities afforded by the digitally enhanced course structure. After HAN's attentively designed and pedagogically well-grounded disagreement, the co-participants took stage to display their alignment with HAN's stance while also minimally diverging from the main niche of her contribution. This was particularly interesting to see because the pre-service teachers did not opt for delivering competing analyses but focused largely on the progressivity of the group analysis. Overall, HAN's disagreement led to a whole-group agreement regarding the teacher's sequential practice and paved the way for moving the LTE activity forward in an entirely reflective manner.

The chapter showed that the video-mediated peer interaction enabled the reflectivity to a great extent. The shared screen made the pre-service teachers' references accessible to each other. They also coordinated their screen-based activities on the shared screen e.g., by moving the cursor next to the line of talk analyzed at certain moments and bodily displaying orientations to the screen. Additionally, they preferred organizing the Analysis and Discussion meeting by compartmentalizing the parts of the short video clip and analyzing turns in their sequential environment in line with the focal subject (i.e., sequence and preference organization) within the fully online course. In light of these findings, it can be claimed that the video-mediated peer interaction maximized the pre-service teacher learning opportunities in a technically feasible, pedagogically sound, interactionally rich, and a truly reflective environment, which calls for a greater attention to the affordances of using classroom recordings and critically analyzing them in groups for preparing pre-service teachers to the interactional realities of L2 classrooms. The CALTE perspective put into practice in digital spaces seemed to prove an efficient way of achieving this goal. In future implementations of the model, LTE professionals can consider designing similar technology-rich environments by establishing transnational partnerships with LTE institutions sharing convergent teacher learning objectives. By doing so, the affordances of video-mediated interactions would be maximized with diverse transcultural teacher learning opportunities as a result of transcending the institutionally defined borders of LTE practices.

References

Badem-Korkmaz, F., Ekin, S., & Balaman, U. (2022). Pre-service language teachers' resistance to teacher trainer advice on task design for video-mediated L2 interaction. *Classroom Discourse, 13*(2), 212-230. https://doi.org/10.108 0/19463014.2021.2020144

Baecher, L., Kung, S.-C., Ward, S. L., & Kern, K. (2018). Facilitating video analysis for teacher development: A systematic review of the research. *Journal of Technology and Teacher Education, 26*(2), 185–216.

Balaman, U. (2019). Sequential organization of hinting in online task-oriented L2 interaction. *Text & Talk, 39*(4), 511–534. https://doi.org/10.1515/ text-2019-2038

Balaman, U. (2023). *Conversation analytic language teacher education in digital spaces*. Palgrave Macmillan.

Balaman, U., & Sert, O. (2017). The coordination of online L2 interaction and orientations to task interface for epistemic progression. *Journal of Pragmatics, 115*, 115–129. https://doi.org/10.1016/j.pragma.2017.01.015

Blell, G., & von Bremen, F. (2020). Assessing pre-service teachers' reflective classroom observation competence in English language teaching. In F. Lenz, M. Frobenius, & R. Klattenberg (Eds.), *Classroom observation* (pp. 225–244). Peter Lang D. https://doi.org/10.3726/b16732

Blume, C., & Schmidt, T. (2020). All kinds of special: Using multi-perspective classroom videography to prepare EFL teachers for learners with special educational needs. In F. Lenz, M. Frobenius, & R. Klattenberg (Eds.), *Classroom observation* (pp. 201–224). Peter Lang D. https://doi.org/10.3726/b16732

Can Daşkın, N. (2015). Shaping learner contributions in an EFL classroom: Implications for L2 classroom interactional competence. *Classroom Discourse, 6*(1), 33–56. https://doi.org/10.1080/19463014.2014.911699

Can Daşkın, N., & Hatipoğlu, Ç. (2019). Reference to a past learning event as a practice of informal formative assessment in L2 classroom interaction. *Language Testing, 36*(4), 527–551.

Christ, T., Arya, P., & Chiu, M. M. (2017). Video use in teacher education: An international survey of practices. *Teaching and Teacher Education, 63*, 22–35. https://doi.org/10.1016/j.tate.2016.12.005

Dobie, T. E., & Anderson, E. R. (2015). Interaction in teacher communities: Three forms teachers use to express contrasting ideas in video clubs. *Teaching and Teacher Education, 47*, 230–240. https://doi.org/10.1016/j. tate.2015.01.003

Ekin, S., Balaman, U., & Badem-Korkmaz, F. (2021). Tracking telecollaborative tasks through design, feedback, implementation, and reflection processes in pre-service language teacher education. *Applied Linguistics Review, 0*(0). https://doi.org/10.1515/applirev-2020-0147.

Huth, T. (2021). *Interaction, language use, and second language teaching.* Routledge.

Kardaş İşler, N., Balaman, U., & Şahin, A. E. (2019). The interactional management of learner initiatives in social studies classroom discourse. *Learning, Culture and Social Interaction, 23*, 100341. https://doi.org/10.1016/j.lcsi.2019.100341

Kardaş İşler, N., & Can Daşkın, N. (2020). Reference to a shared past event in primary school setting. *Linguistics and Education, 57*, 100815.

Mann, S., Davidson, A., Davis, M., Gakonga, J., Gamero, M., Harrison, T., Mosavian, P., & Richards, L. (2019). *Video in language teacher education (ELT research papers 19.01; p. 48).* British Council, Teaching English.

Mondada, L. (2018). Multiple temporalities of language and body in interaction: Challenges for transcribing multimodality. *Research on Language and Social Interaction, 51*(1), 85–106.

Seedhouse, P. (2008). Learning to talk the talk: Conversation analysis as a tool for induction of trainee teachers. In S. Garton & K. Richards (Eds.), *Professional encounters in TESOL* (pp. 42–57). Springer.

Seidel, T., Blomberg, G., & Renkl, A. (2013). Instructional strategies for using video in teacher education. *Teaching and Teacher Education, 34*, 56–65. https://doi.org/10.1016/j.tate.2013.03.004

Sert, O. (2015). *Social interaction and L2 classroom discourse.* Edinburgh University Press.

Sert, O. (2021). Transforming CA findings into future L2 teaching practices: Challenges and prospects for teacher education. In S. Kunitz, N. Markee, & O. Sert (Eds.), *Classroom-based conversation analytic research: Theoretical and applied perspectives on pedagogy* (Vol. 46, pp. 259–279). Springer International Publishing. https://doi.org/10.1007/978-3-030-52193-6

Sidnell, J., & Stivers, T. (Eds.). (2013). *The handbook of conversation analysis.* Wiley-Blackwell.

van Es, E. A. (2012). Examining the development of a teacher learning community: The case of a video club. *Teaching and Teacher Education, 28*(2), 182–192. https://doi.org/10.1016/j.tate.2011.09.005

Walsh, S. (2006). *Investigating classroom discourse.* Routledge. http://site.ebrary.com/id/10163732.

Walsh, S. (2013). *Classroom discourse and teacher development*. Edinburgh University Press.

Waring, H. Z. (2009). Moving out of IRF (initiation-response-feedback): A single case analysis. *Language Learning, 59*(4), 796–824. https://doi.org/10.1111/j.1467-9922.2009.00526.x

Waring, H. Z. (2021). Harnessing the power of heteroglossia: How to multitask with teacher talk. In S. Kunitz, N. Markee, & O. Sert (Eds.), *Classroom-based conversation analytic research: Theoretical and applied perspectives on pedagogy* (Vol. 46, pp. 281–301). Springer International Publishing. https://doi.org/10.1007/978-3-030-52193-6

Waring, H. Z., & Creider, S. C. (2021). *Micro-reflection on classroom communication: A FAB-framework*. Equinox Publishing LTD.

15

Conclusion: What Did We Learn from the COVID-19 Pandemic?

Karim Sadeghi and Michael Thomas

15.1 Introduction

A health crisis that broke out in late 2019 changed the structure of the world and affected all aspects of individual and social life, leading to a new world order in almost every sphere of life. Well into 2022, the consequences are still being greatly felt across the world and thousands of lives are claimed each day globally. At the time of writing this chapter (March, 2022), more than 500 million people have been affected worldwide and more than 6 million have lost their lives. These statistics put COVID-19 as one of the worst global disasters experienced by human beings so far. Different people have viewed this crisis differently with some regarding it a blessing for the integration of technology into all

K. Sadeghi (✉)
Urmia University, Urmia, Iran
e-mail: k.sadeghi@urmia.ac.ir

M. Thomas
Liverpool John Moores University, Liverpool, UK
e-mail: M.Thomas@ljmu.ac.uk

© The Author(s), under exclusive license to Springer Nature Switzerland AG 2023
K. Sadeghi, M. Thomas (eds.), *Second Language Teacher Professional Development*,
Digital Education and Learning, https://doi.org/10.1007/978-3-031-12070-1_15

aspects of life, and others highlighting the high tolls (which continue to grow on a daily basis). No doubt, health-wise, it has been a catastrophe by any standards; however, the pandemic has also been an opportunity for human beings to stand aside and look back at themselves and the surrounding environment and reflect on the meaning of all new incidents. There have obviously been great lessons that we could learn even from the worst events. This reminds us of a Persian anecdote: Once people asked Luqman Hakim (a wise man in the Quran) how he learned to be so polite, his simple answer was by watching impolite people: 'Whatever they did, I did just the opposite!' This is a simple quote indicating how we can learn the best lessons even from the worst incidents.

Although health-wise, despite giant strides taken, scientists still do not have a final solution to combat COVID-19, we have had to learn how to live and cope with it by following some simple instructions like social distancing and adhering to a more hygienic life-style; from a social-life perspective, we have come to appreciate the physical presence of our family members, our friends, our loved ones and all those around us. As far as human values are concerned, we have learned to be more caring and supportive towards each other and especially those who are in need of such support; and we have learned how short life can be and how unexpected the loss of loved ones and family member can occur. We hope all this has made us much better human beings, despite some world leaders' and politicians' never ending desires for war, destroying humanity, killing human beings and genocide. Will they need worse disasters to learn their lessons?

As far as education and in particular language education is concerned, we have indeed learned some good lessons and are learning more. This book is primarily concerned with the impact of the COVID-19 pandemic and accordingly the emergent use of digital technology on language teacher education and professional development. While digital technology in its various forms and meanings was a regular aspect of, and a mainstay in, some educational institutes in technologically advanced contexts prior to the pandemic (with the earliest attempts of using computer for language education now being over 60 years old, according to Butler-Pascoe, 2011), there was very limited regular use of such technology and more specifically synchronous online course delivery in teacher education

15 Conclusion: What Did We Learn from the COVID-19 Pandemic?

(TE) and professional development (PD) circles. The pandemic, however, turned everything in education upside down, like in every other aspect of life. Immediately after the pandemic and as soon as classes started going online globally since March 2020, the focus of educators, teachers and administrators was primarily on learners and on how to deliver lessons online or off-line with the help of technology during the emergency transition period. Little attention was paid to the needs of practicing and trainee teachers and scant attention was devoted to deploying digital technology for offering teacher training and professional development. Prior to attending to their own professional development needs, most teachers sought opportunities to learn to teach online first (with an eye to putting learners first), and only at a later stage did they start thinking about engaging in individualised and self-initiated professional development activities to enhance their professional competence, given that there were no institutionalised practices and support in place yet, as Gautam (2020) observes.

Given that the opportunities for face-to-face professional development workshops are still very limited even after more than two years of the outbreak of the pandemic, teacher educators began experimenting with such courses from a distance with the help of technology and increasingly many TE and PD workshops are being delivered and taken online nowadays. This volume brings together some of the first experiments language teacher educators were engaged in, offering such courses and workshops for pre-service and in-service teachers as documented in the preceding chapters. Next we offer the major findings coming from reported studies as well as the lessons we have learned for post-pandemic times after a brief reference to some other similar works and early attempts to use digital technology for emergency teacher education published elsewhere.

15.2 Research on Online Language Teacher Education at the Time of the Pandemic

One of the earliest attempts to deliver a fully online course on teacher education during the early months of the outbreak of COVID-19 took place in Hong Kong. Moorhouse (2020) explains his experience, challenges and the lessons learned in adapting a face-to-face initial teacher education (ITE) course (Post-graduate Diploma of Education in primary English language education) to a 'forced' fully online (both synchronous and asynchronous) mode when universities suspended in-institute education in February 2020, an experience not dissimilar to most other contexts where teacher education was forced to change mode. The course participants were all full-time in-service teachers or teaching assistants. While asynchronous mode (which also was in place before the pandemic) included dissemination and storage of readings and other materials like annotated PowerPoints on the institute's Learning Management System (LMS), the synchronous mode included real-time live lessons delivered via Video Conferencing Software (VCS). The adaptation included making the VCS session mandatory (which was optional at the beginning of the programme) and student-centred (which was teacher-fronted with the teacher primarily recapping the content of the PowerPoint) as well as allowing for breakout rooms, group discussions and more structured sessions. All this increased student attendance, participation and interaction. The challenges were that micro-teaching was not easy to facilitate, classes were still rather teacher-fronted and 'bumpy', class discussions included longer silences and shorter responses, and paralinguistic communication was limited as students turned off cameras for privacy. The main lesson that the author learned (which is supported by feedback he received from participants) was that 'the blend between synchronous and asynchronous modes of instruction seem to be a possible way to support learning in ITE when face-to-face instruction is not an option' (pp. 610–611) as well as identifying the need for training tutors how to deliver courses online.

A similar study was conducted with 118 pre-service English as a Foreign Language (EFL) teachers in Turkey. Karatas and Tuncer (2020) examined the sustainability of the development of language skills during a move from normal classroom practices to Emergency Distance Education (EDE) mode. Student feedback on the advantages and disadvantages of such a pre-service teacher education mode identified content- and implementation-related issues of the programme requiring further attention; the findings also suggested that EDE was most advantageous for the development of the writing skill but less advantageous for that of speaking, which was significantly ignored during class communications

15 Conclusion: What Did We Learn from the COVID-19 Pandemic? 293

that were primarily conducted through writing in chat boxes. The authors identify the need for preparedness as the main lesson to learn against future similar emergency transitions: 'what needs to be done is to learn from our mistakes and then plan, design, and implement accordingly ... Otherwise, in the end, reality might take its revenge' (p. 27). Coming from the same context, Ozudogru's (2021) study with pre-service teachers in a state public university found that the challenges (pedagogical, technological and social-emotional) trainee teachers faced far outweighed the opportunities of EDE such as sustainability of education and flexibility of assessment. The suggestions that were made to make such training more effective include shorter live sessions, reducing the number of assignments, and more importantly providing both trainee teachers and their instructors with technological pedagogical knowledge and technical online course delivery skills.

Moorhouse's (2020), Karatas and Tuncer's (2020), and Ozudogru's (2021) reflections are but a very small sample of similar works that resonate well with the experience of most language teacher educators elsewhere, as reported by the contributors to this volume. Although the consensus is now to prepare for a blended form of teacher education and professional development, for this to happen effectively, several prerequisites have to be met: necessary hardware, software and infrastructure should be made available, especially in the case of educators and trainees living in technologically disadvantaged parts of the world; teacher educators should receive technical training on how to deliver courses and workshops online (both synchronously and asynchronously) as well as on how to effectively use the available tools and software; teacher trainees should also receive similar training to be able to make effective use of the digital technology; and educators and trainees should be helped to develop a positive mentality towards the effectiveness of online and blended mode of delivery. For all this to work best, the role of planning and offering computer training is significant; indeed, as Rilling et al. (2005) observed almost two decades ago, such training is needed in pre-service and in-service teacher education when societies transition into an electronic age with most communications, readings, etc. happening online. The need for such an integration of digital technology to teacher education programmes and professional development courses/workshops is felt even much stronger today at a time when physical encounters and group gatherings are still restricted in many parts of the world. Despite this, it is also all very important to acknowledge that however real-time, live seamless online communications may be, the most effective form of interaction is achieved with the actual and physical presence of, and eye contact between, human beings, signifying that fully online courses will lack an important element of human presence.

15.3 Lessons Learned for the Future

As one of the very few books on lessons learned during the pandemic, reflecting on their 20-chapter volume on general teacher education programmes in Canada, Danyluk et al. (2022) identify several important challenges and lessons that seem to hold true for non-Canadian contexts and language teacher education programmes as well, as identified too by some of the contributors to our volume. Some of the significant challenges and opportunities their contributors reported were:

> the isolation and additional stressors [such as] job loss, financial difficulties … began to impact not only preservice teachers' mental health but our own sense of well-being… a steep learning curve not only to adapt our courses for online delivery but to learn new technology and pedagogies.… increased feelings of loneliness… [the pandemic being] not only a crisis but an opportunity that saw teacher educators thinking collaboratively, reflecting on programs and courses, and embracing new discoveries of digital tools, skills, practicum alternatives, and ways of being in the online environment. (pp. 334–337)

The editors also identified the following 'impactful lessons': 'Pay[ing] attention to preservice teacher metal health and wellness; Continue[ing] to re-examine programs and how well they meet the needs of preservice teachers; [and] Attend[ing] to the inequities that resulted from the shift to online teaching and learning' (p. 338). Adding to and resonating with these lessons, below we briefly survey some of the major lessons we have learned through the eyes of the contributors to this volume. Although the

15 Conclusion: What Did We Learn from the COVID-19 Pandemic? 295

challenges and the lessons are related to specific contexts and should accordingly be evaluated within that context before generalisations can be made (as Viana, this volume, attests), there are obviously more global implications which again need constant re-evaluation as the pandemic unfolds.

As a result of the pandemic, although we have learned to use technology as an emergency tool to handle most of our educational needs, as Liontas (this volume) highlights, we have also learned that engaging in dialogic interactions and discussing coping techniques, etc. have contributed to a 'broader appreciation for the fact that a healthy, happy sense of physical and mental wellbeing, even under the most strenuous situations, can keep one's soul fulfilled', signifying the need to attend to learner and teacher well-being (in all its senses) if technology is to work efficiently. Technology-wise, many contributors to the volume recommend the need for offering both trainees and educators the required digital knowledge, competency and training or digital literacy (what White et al., this volume, refer to as didactic and technical digital competence). Li (this volume) sees a need for developing teachers' competence in pedagogy and assessment while delivering online classes. The same undoubtedly can be extended to teacher educators who need the required minimum skills in developing, implementing and evaluating courses with the help of digital technology.

Most contributors also emphasise the role of planning a blended mode of delivery rather than relying on entirely live and campus/school-based traditional teaching. Mullen et al. (this volume), for example, advocate 'a more permanent blended learning approach … rather than the internet serving as a hastily-constructed backup method of delivery', which in essence means planning and preparing well in advance before we find ourselves in the middle of another health crisis. Along these lines, Burns et al. (this volume) advise that general teacher professional courses need extensive reconsideration such that 'just-in-time' rather than general models of technology training should be available when needed since, as recognised by White et al. (this volume), teachers' IT needs change constantly. Institutions, according to Burns et al., should have '"go-to" staff' who can skilfully support teachers with technology when needed and should appreciate that 'pedagogy drives the use of technology and not the reverse'. This signifies a more significant place for (technological) collaboration among teachers, as well as between teachers and other school staff in their professional learning journey. Tele-collaborative learning, as Dooly (this volume) identifies, is an appreciable consequence of the pandemic.

One more main lesson we learned during the pandemic was, as identified by Solares-Altamirano (this volume), learning about learning, or leaning to learn (as tagged by Tarnanen et al., this volume). Indeed we had to try out new teaching methods, use new technology, conduct research without appropriate research designs and data collection methods and the like. This has been significant in that teachers and teacher educators had to find their way and survive amid a crisis, had no other option than believing themselves, found benefit in both seeking and offering help and advice, and collaboratively and innovatively used whatever at their disposal to defend their territory. In addition to making teachers and teacher educators more autonomous and responsible, this has in turn meant that we as teachers and teacher educators have learned to be more flexible and versatile. As Carlson and Serrano (this volume) highlight, despite being a disaster, the pandemic has afforded several opportunities as well: we have learned that TE 'does not need to be a one-size-fits-all, face to face experience' and that other modalities like remote (online and offline) and hybrid are alternatives. These new opportunities will not only allow access to educators from whose expertise and experience most people will otherwise be unable to benefit (for distance and cost considerations) but at the same time allow 'more teachers of color and of indigenous background to complete these programs' as evidenced by Carlson and Serrano (this volume). A further opportunity observed by Balaman (this volume) is the truly reflective and interactionally rich environment that digital technology (video-mediated peer interaction) affords pre-service teachers. We have at the same time learned that face-to-face and virtual learning and teaching modes should not be regarded as competing but complementary modes and that adopting one exclusively may not do learners justice: pedagogically informed and technologically skilled teachers/teacher educators will be in a better position to decide on the right time and level of marriage between the two modes of delivery when need arises.

15 Conclusion: What Did We Learn from the COVID-19 Pandemic?

The experience with technology amid COVID-19 crisis has also offered lessons to learn for administrators and policy-makers. As Meniado (this volume) recognises, before digital technology can facilitate language and teacher education, there is a need for required infrastructures to be in place. The hardware computing equipment, internet speed and bandwidth as well as relevant software and resources are only some of the issues that should be heeded by governments well before another crisis hits in. The availability or lack of these resources in a certain context and the access chances for all trainees and educators have important social justice and equity implications worthy of immediate attention. Adding a global focus to teacher education programmes (as Ene, this volume, highlights) can contribute to the success of the course as well as raising awareness among student teachers on issues of global concern such as wars (physical, economic, cyber, political, etc.), environmental affairs and other social inequalities threatening life for everyone.

Despite what technology has to offer in both planned and emergency teacher education programmes (and other spheres of life), an essential need of human beings to socialise and build relationships will always be missing in wholly online interactions since above all human beings are social animals. Before there is another disaster further limiting such relationships, we have an ethical, individual, social and legal responsibility to adhere to health regulations to prevent further catastrophes from taking place, which could further damage education systems and provisions around the globe.

References

Butler-Pascoe, M. E. (2011). The history of CALL: The intertwining paths of technology and second/foreign language teaching. *International Journal of Computer-Assisted Language Learning and Teaching, 1*(1), 16–32.

Danyluk, P., Burns, A., Hill, S. L., & Crawford, K. (2022). Conclusion: What have we learned: Adaptations, recommendations, and silver linings. In P. Danyluk, A. Burns, S. L. Hill, & K. Crawford (Eds.), *Crisis and opportunity: How Canadian bachelor of education programs responded to the COVID-19 pandemic* (pp. 334–340). Canadian Association for Teacher Education (CATE).

Gautam, G. R. (2020). English language teacher professional development during COVID-19 in Nepal. *Interdisciplinary Research in Education, 5*(1), 103–112. https://doi.org/10.3126/ire.v5i1&2.34739

Karatas, T. O., & Tuncer, H. (2020). Sustaining language skills development of pre-service EFL teachers despite the COVID-19 interruption: A case of emergency distance education. *Sustainability, 12*(8188), 1–34. https://doi.org/10.3390/su12198188

Moorhouse, B. L. (2020). Adaptations to a face-to-face initial teacher education course 'forced' online due to the COVID-19 pandemic. *Journal of Education for Teaching: International Research and Pedagogy, 64*(4), 609–611. https://doi.org/10.1080/02607476.2020.1755205

Ozudogru, F. (2021). Turkish preservice teachers' experiences with emergency remote teaching: A phenomenological study. *Issues in Educational Research, 31*(1), 166–187.

Rilling, S., Dahlman, A., Dadson, S., Boyles, C., & Pazvant, O. (2005). Connecting CALL theory and practice in preservice teacher education and beyond: Processes and products. *CALICO Journal, 22*(2), 213–235.

Index[1]

A

Accessibility, 171, 176, 182
Action research (AR), 82–85, 87, 88, 91, 92, 97, 210, 218, 223
Action research facilitation, 82, 83
Active learning, 202
Affordances, 51
Asian EFL teachers, 57–74

B

Blended learning, 37–53

C

CALL, 44–46, 49, 229–245
Challenges in using technology, 97
Chinese, 131, 132, 134, 137–143

Classroom interactional competence, 269–284
Collaborative interaction, 255, 263
Collaborative orientation, 250, 251, 265
Communication technology, 250
Community of Practice (CoP), 15, 26, 28, 30
Competence, 229, 231–234, 236, 237, 239, 245
Context, 102, 103, 105–110, 115, 120, 121
Conversation Analysis (CA), 269, 270, 272, 273, 283
Conversation Analytic Language Teacher Education (CALTE), 269–272, 283, 284
Cooperative learning, 199, 202
Corpus compilation, 108, 118

---

[1] Note: Page numbers followed by 'n' refer to notes.

© The Author(s), under exclusive license to Springer Nature Switzerland AG 2023   **299**
K. Sadeghi, M. Thomas (eds.), *Second Language Teacher Professional Development*,
Digital Education and Learning, https://doi.org/10.1007/978-3-031-12070-1

300   Index

Corpus tools, 114
Co-teaching, 192, 193, 200–204
COVID-19, 13, 19, 37–44,
    49–53, 147
COVID-19 challenges, 58, 65
COVID-19 coping strategies, 66
COVID-19 pandemic, 101–121,
    192, 205
Criterion-referenced assessment,
    221, 222
Critical participatory action research
    (CPAR), 15, 16, 20, 26, 32, 33

D

Data-driven learning (DDL),
    104, 105
Dialogic interactions, 24, 31
Digital competences, 125–144, 266
Digital platforms and
    resources, 48, 50
Digital tools, 126–142, 144
Discursive strategies, 250, 263,
    265, 267

E

Effectiveness, 169, 171
eLearning technology, 15, 18
Emergency remote teaching, 88,
    91, 95–98
Engagement, 170
English, 126, 131, 132,
    134, 137–142
English language learner,
    192–196, 203
English language teaching and
    learning, 102, 103, 105, 106

English language teacher education
    (ELTE), 8, 101–121, 271
Ethics, 110

F

Feedback, 171, 174, 175,
    180–181, 185
First language, 210
Flexibility, 171, 182, 185
Focused task, 151
Focus-on-form, 152, 153
Formative assessment, 212, 216, 217

G

Global (learning), 229–245

H

Hybrid learning
    environment, 209–225

I

Input, 171, 179
In-service, 229, 233–237, 239,
    240, 242–245
In-service teacher training, 57
Instructional design, 147–165
Instructional strategies, 199
Intercultural, 231–234, 236–239,
    243, 245
Internationalization, 232
International students, 81,
    82, 84, 87
Interpersonal relationships,
    113, 117–119

Index

Interview, 128, 129, 131, 132, 137–142
Iterative problem-solving process, 15, 20

K

Knowledge base, 269–272, 283
Knowledge constructs and meaning-making processes, 15
Kruskal-Wallis test, 133, 133n2

L

Language acquisition, 191–205
Language awareness, 104
Language teacher education (LTE), 269–271, 279, 283–284
Language teaching, 130, 132, 133, 137, 139–140
Learning engagement, 203

M

Mindfulness through consciousness, 28, 29, 32, 33
Motivation, 169–171, 186
Multiliteracy, 209, 213–216, 219, 222

O

Online, 229–245
Online collaborative learning, 266
Online corpora, 110
Online Education (OE), 148, 149, 151, 157, 159, 161, 163, 164
Online learning, 13, 15, 16, 19, 20, 192

Online professional learning, 70
Online teaching, 38, 39, 42, 43, 45–49, 52, 53, 83, 87, 88, 91–93, 130, 138–143
On-offline ecosystem, 249

P

Pandemic impact on education, 37
Pedagogical practice, 97, 105, 113–116
Pedagogical process, 15, 30
Post-pandemic education, 49–52
Practice development, 14
Pre-service, 229, 233, 234, 236, 237, 239–245
Preservice teacher, 192–205
Professional development (PD), 57, 62, 64, 65, 69, 209–212, 217, 223
Professional development activities, 62, 64, 66, 67, 69, 70
Professional development during pandemic, 58, 65–67, 69
Professional learning, 209–225
Project-based language learning, 252
Psychosomatic health and wellbeing, 17, 31

Q

Questionnaire, 131–133, 138

R

Reflection, 210–212, 217–223
Resources, 171, 172, 176, 179, 182, 183, 185

302 **Index**

S

Secondary data analysis, 109
Second language, 210
Self-assessment, 216–219, 221–224
Self-determined learning, 70
Self-directed learning, 59, 70
Senior high/upper secondary school, 126, 128, 130
Socio-economic inequalities, 117
Spanish, 131, 132, 134, 137, 139–143
Student teacher, 209–225
Sweden, 125–144
Synchronous online instruction, 19

T

Task, 149–154, 160, 161
Task-based language teaching, 149
Task-supported language teaching, 151–154
Teacher agency, 170, 183
Teacher development, 58–62, 65–67, 70–72, 171, 172, 181, 182, 185
Teacher education, 192, 196, 204, 210–212, 214–216, 218, 222, 224, 225, 249, 266
Teacher emotions, 88
Teacher learning, 185, 269–284
Teacher professional development, 91, 98
Teacher research, 84
Teachers' beliefs, 182
Teacher training, 37–53, 229–245
Teaching English in difficult circumstances, 102
Teaching English to Speakers of Other Languages (TESOL), 229–245

Technological pedagogical content knowledge (TPACK), 178, 183
Technology, 109, 113, 116, 119
Technology affordances and constraints, 19, 27
Technology-enhanced professional development, 64, 65
Technology-enriched pedagogy, 210
Technology in online teaching, 92, 93
Technology integration, 175, 176, 178
Technology-supported professional development, 61, 62
Telecollaboration, 249–267
Training, 176, 180, 182–184, 186
Transcription, 252, 255, 257
Translanguaging, 214
Turn-taking, pauses, 265
21st century skills, 250

V

Video club, 271
Videography, 271
Video-mediated interaction, 271, 272, 284
Video use, 271
Virtual Exchange, 250, 251

W

White, J. R., 131, 140, 142
Work-based learning, 63, 70
World 101, 229–245

Z

Z value of sign test, 133